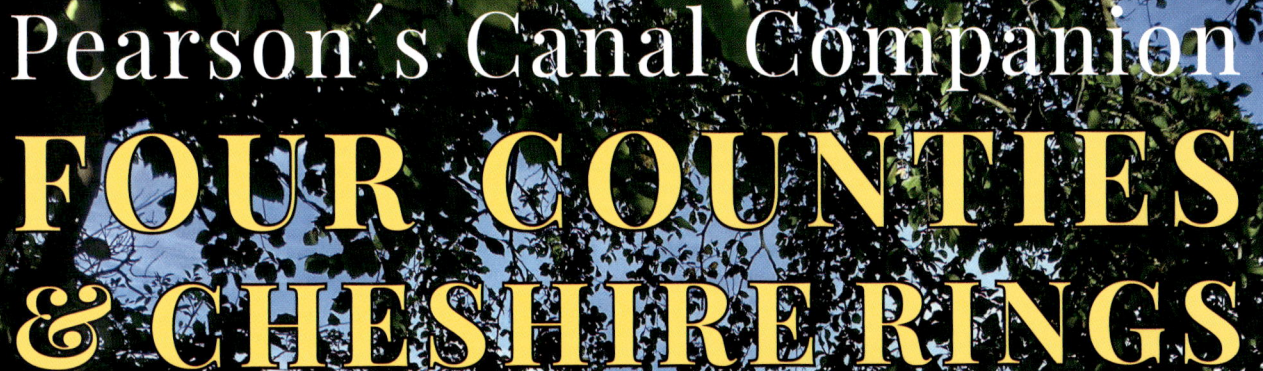

Pearson's Canal Companion
FOUR COUNTIES & CHESHIRE RINGS

In fond memory of Eileen Lester of Gailey Roundhouse 1933-2022

Published by Wayzgoose
www.jmpearson.co.uk
enquiries@jmpearson.co.uk

Copyright: Michael Pearson
1st Combined Edition 2024
ISBN 978 1 3999 8869 8

LOCK-WHEELING

My Potteries baptism occurred in a tenebrous Hanley cinema, of all places. A thousand Stokies, munching their way through a matinee performance of *The Sound of Music*. 'Sooch' was the first word in their inimitable dialect I felt confident enough to translate. Three coruscating hours later - having climbed every mountain, having forded every stream, still trying to solve a problem like Maria - we filed out beneath a fumacious Six Towns sky. A decade after its passage through Parliament, the Clean Air Act was still 'work in progress' where that loose affiliation of insular, infighting communities was concerned. North Staffordshire invariably arrives late at a party. If, that is, it condescends to attend at all.

Ovens were belching, steam locomotives panting, elephantine PMT half-cabs lumbering through late afternoon streets, conveying weary shoppers home to such exotica as Fegg Hayes, Talke Pits, and blunt, uncouth Sneyd. Uninvited, a virus took up residence in my blood stream.

Further Potteries epiphanies ensued, foremostly the novels and short stories of Arnold Bennett. Auspiciously, *Clayhanger* opens with its titular character observing, from a 'steep-sloping, red-bricked canal bridge', a 'long narrow canal-boat roofed with tarpaulins' approach from the north, towed by 'an unhappy skeleton of a horse', floundering its way through a 'morass of sticky brown mud'. That I acquired my copy of that lost masterpiece on precisely the same day (24.08.70) as that most seminal of canal books, L. T. C. Rolt's *Narrow Boat*, owed more to synchronicity than coincidence. But if Bennett satisfied my literary appetite for the region, its trademark bottle kilns provided visual manna. Flattering myself I could paint - I was, after all, about to be awarded my alma mater's prestigious Art Prize - I began experimentally adding bottle kilns to Lowryesque landscapes, culminating in an enormous 'canvas' consisting solely of kilns in diminishing, monochromatic perspective, afforded a Salvador Dali inspired title: *The Ovens of Human Tranquility*. Pretentious? Moi?

By the time of my next encounter with the Potteries, I had ascended to the hormone-charged heights of the Lower Sixth. Newly equipped with a second-hand 35mm SLR Praktica - whose Iron Curtain origins pleased me inordinately - I swooped from Longton's elevated railway station one rainswept day, determined to emulsify the genius loci of the district on film. Industrial environments were not exactly new to me - my hometown's aromatic breweries, South Derbyshire's collieries and salt-glazed sanitary-ware works, York's Layerthorpe bowels - but this was an eye-opener, a dissolution beyond redemption. Peregrinating with the zeal of a would-be Bill Brandt, I scrambled across wastegrounds to the rear of Foley's Pottery, discovering a suitably decrepit building through which to frame two kilns enhanced by the presence of a slag heap looming, pyramid-like in the distance. An enduring love of the Potteries - subsequently bolstered by cheese & bacon oatcakes and Wrights steak pies - was consummated.

An equally intense affection for Manchester transpired. Floundering, after two abortive terms at Derby Art School, my father adroitly pointed me in the direction of his own form of employment, printing. Inherently acquiescent, I signed up for a three year course in Print Technology at Manchester Polytechnic. A congenial bunch of misfits, my peers consisted of school-leavers eschewing university; a trio of what we would now term 'mature' students, factory floor artisans with ambitions of scaling the managerial ladder; a cohort from Nigeria, under the delusion that the empire still existed; and a bewhiskered character with a high-pitched voice who never attended lectures or workshops, but who came 'top' at the end of every term. The most remarkable score awarded me was 6 out of 100.

My heart - as you might by now have surmised - wasn't in it. My heart was playing truant: scouring the city's backstreets for the ghosts of Cardus, Spring and Valette; perusing the subterranean shelves of Gibbs secondhand bookshop; or in attendance at the Free Trade Hall where, on Thursday nights, the Hallé soldiered on in a post-Barbirollian coda.

Manchester my Manchester - gravured within my soul.

Contents

Four Counties Ring
Maps 1 - 27 Pages 5 - 68

Caldon Canal
Maps 28 - 30 Pages 69 - 80

Cheshire Ring
Maps 31 - 53 Pages 81 - 146

Weaver Navigation
Maps 54 - 57 Pages 147 - 154

Information
Pages 155 - 157

Boating Directory
Pages 158 - 159

Acknowledgements
A good deal of water has flowed under the hump-backed bridges of the canals featured in this guide in the 42 years which have elapsed since we first covered them, and we have grown to think of our loyal readers as an extended family of fellow travellers, deserving of as much gratitude as anyone. But where this newly combined edition is concerned, we are especially beholden to Andrew Denny, John Eyres, Liz Hawkes, David Hymers, Stan & Judy King, Chris & Terry Rigden, Peter Silvester, Jenny Tyte, and Colin Warne for their much valued input. Special thanks go to Meg Gregory for her inspirational cover; Karen Tanguy for painstakingly and good-humouredly editing Lock-wheeler's protean text and maps; Tamar Lumsden for her increasingly welcome contributions; and Jackie Pearson for postponing retirement! Finally, much gratitude to all at the admirable Short Run Press of Exeter, who have forgotten more about printing than Lock-wheeler ever learned.

FOUR COUNTIES RING

SHROPSHIRE UNION CANAL Autherley Junction 3mls/1lk/1hr

QUITE what shade of grey you'd call Bridge 1 nowadays is anybody's guess, but once upon a time it formed a pristinely whitewashed welcome to the Shropshire Union (nee Birmingham & Liverpool Junction) Canal a 39-mile odyssey as exhilarating as any that the inland waterways system has to offer. Sam Lomas would shudder. He was toll-keeper, general factotum and major-domo of Autherley Junction back when the canal still worked for a living. One imagines he would have painted the bridge - single-handedly, at his own expense - rather than let it look neglected.

Chances are you'll be eager to get on with your journey, but Autherley repays exploration. One of Thomas Telford's distinctive lock cottages stands back from the stop lock. You'll encounter others on your voyage north, but quite what the purpose of the lofty and bulky chimney was, is open to conjecture; though it still boasts a fine trio of salt-glazed pots. Other ancillary buildings erected by the original canal company remain in use as part of Napton Narrowboats' hire base.

'This doesn't bode well,' we can hear you thinking aloud, as you attempt to extricate yourself from Wolverhampton's northern outskirts, hemmed in by sewage works, solar panels and housing estates. Keep faith, you'll soon find the kind of back of beyond landscape other, less discerning folk fly thousands of carbon-emitting air miles to embrace. Moreover, don't knock that sewage plant, it provides the canal with millions of gallons of suitably treated water on a daily basis, a fact which keeps it well-topped-up when others display a marked tendency to run dry.

Old photographs show 'The Shroppie' stretching bleakly away from 'Cut End' across a flat and empty tract of land towards a low and undistinguished horizon. This, however, is no longer the case, for where houses haven't been built, there are swards of open public space, 'landscaped' indiscriminately with trees and vegetation. 'Green is good' the planners will tell you, but not necessarily when the result is anonymous.

From Bridge 2, Reapers Walk leads to a convenience store, an Indian takeaway, buses into Wolverhampton, and a surprising survival ... a 17th century dovecote, sole remnant of Barnhurst Farm, a sizeable property which had once belonged to wealthy wool merchants, but lamentably demolished in the 1970s to make way for the housing estate.

Wolverhampton Airport was established between the Shropshire Union and Staffordshire & Worcestershire canals on land previously used as a sewage farm. Amy Johnson flew demonstration flights to mark the official opening on 25th June 1938. During the Second World War the aerodrome was employed as an Elementary Flying Training School, and amongst its intake were contingents of Turkish, Iraqi and Iranian pilots. One can't help but wonder if many of the finer points of flying technique were lost in translation. After the war the aerodrome gradually returned to civilian use. In the 1950s, Don Everall Aviation enterprisingly operated scheduled flights to the Isle of Man and Channel Islands. The Ealing feature film, *The Man in the Sky*, staring Jack Hawkins and Elizabeth Sellars, was largely shot on location here in 1956. Closed in 1971, housing occupies the airport's site.

Cast iron mileposts measure distances between Autherley, Norbury and Nantwich, and by the time you reach the first of these the towpath has changed sides at Bridge 3, an imposing roving, or 'change-line' bridge. Wolverhampton Boat Club built their premises in 1966, having previously been eponymously based at Autherley; and, by all accounts, a sociable club it is too.

Industrial units east of the canal - now occupied by furniture makers and a chicken processing plant - once belonged to the aircraft makers,

Autherley Stop Lock

Boulton Paul. Over a thousand WWII Defiant fighters were built here, a design whose reputation for unreliability has been somewhat rehabilitated in recent years. During the war a dummy factory was erected on the outskirts of Brewood to mislead enemy planes. One Junkers Ju88 did manage to attack the Boulton Paul works, however, though the five bombs it dropped hit the neighbouring sewage farm instead. Its mission ended even more ignominiously, being shot down over Nuneaton. Incidentally, the canal still narrows at the site of stop gates, placed beyond Bridge 4 to minimise flooding were the canal to be breached by bomb damage.

An embankment carries the canal over the River Penk as a rural atmosphere is firmly established. There is access from Bridge 4 (or, indeed 5) to Pendeford Mill Nature Reserve, amongst whose attractions is a yew tree reputedly two thousand years old. Presumably its presence inspired the name of Old Tree Nursery, a centre for mental health and work placements in gardening and horticulture.

A sequence of narrows and widenings ensues as the canal cuts through a band of Keuper Sandstone. Canalside cornfields are woven with a poppy trim. The M54, which links Telford to the M6, spans the canal, on a section completed in 1983. Briefly, the towpath is commandeered by the Monarch's Way, a 615 mile long approximation of King Charles II's convoluted escape route from Worcester to Brighton via Bristol and Yeovil in 1651. No motorways in those days.

2 SHROPSHIRE UNION CANAL Brewood & Stretton 4mls/0lks/1½hrs

GETTING into its characteristically loping stride, the old Birmingham & Liverpool Junction component of the Shropshire Union Canal forges north in a series of cuttings and embankments, known respectively as 'rockings' and 'valleys' to generations of working boatmen. As originally built - it was opened throughout in 1835 - its course across this agricultural landscape would have resembled an open wound. Long ago, however, absorbed into nature's rich tapestry, the canal now looks as if it has always been there, especially in this era of reduced maintenance regimes.

Having grown accustomed to the functional lines of Telford's overbridges, Bridge 10's ornamentation comes as a surprise. Known as Avenue Bridge, it was built to carry the carriageway to Chillington Hall. The advent of the canals heralded many similar attempts at ornamentation and disguise, where powerful landowners would only condescend to permit a waterway to cross their parklands if suitable steps were taken to adorn the otherwise purely functional architecture of the new trade route. Chillington itself lies about a mile and a half to the west in grounds landscaped by Capability Brown. En route you encounter Giffard's Cross, where in the sixteenth century one of the Giffards (who have inhabited the estate for over eight hundred years) is said to have shot a marauding panther.

'Brood' is one of the prettiest villages on the Shropshire Union, if not the canal system as a whole. This is Mike Webb country: or perhaps that should be, 'Espionage Webb', as he was affectionately known on account of the meticulous records he kept of boat movements during the post-war years, when he was growing up in Brewood and attending the local

1: Countrywide Cruisers
2: Industry Narrowboats

⚠ 1 One-way working in narrow sections

for details of facilities at Brewood turn to page 10

grammar school, where he and his chums fell into the habit of collecting boat names because there was no nearby railway line at which to train-spot. But Mike's greatest legacy - painstakingly nurtured by his widow, Maria - is the photographs he took of working boats in the late 'fifties and early 'sixties. A retrospective collection of them appears in *The Twilight Years of Narrow Boat Carrying* available from Audlem Mill Canal Shop (Map 9). Mike's funeral took place in Brewood in 2012. Fittingly his coffin arrived by boat. A bench just south of Bridge 14 commemorates this gentle soul together with a suitably illustrated memorial in the churchyard.

Countrywide Cruisers occupy Brewood Wharf. A gas works stood here from 1872 until the First World War, supplies thereafter coming from a much larger works in Stafford. Electricity didn't arrive in Brewood until 1928. For two or three miles the towpath is made busier than usual by walkers doing the Staffordshire Way, a long distance footpath which encounters a good many canals between Kinver and Mow Cop. Belvide Reservoir is one of the main sources of water supply for the Shropshire Union Canal. It is also, under the auspices of the West Midland Bird Club, a magnet for ornithologists. Broom Hall, east of Bridge 16, was the home of William Carlos who hid King Charles II in the oak tree at nearby Boscobel after the Battle of Worcester in 1651.

A sturdy, yet elegant aqueduct of iron, brick and stone construction carries the canal over Watling Street, a route initially forged by ancient Britons between the channel ports and the north-west, which subsequently became one of the most important Roman roads. When road numbering was introduced after the First World War it was designated the A5, linking London with Holyhead.

As a tyro guidebook compiler in the 1980s, the gnarled author of this guide erroneously drew attention to the intriguing juxtaposition at this point of Telford's Birmingham & Liverpool Junction Canal with his Holyhead Road. Fortunately, for the sake of historical accuracy, the truth later dawned on him that Telford had driven his road through the Black Country, leaving the Watling Street at Weedon in Northamptonshire and rejoining it at Oakengates in Shropshire. We live and we learn!

From the perspective of the canal traveller - especially boaters - the crossing seems over in a flash. Best, perhaps, to pause, and take the steps leading down to road level to appreciate the structure more fully (though do beware the traffic, hurtling by at speeds the canal builders, let alone the romans, could scarcely have envisaged). Eight impressive cylindrical pillars - turrets, almost - frame substantial curved retaining walls which support the iron trough that spans the road, bearing Telford's name and dated 1832. It's long overdue a fresh coat of paint, though one supposes that would entail closing the A5, perish the thought!

Until the mid-1950s, the Aqueduct Inn stood at Stretton Wharf, its gable ends signwritten to the effect that 'teas are provided and parties catered for'. Vivian Bird referred to it in passing when journeying northwards in 1953 to load oil at Ellesmere Port with the Thomas Clayton pair, *Towy* and *Kubina*, as described in *By Lock and Pound*, an eminently readable account of The Shroppie being used as a working waterway.

Brewood   Map 2

Probably because it is so close to the county boundary, Brewood feels more like Shropshire; there being a 'west country' richness about it which comes as a surprise considering its proximity to Wolverhampton. Furthermore, there is a timelessness about 'Brood' which seduces you into spending longer here than you might have planned. Winding lanes of gracious houses lead to the old market place, enhancing one corner of which is 'Speedwell Castle', a Gothic fantasy erected in the 18th century on the winnings of a racehorse named Speedwell. The tall-spired parish church is notable for its Giffard family tombs. In the south-east side of the churchyard a stone backed by the carved image of a narrow boat pair commemorates Mike Webb, whilst elsewhere lies the grave of Hugh Rose, a Scots engineer who came here to build the canal. A plaque in the Market Place recalls that the engineering contractor, Thomas Andrew Walker, was born in Brewood in 1828. Among his achievements were the Manchester Ship Canal, Severn Tunnel and London's District Line. The Roman Catholic church, by Bridge 14, is the work of no less a Victorian architect than A. W. N. Pugin.

Eating & Drinking

BRIDGE INN - Bridge 14. Tel: 01902 903966. Former boatmans' pub. Marston's & guest ales. Home cooked food. Open from noon. Useful laundry. ST19 9BD
THE CURRY INN - Church Street. Tel: 01902 850989. Eat in or take-away Indian. Opens 5.30pm. ST19 9BT
LAZY DAYS - Stafford Street. Tel: 01902 850038. Pleasant little cafe open Tue-Sat 9am-3pm, Sun 10am-2pm. ST19 9DX
THE OAKLEY ARMS - Kiddemore Green Road (1 mile west of Bridge 14). Tel: 01902 859800. Brunning & Price pub/restaurant housed in a former country

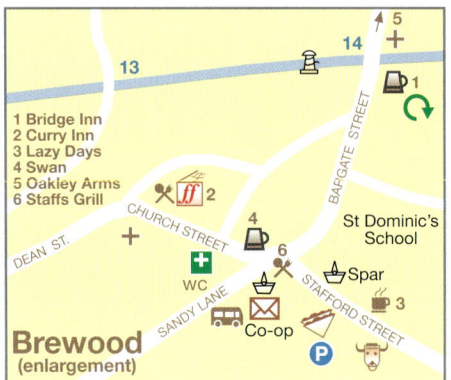

club whose owner's twin daughters both married members of the rock group Deep Purple. Food served throughout from noon daily. ST19 9BQ
STAFFORDSHIRE GRILL - Market Place. Tel: 01902 850123. Country pub/steak house. Rooms. ST19 9BS
SWAN - Market Place. Tel: 01902 850330. Traditional village local open from 11.45am daily. ST19 9BS

Shopping

Spar (with cash machine) and Co-op (inc post office). Try the Village Bakery (Tel: 01902 850196) for cakes and filled baps. Butchers W. Maiden & Son (Tel: 01902 850346) are easily missed at the far end of Stafford Street. Established in 1946, you can see pies being made on the premises and take away that Black Country delicacy, 'gray paes' or Staffordshire oatcakes.

Things to Do

CHILLINGTON HALL - about a mile and a half west of Bridge 10. Tel: 01902 850236. Guided tours on selected dates. Holiday Lets. WV8 1RE
BOSCOBEL HOUSE/WHITE LADIES PRIORY - English Heritage properties well worth a detour approximately three miles west of Brewood.

Connections

BUSES - Select services 877/878 trundle back and forth between the market place and Wolverhampton at roughly hourly intervals Mon-Sat, with some services continuing via Wheaton Aston to Stafford.
TAXIS - Codsall & Perton Cars. Tel: 01902 844944.

Wheaton Aston   Map 3

Twinned with the sizeable town of Wheaton, Illinois, Wheaton Aston was once a small farming community but is now a somnolent suburban enclave. St Mary's little Victorian church is distinguished with some glass by Charles Eamer Kempe, a prolific manufacturer of stained glass, inspired by William Morris and trained by George Frederick Bodley.

Eating & Drinking

THE HARTLEY - Long Street (Bridge 19). Tel: 01785 840232. Rebranded canalside pub with a snazzy canal-inspired colophon. Food served lunchtimes daily, evenings (from 5.30pm) Wed-Sat, plus breakfast on Sats 9-11am. Good choice of regional ales. ST19 9NF
COACH & HORSES - High Street. Tel: 01785 841048. Village local. ST19 9NP

Shopping

A Premier convenience store, with post office counter, is just three or four minutes away from the canal and opens 6am-9pm daily. Deeper into the village there's a small pharmacy and the Church Stores Spar which does a nice line in hot snacks too. Turner's quaint canalside garage stocks Calor gas, diesel and boating accessories. Free range eggs from Bridge Farm close to Bridge 19.

Connections

BUSES - Select services 877/878 run approx half a dozen times Mon-Sat, to/from Wolverhampton (via Brewood) and Stafford.

3 SHROPSHIRE UNION CANAL Wheaton Aston 4mls/11k/1½hrs

NOTHING epitomises rural England quite so much as the ripe smell of muck-spreading, and there is plenty of opportunity to savour this fragrant bouquet as the canal traverses a landscape almost entirely given over to agriculture. Wheaton Aston Lock is of a solitary disposition, the only one in twenty-five miles of canal; a telling measure of Telford's advanced engineering techniques. As originally built, the locks on the B&LJ were equipped with mitred pairs of gates at both ends of each chamber. Much extended, one of Telford's trademark tollhouses lurks behind a high hedge alongside the lock.

Dated 1956, a Francis Frith postcard of the canal at Wheaton Aston shows GPO telegraph poles marching purposefully along the towpath - as indeed they once did throughout the course of the Birmingham & Liverpool Junction - and occasionally one comes upon a truncated pole in the undergrowth.

The canal penetrates the deciduous heart of Lapley Wood, and there's another typically bosky Shroppie cutting by Little Onn, but elsewhere the embankments offer wide views eastwards towards Cannock Chase. How astonishingly remote and unpeopled the landscape seems. The West Midlands conurbation is less than a dozen miles to the south, yet moor for the night between Wheaton Aston and Little Onn, and you'll have only the occasional eerie hoot of a hunting owl, or the distant silent wash of headlights on a country lane, for company. Something of this sense of isolation must explain the survival of Mottey Meadows, alluvial flood meadowlands, unploughed for centuries, whose name apparently derives from the French word for peat - *motteux*.

Intriguingly, old maps depict the existence of a gunpowder magazine at the point where the canal bears due north beyond Bridge 20. One of the canal's lengthy embankments carries it across a sequence of culverts which provide access between neighbouring fields. It also spans a brook which flows eastwards into the River Penk, registering the fact that this is the watershed between the Trent and the Severn. The ghost of a Roman Road bisects the canal at the southern end of Rye Hill Cutting.

Abandoned wartime aerodromes inevitably have their ghosts, and in decay accumulate a patina of lore and legend, hard to equate with the often mundane use to which they were put after closure. Wheaton Aston was opened in 1941 and became one of the RAF's largest training units. After the war it became a resettlement site for refugees. Many found work in the Cannock and North Staffordshire coalfields, or in the latter's pottery industry. The camp closed in 1965 and subsequently became a pig farm. Stroll westwards along the lane from Bridge 24 and you'll find poignant remnants of both the camp and the airfield; not least an old control tower.

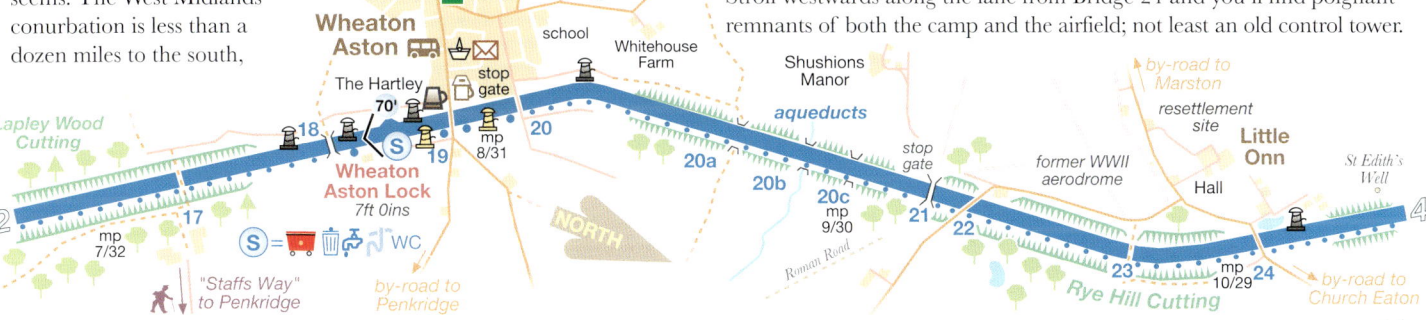

11

4 SHROPSHIRE UNION CANAL Gnosall 4½ mls/0lks/2hrs

PERSISTING in its self-absorbed hike across the empty landscapes of west Staffordshire, The Shroppie even attempts to shun the little town of Gnosall, the name of which recalls to mind that old comic song by Flanders & Swann about The Gnu. In this case, you don't say Ger-no-sall, you say No-zull, or Knows-all.

Near High Onn, the buildings of two wharves remain intact. One - now converted into a most desirable home - belonged to Cadbury's, the other to a local landowner, suggesting that there was once a degree of agricultural traffic on the canal. Logs, kindling and coal are on sale at the latter and winding permitted courtesy of the owner.

Bridge 26 is of the 'turnover' type, where the towpath changes sides, uniquely, on this occasion, bearing a public road as well. Bridge 31 is equally unusual in that it carries two farm tracks separated by a central stone wall. Deep shadowy sandstone cuttings, spanned - like leaping squirrels - by lichened red or grey stone bridges of simple balance and unaffected dignity, lead to the eighty-one unlined yards of Cowley Tunnel (No.33); the only one on the Shropshire Union. Cuttings such as this are apt to play aural and olfactory tricks. The blended aromas of bacon and diesel hang enticingly in the air and voices carry further than you'd think: so be inclined to temper your remarks concerning the odd looking couple on that boat you just passed.

Gnosall's canal environment is zealously cared for by its Parish Council. There are several visitor moorings of 48 hour duration, plus a generous 5 days beyond Bridge 35A. A small holding, inhabited by goats and ducks and chickens (kept in order by a noisy cockerel), adds bucolically to the scene.

Bridge 35A - curiously rectangular and reminiscent of the one at Welton on the Leicester Section of the GUC - used to carry a railway over the canal, but now forms the course of the Stafford & Newport Greenway, part of The Way For The Millennium, a forty mile long distance footpath connecting two extremities of Staffordshire, Newport to the west and Burton-on-Trent to the east. Historically, the railway was unusual in that it was actually built by the Shropshire Union Canal Company, apparently hedging their bets on the transport mode of the future. When, in 1847, they leased themselves to the London & North Western Railway, few shareholders would have backed the canal to outlast the railway. Now it forms a nice, traffic-free route for a jog before or after boating. In his detailed history of the line, *The Shropshire Union Railway*, Bob Yate alludes to Gnosall's timber built station

'Passengers No More'
1: Gnosall - closed 7.9.64

buildings, likening them to a barn: 'the platforms boasted some of the finest station gardens in the country for many years'. The last Station Master, Stanley Griffiths, was only twenty-one when Beeching and Marples conspired to close the line on 7th September 1964

A couple of miles west of the canal at Bridge 37 lies Aqualate Mere which, at about a mile long, is the most extensive natural lake in the region. For its size it is remarkably shallow, having been scoured by retreating glaciers, and is notable in geological circles for its rare Esker deposits. Bitterns are regular visitors to its extensive reedbeds. Footpaths and bridleways provide access to the site which is managed as a National Nature Reserve by Natural England.

On a clear day the embankments north of Gnosall reveal that famous Shropshire landmark, The Wrekin, 15 miles to the south-west; a slumbering hunchback of a summit, 1335ft high. A. E. Housman celebrated it in *A Shropshire Lad* - 'his forest fleece the Wrekin heaves' - and Salopians raise their glasses in a toast to: "All friends around the Wrekin".

Church Eaton (Map 4)
Eating & Drinking
ROYAL OAK - High Street (approx 15 mins walk east of Bridge 25). Tel: 01785 823078. Community-owned pub open from 5pm weekdays; 3pm Saturday and noon Sunday. Wye Valley beers, no food. ST20 0AJ

Gnosall Map 4
Gnosall Heath thrived with the coming of the canal and the railway not long afterwards, Gnosall stood back and watched with alarm, the onset of Progress. Two pubs slaked the thirst of passing boatmen, a steam powered flour mill, a saw mill, and a smithy took advantage of the new transport mode, whilst an Ebenezer Chapel kept a sense of proportion amidst all the excitement. Nowadays the pubs pander to pleasure boaters and passing motorists and the flour mill and chapel have become private residences. Half a mile east of the canal, Gnosall slumbers on its hilltop, the substantial parish church of St Lawrence (clerestoried nave and Norman pillars) being its most notable (though invariably locked) landmark.

Eating & Drinking
THE BOAT - Wharf Road (Bridge 34). Tel: 01785 822208. Marston's/Banks's pub with curved wall abutting the bridge. Opens noon daily. Meals served lunchtimes and evenings (from 5.30pm) Tue-Sat. and from noon until 4pm on Sundays. ST20 0DA
THE NAVIGATION - Newport Road (Bridge 35). Tel: 01785 824562. Cosy pub open from noon daily. Food served weekdays lunchtime and evenings (from 5pm), throughout at weekends. ST20 0BN

Three more pubs to chose from in the village. Fish & chips on A518 open daily (except Sundays), both sessions. Tel: 01785 822806. No less than three take-aways: Bengal Spice (Tel: 01785 823248); Gnosall Kitchen (Tel: 01785 823388); and Jia Jin Chinese/English (Tel: 01785 824388).

Shopping
Convenience store (with cash point) by Bridge 34. Another convenience store on way into Gnosall and Co-op in village itself. Gnosall Laundry Services (Tel: 0794 300 6222) provide handy launderette services, plus ironing and dry cleaning, close to Bridge 34.

Connections
BUSES - Arriva service 5 half-hourly (hourly Sun) to/from Stafford and Telford.

Norbury Junction Map 5
Just as much a magnet for motorists as boaters. The tall boiler room chimney; a bell on the roof of the workshop, rung at the commencement of each working day; three pairs of staff cottages; and the Section Inspector's villa, *Ferndale*, retain much of the magic of Norbury Junction's heritage. BIFoR, the Birmingham Institute of Forest Research has a facility in nearby Shelmore Wood studying the effect of carbon dioxide emissions on woodland. Sworn adversaries, Pevsner and Thorold nevertheless share an enthusiasm for St Peter's, Norbury, half a mile to the north-west, notably the effigy of a cross-legged knight.

Eating & Drinking
OLD WHARF TEA ROOMS - canalside Bridge 38. All-day, all year licensed cafe; sizeable portions of homely cooking. Tel: 01785 284292. B&B and s/c accommodation also available. ST20 0PN
JUNCTION INN - canalside Bridge 38. Tel: 01785 284288. Opens noon. Food lunch and evenings (from 5.30pm) Mon-Fri, and from noon Sat & Sun. ST20 0PN

Shopping
Excellent boatyard shop: provisions, off-licence, gifts, chandlery and a wide choice of canal books.

High Offley Map 5
ANCHOR INN - canalside Bridge 42. Tel: 01785 284569. Famously unspoilt *Good Beer Guide* listed boatman's pub which has been in the same family for generations. Devizes-brewed Wadworth 6X from the jug. Catering is restricted to sandwiches, but what delightfully innocent and simple sandwiches they are. Real pub, real ale, *real* treasure! ST20 0NB.

13

5 SHROPSHIRE UNION CANAL Norbury Junction 4mls/0lks/1½hrs

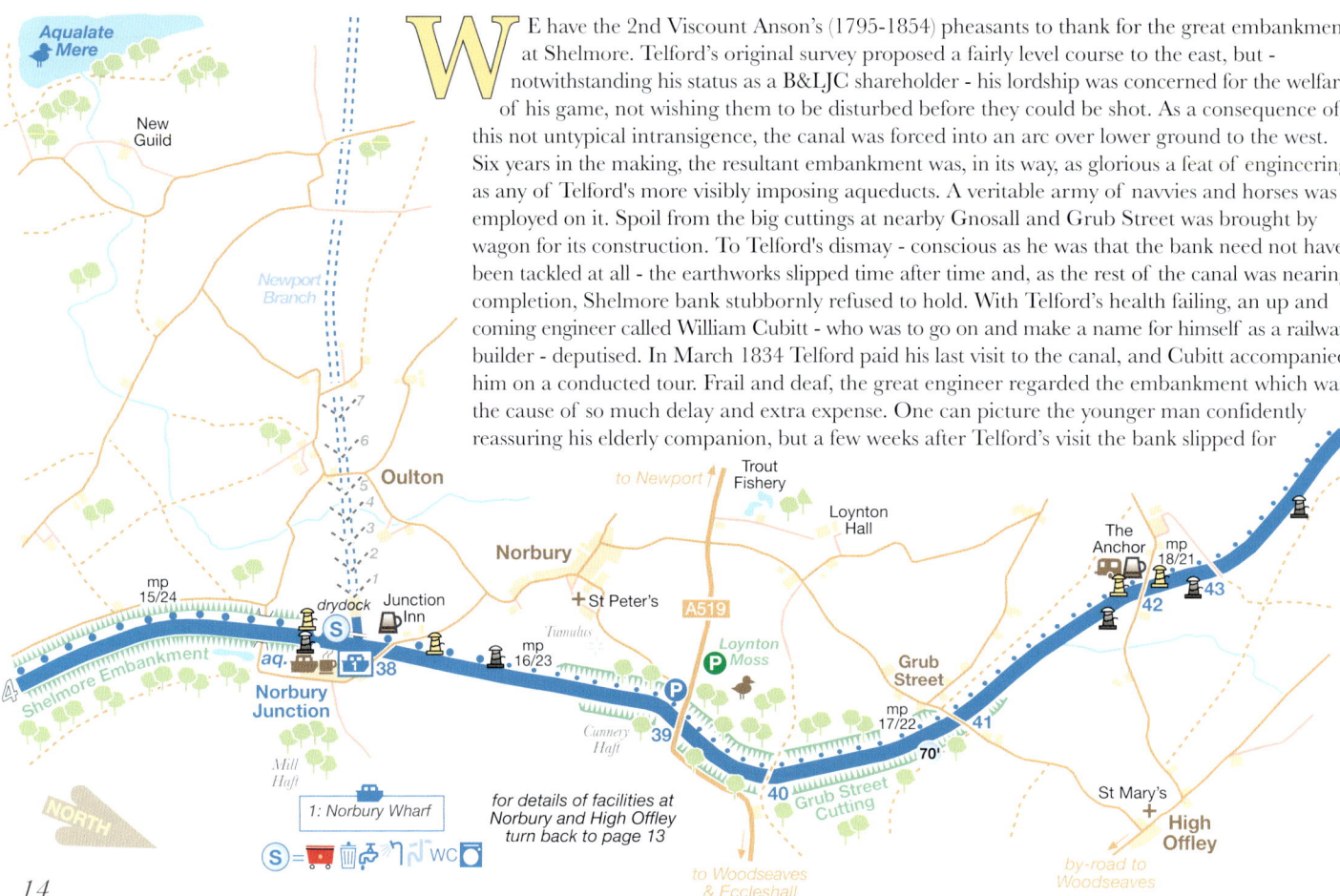

We have the 2nd Viscount Anson's (1795-1854) pheasants to thank for the great embankment at Shelmore. Telford's original survey proposed a fairly level course to the east, but - notwithstanding his status as a B&LJC shareholder - his lordship was concerned for the welfare of his game, not wishing them to be disturbed before they could be shot. As a consequence of this not untypical intransigence, the canal was forced into an arc over lower ground to the west. Six years in the making, the resultant embankment was, in its way, as glorious a feat of engineering as any of Telford's more visibly imposing aqueducts. A veritable army of navvies and horses was employed on it. Spoil from the big cuttings at nearby Gnosall and Grub Street was brought by wagon for its construction. To Telford's dismay - conscious as he was that the bank need not have been tackled at all - the earthworks slipped time after time and, as the rest of the canal was nearing completion, Shelmore bank stubbornly refused to hold. With Telford's health failing, an up and coming engineer called William Cubitt - who was to go on and make a name for himself as a railway builder - deputised. In March 1834 Telford paid his last visit to the canal, and Cubitt accompanied him on a conducted tour. Frail and deaf, the great engineer regarded the embankment which was the cause of so much delay and extra expense. One can picture the younger man confidently reassuring his elderly companion, but a few weeks after Telford's visit the bank slipped for the umpteenth time, and by the time Telford died, on 2nd September, his last canal remained uncompleted. Not until the following January was Shelmore Bank considered solid enough for the canal to be put in water and for the first boat to gingerly proceed across. Tall trees mask the immensity of the embankment nowadays, curtailing what would otherwise be panoramic views.

Sadly - for all abandoned routes tug at the heartstrings of keen canal travellers - Norbury is no longer a junction, though the name lives on, and a roving bridge spanning an arm which leads to a drydock at least sustains the illusion of another canal heading off into the unknown. The Newport Branch was abandoned by the LMS Railway in 1944, yet exploration of the country roads west of the canal will reveal overbridges and the poignant remains of lock chambers. John and Sally Seymour walked down it one Sunday morning in 1963 as described in *Voyage into England*.

Formed in 2000, the Shrewsbury and Newport Canals Trust aim to 'protect, conserve and improve' the route and its branches with the ultimate goal of restoring a continuous navigable waterway linking Norbury Junction with Shrewsbury. Several short sections of the canal remain in water at Newport, some five miles to the south-west of Norbury, and the Trust are busily restoring Wappenshall Wharf on the outskirts of Telford.

Even without a proper junction to its name, Norbury remains a busy

Norbury Junction

canal location, popular with day-trippers of all persuasions. British Waterways had a Section Office and maintenance yard here providing employment for thirty men engaged in the day to day upkeep of the canal. Nowadays, much of the Canal & River Trust's maintenance is undertaken by contractors; to the detriment, many argue, of the canal's upkeep.

Leaving Norbury astern, lines of moored boats usher the canal into a cutting. Staffordshire's Grub Street is not synonymous with the lower echelons of the literary trade. No, this Grub Street is known in canal circles as the location of another of the Shroppie's trademark cuttings. For over a mile the canal is wrapped in a thick coat of vegetation, again, like Shelmore, hiding the sheer size of the eighty foot deep cutting, whose most unusual feature is the double-arched bridge which carries the A519 across the canal. The tiny telegraph pole is a survivor from the line which once marched beside the Shroppie. A black, monkey-like creature is reputed to have haunted Bridge 39 ever since a boatman was killed here in the 19th century. Working boatmen referred to haunted places as 'frightenings'.

Loynton Moss is administered by the Staffordshire Wildlife Trust. Its entrance lies a short distance west of Bridge 39, and whilst the A519 can be busy, there's a broad enough verge on which to shelter from the most aggressive of speed-merchants. The moss is essentially a wetland landscape supporting a wide range of species, though visitors are warned that mosquitos are prevalent throughout the summer months.

6 SHROPSHIRE UNION CANAL Shebdon & Knighton 4mls/0lks/1½ hrs

STAFFORDSHIRE morphs into Shropshire as the canal continues to traverse an uncluttered countryside almost entirely given over to agriculture. It can come as a surprise to find so remote a landscape in the 'crowded' middle of England. For all our obsession with building on greenfield sites, there are still empty pockets of England to be encountered by happenstance.

To the west of Shebdon Wharf, Batchacre Hall was home to - in the words of Henry Thorold - the 'eccentric bachelor politician' Richard Whitworth (1734-1811), an early advocate of canals. Such was his enthusiasm for all things watery, he constructed a lake in the grounds on which historic naval battles were re-enacted, together with a trial length of canal. Batchacre Hall is now a farmhouse and livery stable.

Blithely we pleasure boaters sail across embankments and through cuttings with no more thought for their construction than if we were driving down the M6. But imagine the impact of Telford's brash new canal on the surrounding early nineteenth century landscape. Put yourself in the position of the occupant of Batchacre Park. Up until 1830 dawn rose across the open pasturelands throwing light through his east-facing windows. A year later his view of the rising sun was cut off forever by an embankment twice the height of the farmhouse. No wonder the landowners of this rural corner of Staffordshire had their misgivings, and the canal company paid dearly in compensation for the land they acquired. A series of leaks in the vicinity of Shebdon brought about closure of the canal in 2009, but soil-blending techniques have consolidated the bank for the foreseeable future. West of the canal, there are good views of The Wrekin, with the Clee and Breidden hills prominent on the far horizon.

Cadbury, the chocolate manufacturers, opened a factory at Knighton in 1911 to process milk collected from the dairy farming hinterland of the Shropshire Union Canal. Canal transport was used exclusively to bring countless churns gathered from numerous wharves along the canal; from simple wooden stages at the foot of fields, to the sophistication of Cadbury's own milk concentration depot at High Onn. Sugar and coal were other commodities transported by boat to Knighton. The last boatman to trade to Knighton was Charlie Atkins senior; eponymously nicknamed 'Chocolate Charlie'. He carried the final cargo from Knighton to Bournville in 1961. Sadly, the works, latterly manufacturing unbranded powdered drinks, was due to shut down in 2024, and the survival of its iconic canalside buildings must be in doubt.

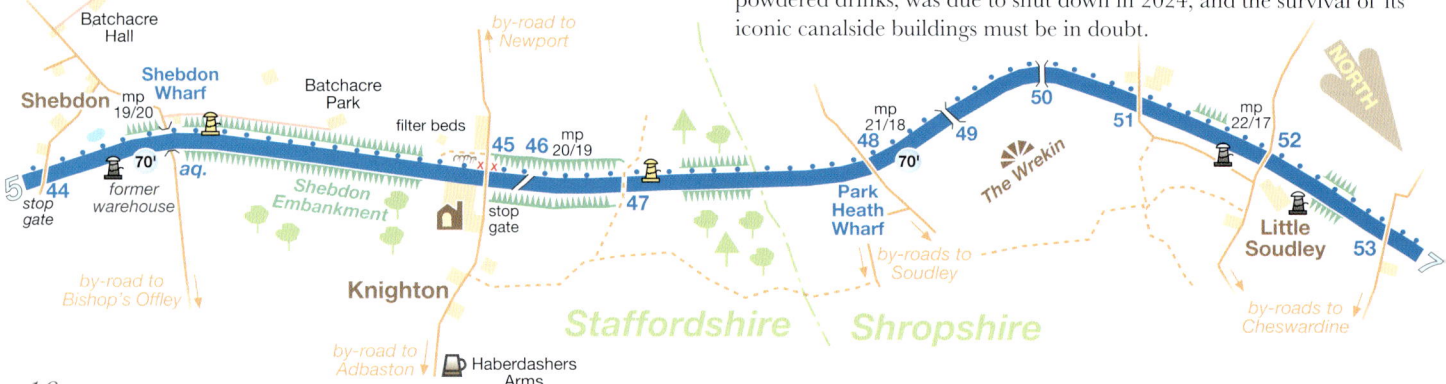

7 SHROPSHIRE UNION CANAL Goldstone & Tyrley 4mls/5lks/2hrs

THE Shroppie flirts with the county boundary as Staffordshire gives Shropshire a subtle dig in the ribs. The landscape, however, is impervious to the machinations of local government, remaining aloof and typically inscrutable: a tall, dark, silent canal, this Shropshire Union; much given, punningly, to 'brooding'.

Woodseaves is another prodigious cutting: almost a hundred feet deep in places. These cuttings proved just as troublesome to Telford and his contractors as the embankments. In its raw, newly completed state, it must have corresponded to the canal at Corinth. Brittle at best, frequent rock falls were a fact of life, and indeed still are, as occasional lumps of fragmented rock imply. The towpath has been impassable for some years. Whilst boaters occasionally feel their craft encountering submerged debris as well. Speed, in any case, is restricted to 2mph. Too fast, one imagines, for any botanists in your party, anxious to identify the huge variety of species on view. A feature of Woodseaves is its pair of high bridges, spanning the canal-like portals to the mysterious chasms of another world.

Tyrley (pronounced 'Turley') Wharf was a point of discharge and collection for the local estate at Peatswood; Cadburys also used to collect milk from here and take it by boat to their works at Knighton. The buildings date from 1841 and were erected in a graceful Tudor style by the local landowner. Nowadays, its commercial significance a thing of the dim and distant past, it would be difficult to imagine a more picturesque location. Why, even the former chapel is now used for the manufacture of rocking horses!

A flight of five locks - the last to be faced southbound for seventeen miles - carry the canal down into, or up out of, Market Drayton. The lower chambers are located in a shadowy sandstone cutting across which branches intertwine to form a tunnel of trees. Chiaroscuro lighting effects challenge photographers. Damp, and rarely touched by sunlight, all manner of mosses and ferns flourish in this conducive environment. Crepuscular bats leave their tree bole roosts to hunt for insects, acrobatically twisting and turning over the luminous pounds between the locks. Bridge 61 is known as Tyrley Castle in deference to an 11th century fortification recalled now solely by the name of a farm to the west. Berrisford Aqueduct carries the canal over a by-road on the approach to Market Drayton. We can recommend descending the steps from its southern end to appreciate the imposing nature of this sandstone structure from below.

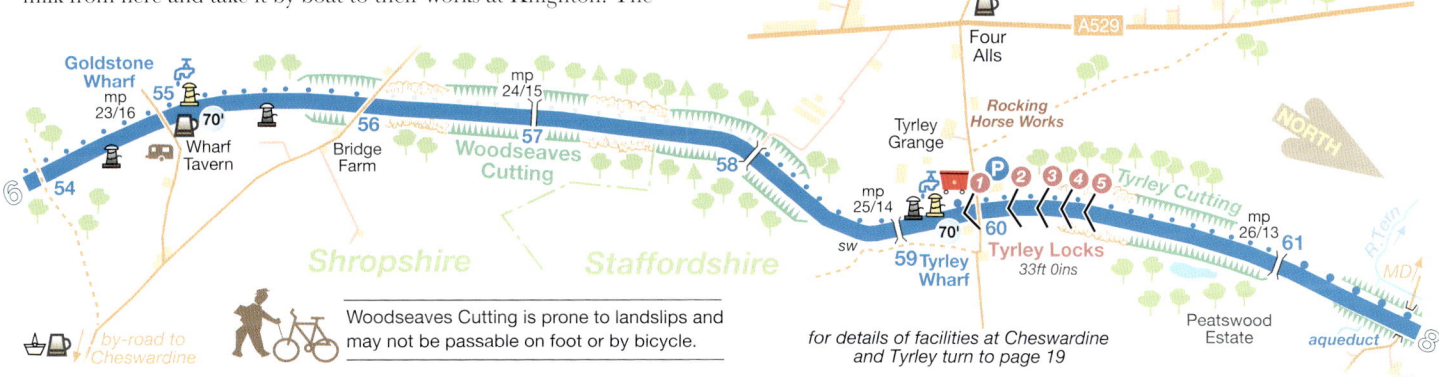

Woodseaves Cutting is prone to landslips and may not be passable on foot or by bicycle.

for details of facilities at Cheswardine and Tyrley turn to page 19

17

8 SHROPSHIRE UNION CANAL Drayton & Adderley 4mls/5lks/2hrs

MARKET DRAYTON was the largest, in fact the *only*, town encountered by the old Birmingham & Liverpool Junction Canal on its route from Autherley to Nantwich. Naturally, a sizeable wharf was provided for dealing with local cargoes; though the canal's monopoly on local trade lasted only thirty years before the railway reached the town. It is sometimes difficult, in these days of the all too ubiquitous HGV, to appreciate the importance of the canal wharf and the railway goods yard to the past prosperity of small towns like 'Drayton. They must have been the hub of local life, few businesses would have been able to carry out their trade without regular recourse to the wharfinger and the stationmaster. From the opening of the canal until the First World War no commodity, apart from local agricultural produce, could have arrived at Market Drayton, or been dispatched, without the involvement of these important gentlemen. One of the wharf's earliest tenants was William Hazeldine, the ironmaster affectionately nicknamed 'Merlin' by Telford.

The wharf remains a busy place, with boating facilities on the towpath side and a basin opposite. Talbot Wharf belongs to the Machin family who for many years ran their Holidays Afloat hire fleet from here. Some of the wharf's buildings are rather dilapidated, but at the northern end of the basin the attractive, if oddly shaped, Betton Mill is now occupied by offices and apartments. When first erected in 1906 it was used to store cheese.

The canal widens north of Bridge 63, being overlooked, on the offside, by a housing development with private moorings. This was the site of Ladyline, one of the leading lights of the 1960/70s boom in canal leisure boating.

North of 'Drayton the canal makes a quick getaway. Palethorpes factory churns out 55 million sausage rolls per annum. Yet to materialise, plans were announced in 2020 for a new marina and housing development at Victoria Wharf.

The five locks of the Adderley flight limber you up for (or warm you down after) the fifteen of Audlem. In 1980 they ran to a resident lock-keeper - who went by the delightfully bucolic name of Frank Butter - and were so beautifully maintained and manicured that they won first prize in the National Lock & Bridge Competition. A privet hedge beside the third lock down indicates the site of a demolished lock-keeper's cottage, whilst a bench by Lock 4 commemorates canal stalwart Ike Argent.

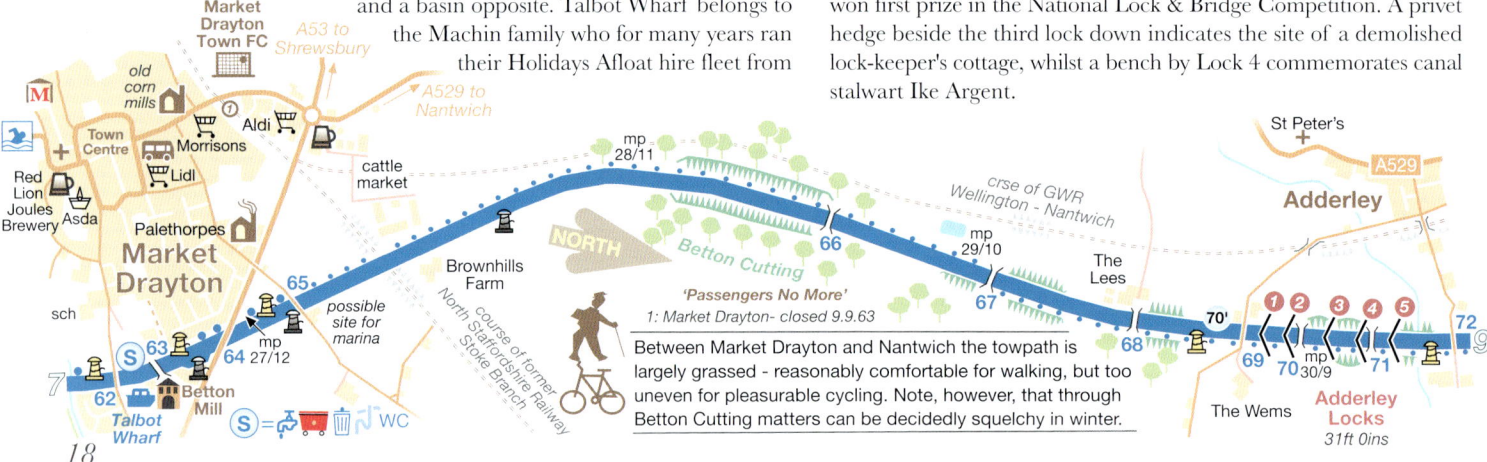

18

Cheswardine (Map 7)

Cheswardine lies a country mile to the east - say 25 minutes on foot - of the canal and can be accessed from bridges 52-55. High Street ascends to the parish church of St Swithin's much rebuilt by the Gothic Revival architect John Loughborough Pearson, best known for Truro Cathedral. 'Stately ... but not specially distinguished' was Pevsner's put down regarding the former. Now a care home, neo-Elizabethan Cheswardine Hall was erected in 1875 for the Newcastle-under-Lyme MP, Charles Donaldson-Hudson.

Eating & Drinking
WHARF TAVERN - Goldstone Wharf (Bridge 55). Tel: 01630 661226. A popular port of call throughout the boating season for good pub grub. Caravan and camp site, self-catering and spacious garden. TF9 2LP. *There are two pubs in the centre of the village: Fox & Hounds (Tel: 01630 661244) and Red Lion (Tel: 01630 661234).*

Shopping
A community shop can be found on Podmore Road - ask locally for directions. It's open from 8.30 to 11am daily, plus 2-4pm on Fridays.

Tyrley Map 7
Eating & Drinking
THE FOUR ALLS - Woodseaves (10 minutes walk west of Tyrley Wharf). Tel: 01630 652995. Food served Mon-Fri 12-3pm and 5-8.30pm; Sat 12-8.30pm and Sun 12-5pm. TF9 2AG.
The Rocking Horse Works can be contacted on 01630 653194.

Market Drayton Map 8

We've long had a soft spot for Market Drayton, its narrow thoroughfares, pretty buttercross, and - Pearsons being Pearsons - the old corn mills opposite Morrisons at the far end of Cheshire Street. In more touristy climes 'Drayton would undoubtedly be better known. But this is sleepy Shropshire, and the town only really comes to life on a Wednesday when the ancient market is in full swing and country folk gather to seek out a bargain and a gossip. Though perhaps not quite as bucolic as of yore, this remains the town's real strength, along with its plethora of half-timbered houses which mostly date from the aftermath of a fire that swept through the place in 1651. Drayton's most famous son was Robert Clive, best remembered here for scaling the sturdy tower of St Mary's and for blackmailing local shopkeepers - ideal escapades in preparation for a career in diplomacy and military leadership. He established British rule in the Sub Continent and became known as 'Clive of India'. A pair of large food factories - Palethorpes and Muller - provide the main employment, whilst Billingtons make gingerbread, a delicacy long associated with the town, in a business park on the northern outskirts.

Eating & Drinking
CLIVE & COFFYNE - Shropshire Street. Tel: 01630 657523. *Good Beer Guide* listed pub featuring Hobsons and Hancocks ales. Coffynes are mutton pies! TF9 3BY
JONES'S - High Street. Tel: 01630 652042. Comfortbale family run coffee shop open 9am to 4pm ex Sun. the owners also run a vineyard at Colehurst, a couple of miles SW of Market Drayton. TF9 1QB
FOODSHION - Cheshire Street. Tel: 01630 658382. Chinese, Asian & Thai cuisine to eat in or take-away from 4.30pm daily ex Tue. TF9 1PD
NOMAD - High Street. Tel: 0730 092 1263. Informal cafe bar with Mediterranean feel. Open Wed-Sat from noon. TF9 1QB
RED LION - Great Hales Street. Tel: 01630 652602. Joule's Brewery was originally in Stone (see Map 20) but closed in 1974. The name, happily, was revived in 2010 and their beers are brewed here in Drayton using local mineral water. *GBG* listed, the Red Lion is the 'brewery tap' and a fine establishment it is too, atmospherically wood-panelled. Opens 11am, food served Mon-Sat 12-3pm and 5-9pm. Roasts on Sunday 12-5pm. Complimentary sausage rolls on Fridays ... 'until they're gone'! TF9 1JP

Shopping
Drayton Deli is a good food shop beside the handsome Buttercross - Pearsons can vouch for their pasties - whilst The Fields Kitchen on Church Street is an alternative source of local produce. Both are outlets for Billington's gingerbread; best savoured with port, apparently. The Post Office is on High Street adjoining the former Corbet Arms Hotel where Thomas Telford stayed when overseeing construction of the Birmingham & Liverpool Junction Canal. See map for supermarkets.

Things to Do
FESTIVAL DRAYTON CENTRE - Frogmore Road. Tel: 01630 654444. Community theatre/cinema, hub and coffee shop serving local produce. TF9 3AX
MUSEUM & RESOURCE CENTRE - Shropshire Street. Open Wed & Sat mornings from May to October. Admission free. Local history nostalgically displayed in an old shop. TF9 3DA

Connections
BUSES - Arriva service 64 operates approx bi-hourly Mon-Sat to/from Shrewsbury and Hanley (Stoke-on-Trent) via Newcastle-under-Lyme.
TAXIS - Drayton Cars. Tel: 01630 653200.

Adderley Map 8
Scattered village which once boasted a railway station. The isolated church largely dates from 1800 and is under the care of the Churches Conservation Trust. Lovely ironwork tracery on clear glass windows and a mounting block for equestrian worshippers.

9 SHROPSHIRE UNION CANAL Audlem 4mls/15lks/4hrs

'THOSE trademark 'Shroppie' grey and white balance beams could do with a lick of paint', we said out loud on the occasion of our most recent survey, but the Audlem flight remains a pleasure: whether you are working up or down it, or simply spectating. Thirty-one miles out from Autherley, northbound travellers encounter Cheshire for the first time. Then fifteen locks, snuggled in a brackeny cutting of larch and Scots pine, drop the canal the best part of a hundred feet. Needless to say, the flight can be busy, and at such times patience, courtesy and good humour have their rewards. To paraphrase some old advice: be nice to people when you're working up lock flights, because you might meet the same people coming down. One or two of the lock chambers have retained their keeper's cottages, others have lost them, though at Lock 8 you can still smell the scents of garden flowers. Back in the present day, cakes, pies, ice cream - and other morale-boosting edibles - are often available from Panda's Pantry at Lock 1.

The barrel-roofed building by Lock 10 was used by stonemasons, blacksmiths and carpenters engaged in maintenance. Towards the foot of the flight - known to old boatmen as the Audlem "Thick" - you pass Audlem Wharf, one of the prettiest ports of call on the Shropshire Union, with a former warehouse restored as a popular pub and the adjacent lofty Kingbur Mill converted into a superb gift shop. The mill was built during the First World War by H. Kingsley Burton, hence the name. It produced animal feeds; boats brought in raw materials and took away sacks of feed. Old photographs depict a covered gantry which spanned the roadway and jutted out over the canal to facilitate loading and unloading. The mill ceased working in the nineteen-sixties and was converted into a canal shop in the 'seventies by the late John Stothert, much of its internal fittings and machinery being atmospherically retained.

Shadowing the Shropshire Union - which belonged to the London & North Western Railway by the time the railway age was in full swing - the rival Great Western company's Wellington to Nantwich and Crewe route was a useful means of competition. The crane which adorns the wharf outside the Shroppie Fly pub belonged at the railway station before it was re-sited. Audlem station closed in 1963, but not before it had been immortalised by Flanders & Swann in their melancholy elegy to the Beeching axe, *Slow Train*. George Dow, the railway public relations officer, historian and early designer and advocate of diagrammatic maps, lived in Audlem for many years, his close friend Hamilton Ellis being a regular visitor. What a shame the latter wasn't cajoled into portraying the flight in one of his inimitable oil paintings, after

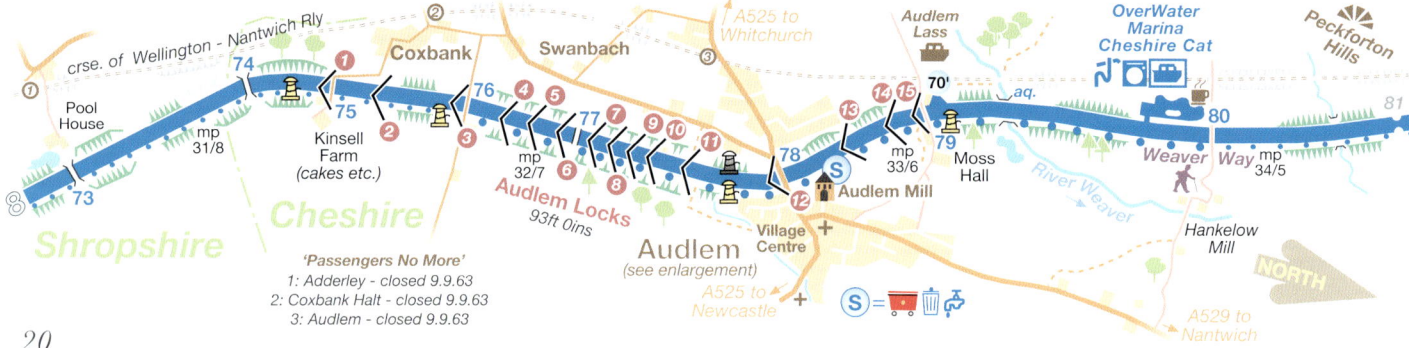

'Passengers No More'
1: Adderley - closed 9.9.63
2: Coxbank Halt - closed 9.9.63
3: Audlem - closed 9.9.63

all it was in railway ownership for a century. Beside the bottom lock community allotments are nurtured. Then, passing a well preserved stable block - where Jane Marshall runs Roses & Castle Workshops - the canal, wide with concrete banking but deceptively shallow, bounds across the strippling River Weaver on a high embankment.

One of the crazier notions of the Ministry of War Transport during the Second World War was to make the Weaver navigable by 100 ton barges to this point, beyond which a lift would carry them up to the level of the Shropshire Union. OverWater is one of the new breed of 'farmland' marinas which have proliferated on the canal system since the millennium. A waterbus service links the marina with Audlem on summer weekends. Bridge 80 retains its early British Waterways era blue and yellow number plate, immediately to the south, a drainage paddle is embossed 'SUC Ellesmere 1928'; minor artefacts of enduring value.

Audlem Map 9

Lovely old Audlem has grown in confidence and commerce in the forty odd years we've known it, and its annual Festival of Transport and Gathering of Historic Boats in July only serves to put it even more firmly on the map. Yet the village seems comfortable with its burgeoning popularity, and assimilates visitors without descending into self-conscious parody. Highlights include the ancient buttermarket, parish church, and two particularly handsome non-conformist chapels.

Eating & Drinking
AYAAN'S - Tel: 01270 812226. Shropshire Street. Open daily (ex Tue) from 5pm for take-away: kebabs, burgers, chickens. CW3 0AE
THE BRIDGE - canalside Bridge 78. Tel: 01270 812928. Marston's, food daily 12pm-8pm. Nice etched windows pertaining to Marston & Thompson ... though who remembers Thompson now? CW3 0DX
LITTLE TAPAS - Shropshire Street. Tel: 0799 978 1005. Wine bar open Thur-Sat from 5pm. CW3 0AE
LORD COMBERMERE - The Square. Tel: 01270 483098. Re-opened village centre pub. CW3 0AQ
No.11 - Cheshire Street. Tel: 01270 910835. Tea room open Tue-Sat 9.30am-4pm. CW3 0AH
PICCOLA - Cheshire Street. Tel: 01270 447559. Italian restaurant open Wed-Sat from 5pm. CW3 0AH
THE SHROPPIE FLY - canalside Lock 13. Tel: 01270 421396. Warehouse conversion with boat-shaped bar

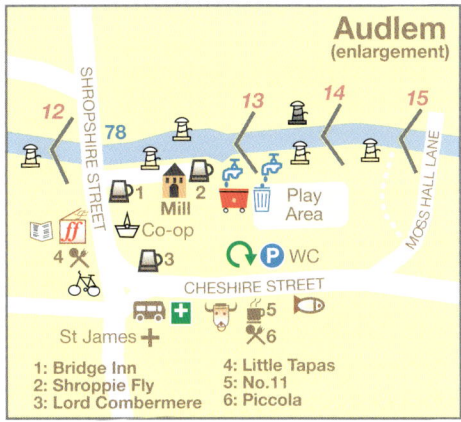

and outdoor canalside seating. Food served Mon-Fri 12-2.30pm and 5.30-8.30pm. At weekends breakfasts are provided between 9 and 11am and food thereafter from noon. CW3 0DX
VILLAGE CHIPPY - Cheshire Street. Fish & chips. Tel: 01270 811777. Open daily ex Sun. CW3 0AH

Shopping
It's amazing to find a village with so many outlets. Indeed, shopping here is a pleasure rather than a stressful chore. Oxtail & Trotter's butchery (Tel: 01270 811793) on Cheshire Street is excellent, but there's also a well-stocked Co-op (ATM) open daily 7am-10pm, a Boots pharmacy, and a bicycle shop - Tel: 01270 812503 - should you need running repairs. A mobile fish van calls on Thursday mornings. Laundry facilities and cafe at OverWater Marina by Bridge 80.

Things to Do
AUDLEM MILL CANAL SHOP - Tel: 01270 811059. Christine and Peter Silvester operate one of the best canal shops on the system and are congenial mines of local information to boot. As well as a wide range of gifts, crafts and needlework, the mill stocks an unrivalled range of canal books, and a growing list of self-published titles. Deservedly popular, is Peter's self-penned guide *Audlem Locks - A Walk Through History*. Events are held throughout the year. CW3 0DX
HACK GREEN SECRET NUCLEAR BUNKER - Hack Green, Map 10. Tel: 01270 629219. Open 10.00-5.00 daily during summer season - telephone for other times. Admission charge/annual pass. Eerily authentic, if chilling, visitor centre in its original macabre setting. Brings home the terrifying power of nuclear weapons and the government's state of readiness. Refreshments in a NAFFI canteen and souvenir shop. CW5 8AL

Connections
BUSES - D&G service 72 to/from Nantwich roughly half a dozen times per day Mon-Sat. The route is a circular one: outward from Nantwich via Wrenbury on the Llangollen Canal.

21

10 SHROPSHIRE UNION CANAL Hack Green 4mls/2lks/2hrs

GRUB Street, *Hack* Green: is the Shroppie scoring literary points? Itinerant canal writers apart, there are two isolated locks and the remnants of a stable at Hack Green, recalling the practice of frequent changing of horses on the 'fly' boats which travelled day and night with urgent, perishable cargoes, the sort of canal age equivalent of a lorry pull-in now.

This is the Cheshire Plain and dairy farming has long been a vital part of the area's economy - though for how much longer one might wonder, given the precarious state of agriculture in the 21st century. Making a profit from milk is notoriously difficult these days, no wonder farmers are being encouraged to replace cows with canal boats as demonstrated by a growing number of new marinas in the area.

When we first explored this canal in the early Eighties we were blissfully unaware of Hack Green's nuclear bunker, a Second World War radar station secretly designated to play a role as a Regional Government Headquarters in the event of a nuclear war. Deemed redundant at the end of the Cold War, it has somewhat bizarrely become a tourist attraction.

Adroitly changing the subject, let us recall how trade survived on this canal until the 1960s; which must be some sort of testimony to the viability of canal carrying. Perhaps in the final analysis attitudes rather than economics prevailed. One of the most celebrated traffics on the Shroppie in latter years was Thomas Clayton's oil run from Stanlow on the banks of the Mersey to Langley Green, near Oldbury in the Black Country. The contract commenced in 1924 and the Clayton boats, with their characteristic decked holds, and river names, were a mainstay of trade on the canal for thirty years. Even post-war, a thousand boat-loads per annum were being despatched from Stanlow, some remaining horse-drawn until the early Fifties. But, in common with other canals, the Shropshire Union lost its final freights to the motor lorry; then, for many, with the disappearance of its working boats, something died on the Shroppie, some intangible component of canal heritage that no amount of preservation, nor hectic holiday trade, can ever quite compensate for. On the outskirts of Nantwich the canal passes beneath the Crewe to Shrewsbury (and South Wales) railway line.

'Passengers No More'
1: Coole Pilate Halt - closed 9.9.63

Though unsurfaced for the majority of its length, the Shropshire Union towpath can be fairly comfortably walked, though footwear can quickly become wet and muddy, especially in cuttings during the winter months. Cyclists will find the going bumpy in places, and should at least plan for the possibility of punctures.

11 SHROPSHIRE UNION Nantwich, Hurleston & Barbridge 5mls/0lks/2hrs

THE character of the Shropshire Union Canal changes perceptibly at Nantwich: northwards lie the broad, winding waters of its earlier constituent, the Chester Canal, opened in 1779; southwards the direct and narrow Birmingham & Liverpool Junction Canal, upon which work began here in 1827, though five years elapsed before the embankment settled sufficiently for the canal to be opened. Northbound, it's easy to feel lost without the reassuringly regular appearance of those elegant mileposts which have accompanied you all the way from Autherley.

Long before the advent of the canals, Nantwich was reduced to ashes by the Great Fire of 1583 which lasted for almost three weeks. Four bears, thoughtfully released for their own safety, are said to have 'considerably hampered' attempts to douse the flames! Concerned for the area's salt industry, Queen Elizabeth donated a thousand pounds towards the town's rebuilding fund. Sixty years later Nantwich sided with the Parliamentarians during the Civil War, the only Cheshire town to do so. In 1644 its citizens were besieged by the Royalists for six weeks. An annual re-enactment celebrates their relief on the 25th January.

The broad embankment elevates the canal above the housing, back gardens and allotments which constitute the periphery of Nantwich. Ironically, these earthworks, together with a cast iron aqueduct over the Chester road, could have been avoided if the owners of Dorfold Hall had not objected to the passage of the canal across their land. A Sculpture Trail has been laid out beside the embankment's refurbished towpath, the main exhibit being in the form of a boat horse built out of reclaimed lock gates. Visitor moorings are provided along the length of the embankment, and they make for a pleasant overnight stay with easy access to the town centre, an enjoyable ten minutes stroll to the east.

The basin and former terminus of the Chester Canal, hints at the more expedient route to the south which Telford would have liked to have used. Nowadays it's pretty choc-a-bloc with boats,

for details of facilities at Nantwich and Barbridge turn to page 25

11A SHROPSHIRE UNION Bunbury & Beeston 4mls/5lks/2hrs

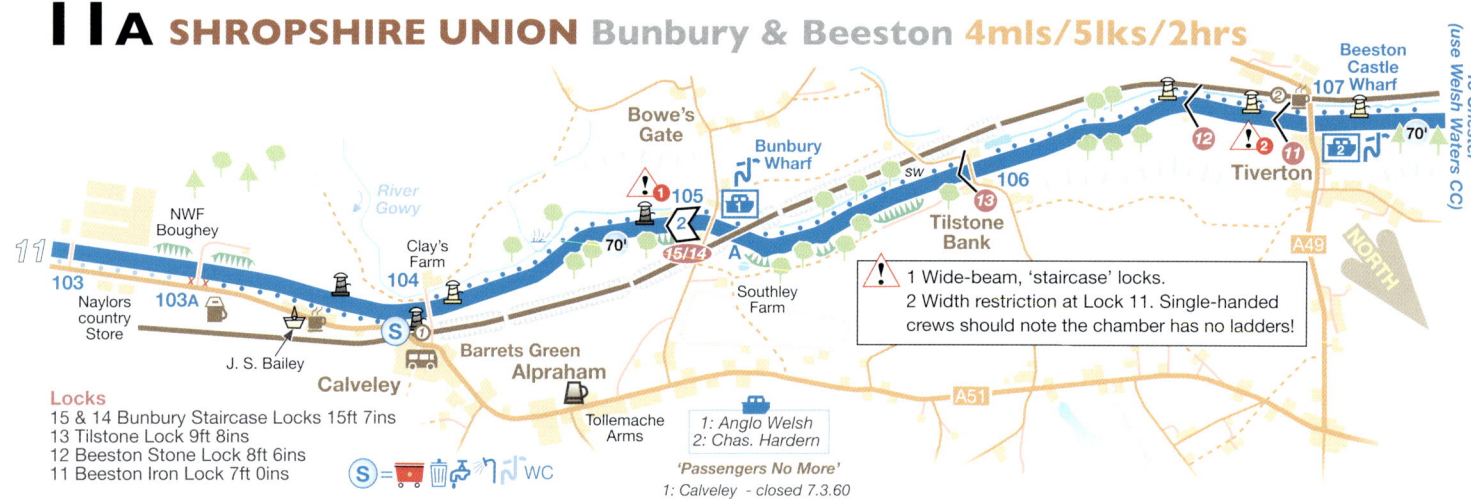

Locks
15 & 14 Bunbury Staircase Locks 15ft 7ins
13 Tilstone Lock 9ft 8ins
12 Beeston Stone Lock 8ft 6ins
11 Beeston Iron Lock 7ft 0ins

1 Wide-beam, 'staircase' locks.
2 Width restriction at Lock 11. Single-handed crews should note the chamber has no ladders!

1: Anglo Welsh
2: Chas. Hardern

'Passengers No More'
1: Calveley - closed 7.3.60
2: Beeston Castle & Tarporley - csd 18.4.66

but there's a certain pleasure to be had from manoeuvring in and out of its narrow confines to fill up with diesel: all a far cry from 1939 when Tom and Angela Rolt couldn't get *Cressy* into the basin because a bar of silt, built up by the passage of motor boats, prevented their entry. Adjoining the basin are the premises of the Nantwich & Border Counties Yachting Club, an organisation whose founder members were early advocates of the use of the canal system for leisure.

Between Nantwich and Hurleston Junction the former Chester Canal passes uneventfully through a landscape typical of the Cheshire Plain. Hurleston and Barbridge are the 'Clapham Junctions' of the inland waterways. Throughout the cruising season the section between them is often frenetic with boats converging and diverging to and from all points of the canal compass. Providentially the old Chester Canal was built to barge dimensions and there is usually plenty of room to manoeuvre. Bridge 98 used to carry the weight of milking herds bound for the neighbouring parlour. Now this has been converted into housing and the pastures given over to maize; a sobering reflection on the profit & loss of agriculture. Hurleston Junction, with its quartet of locks, is the starting point of the Llangollen Canal's serene journey into Wales. It's overlooked by a high-banked reservoir which receives its water supplies from the Llangollen Canal, a factor instrumental in the survival of the waterway back in 1944 when there were proposals to close it.

Barbridge Junction marks the beginning and end of the Middlewich Branch of the Shropshire Union Canal, and it is, along with Middlewich, Great Haywood and Autherley, a pivotal point for all Four Counties Ring travellers. Notwithstanding the A51's thundering traffic, Barbridge is a popular overnight mooring spot, and there's the interest of the junction itself, where once a transhipment shed spanned the main line.

NB: Map 11A (above) is included simply for the benefit of boaters journeying to/from the boatyards and hire bases at Bunbury and Beeston.

Nantwich
Map 11

North or south, there are few English towns of this size nicer than Nantwich. The octagonal tower of St Mary's church, glimpsed across freshly-built rooftops from the high canal embankment, tempts you to moor and get to know Nantwich better. Strolling into town - crossing the River Weaver in the process - the appeal of the town increases as the centre is reached. Welsh Row is a handsome thoroughfare: keep your eyes peeled for the Tollemache Almshouses, Cheshire Constabulary police houses, Primitive Methodist chapel and Town Well House (No.52). In medieval times Nantwich was the chief salt producing town in the county.

Eating & Drinking
AUSTINS - Hospital Street. Tel: 01270 625491. Consciously old fashioned coffee house which transcends kitsch by virtue of its range of comfort food including their very own bangers and mash, cottage pie, omelettes, cakes etc. CW5 5RL
BASMATI - Pillory Street. Tel: 01270 620600. Indian restaurant/take-away housed in railway station booking hall. Open from 5.30pm daily (ex Tue). CW5 5SS
BLACK LION - Welsh Row. Tel: 01270 628711. 17th century half-timbered pub on way into town. Ales from Cheshire brewer Weetwood. Meals served Fri-Sun lunchtimes and Thur-Sat evenings. CW5 5ED
CROWN HOTEL - High Street. Tel: 01270 625283. Teetering, Grade I listed, 16th century timber building providing comfortable accommodation together with a bar and grill open to non-residents. CW5 5AS
CAFE DE PARIS - Hospital Street. Tel: 01270 627562. Charming cafe under authentic French ownership, open from 9am to 4pm daily ex Sun. CW5 5RP
ODDFELLOWS - Welsh Row. Tel: 01270 623572. Marston's pub handy for the canal. CW5 5ET

WATERSIDE CAFE - Nantwich Basin. Tel: 01270 748283. Breakfasts, coffees, lunches and teas from 9am-3.30pm daily ex Mon & Tue. CW5 8LB
ROMAZZINO - High Street. Tel: 01270 619100. Italian restaurant open from noon daily. CW5 5AR
STREET - Welsh Row. Tel: 01270 625539. Open daily from noon for eat in or take-away burgers, burritos, noodles & curries: i.e. 'street food'. CW5 5ED

Shopping
Nantwich's shops are one of its strengths, and it is easy to spend more time - and consequently money - in them than you anticipated. Antique shops and boutiques abound, but it is the food sellers that are most satisfying: butchers like Clewlows (in our top five canal-connected purveyors of pork pies), and fishmongers like Sea Breezes both of whom have outlets in Pepper Street; bakers like Chatwins on The Square, and A. T. Welch's surprisingly narrow yet deep premises on Hospital Street housing butcher, grocer, delicatessen, and coffee merchant counters. Nantwich Bookshop on The Square boasts a coffee lounge. The indoor market hall is open on Tuesdays, Thursdays and Saturdays. Laundry facilities are available at the canal basin.

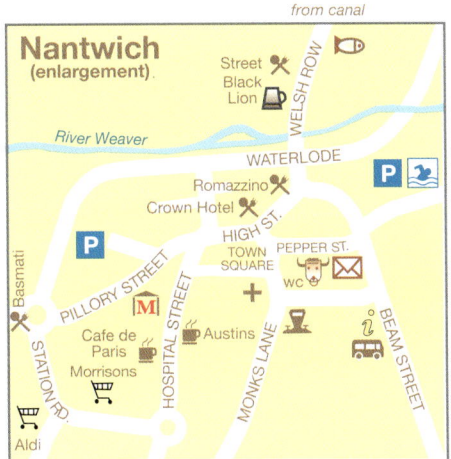

Things to Do
TOURIST INFORMATION - Civic Hall. Tel: 01270 303150 or 628633. CW5 5DG
NANTWICH MUSEUM - Pillory Street. Tel: 01270 627104. Displays of local history. Open 10am-4pm ex Mon & Sun. Free admission. Small gift shop. CW5 5BQ

Connections
BUSES - Arriva service 84 connects at 30 minutes intervals Mon-Sat (bi-hourly Sun) with Crewe in one direction and hourly with Chester in the other.
TRAINS - services to/from Crewe and Shrewsbury.
TAXIS - Direct. Tel: 01270 585000.

Acton
Map 11

A short walk across the fields from Bridge 93 leads to this village whose imposing church repays investigation, for amongst the gravestones you'll come upon that of A. N. Hornby, the English cricket captain whose one-off defeat to Australia at The Oval in 1882 brought about a spoof obituary which referred to the cremated 'remains' of the English game being sent to Australia, hence the origin of 'The Ashes'.

Barbridge
Map 11

Eating & Drinking
OLDE BARBRIDGE INN - Old Chester Road (adjacent Bridge 100). Tel: 01270 528327. Comfortable canalside pub serving Weetwood ales. Food served throughout from noon daily. CW5 6AY

Connections
BUSES - Arriva service 84 as Nantwich.

12 SUC MIDDLEWICH BRANCH Cholmondeston 4mls/2lks/2hrs

REMOTE, and seemingly always windswept, the Middlewich Branch of the Shropshire Union cuts across the grain of the landscape on a series of high embankments. It can be a busy length of canal for, as well as Four Counties Ring traffic, it funnels boats to and from the hugely popular Llangollen Canal, and so consequently its four deep and heavy-gated locks can become bottlenecks at the beginning and end of summer weeks.

Historically, the branch, opened in 1833, belonged to the Chester Canal Company and was engineered by Thomas Telford. Trade was heavy in cargo-carrying days, as after opening of the Birmingham & Liverpool Junction Canal, this became the optimum route between the Black Country and the industrial North-west. Trade also developed between Ellesmere Port on the banks of the Mersey and The Potteries: Cornish china clay in one direction, finished crockery in the other.

In 1888 a curious experiment was undertaken, to see if it was feasible to replace horse-power by laying a narrow gauge railway along the towpath below Cholmondeston Lock, and employing a small steam locomotive called 'Dickie' to haul strings of narrowboats. The concept didn't develop here, laying track was considered cost-prohibitive and there were problems in steering the boats, though it did catch on abroad, especially on the French waterways. Cholmondeston still retains a railway presence, however, in the shape of the Crewe to Chester line, part of the historic route of the Irish Mails to Holyhead.

A high wooded embankment carries the canal across the River Weaver. Four Counties Ring travellers meet the river again near Audlem. It rises on the south-facing slopes of the Peckforton Hills and passes beneath the Llangollen Canal at Wrenbury prior to becoming navigable at Winsford (Map 57), less than five miles downstream of the Weaver Aqueduct. There is nothing spectacular about the canal's crossing of the river, but it takes place in the most agreeable of locations. And, as you pass on your elevated way, it's hard to escape a fleeting sense of regret that the riverbank, being on private land, cannot so easily be explored. When plans were formulated by the Ministry of War Transport in 1942 for an upgraded Weaver-Wolverhampton Waterway (see page 21), it was acknowledged that the aqueduct would have to be rebuilt and enlarged to accommodate the 200 ton barges it was envisaged would operate as far upstream as Nantwich. Sadly, canal history is filled with schemes which never came to fruition, and died-in-the-wool canal enthusiasts can only day-dream of journeys they were never able to make.

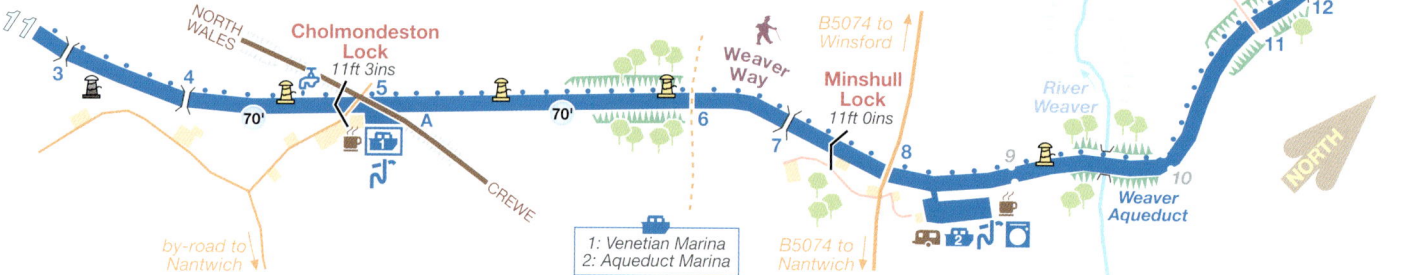

13 SUC MIDDLEWICH BRANCH Church Minshull 4mls/0lks/1hr

TO subconsciously relegate the Middlewich Branch to the back of your mind as an unspectacular, but necessary link in the waterways of the North-West would be unjust, for this is a rumbustious canal, extrovertly ushering you loftily above the snaking valley of the Weaver, presenting you with expansive views towards a horizon bounded by Delamere Forest and the Peckforton Hills. Church Minshull - all russet coloured brick and black & white half timbering - looks, from the canal's elevated position, like a toy village embracing the river's luxuriant banks. Tom and Angela Rolt enjoyed an extended stay here in the fateful Autumn of 1939 while Tom worked for Rolls Royce at Crewe. It was tedious work he didn't enjoy, but the couple revelled in the close-knit community which flourished at Minshull: the blacksmith who shod the local cart horses; and the miller whose water wheels supplied the village with its electricity, continuing to do so right up until 1960.

Several sizeable farms border the canal, their fields filled with dairy herds or cut red by the plough in a ruddy shade of corduroy. The cattle appear not averse to drinking canal water.

Near Bridge 22, woods partially obscure the Top Flash, a subsidence induced lake beside the Weaver. The main London-Glasgow railway crosses the canal, its sleek electric trains swishing by at forty times the speed of your boat. To the south-east lies a forgotten, older transport route, a Roman road which linked the early salt mines at Nantwich and Middlewich. Some interesting old canal horse stables have been converted into living quarters by Bridge 18. Until the Government pulled the plug on the extension to Manchester, HS2 was earmarked to cross the canal between bridges 25 and 26.

The Middlewich Branch's towpath is largely grassy: fine for well-shod walkers but horribly bumpy and uncomfortable for cycling until it reaches Clive Green, east of which it has been upgraded as part NCR 5.

Summary of Facilities

The Badger Inn at Church Minshull (Tel: 01270 522348 - CW5 6DY) is a smartly refurbished country inn easily reached from Bridge 14. Food is served from noon daily throughout. The Verdin Arms (Tel: 01270 522275 - CW10 0LW) is accessible by footpath from Bridge 19. It opens at 5pm but doesn't do food.

Arriva bus service 31 operates hourly Mon-Sat from Church Minshull to Crewe.

14 TRENT & MERSEY CANAL Middlewich 4mls/7lks/3hrs*

£3 MILLION was spent on restoring the canal following a breach below Stanthorne Lock in 2018. The bulk of that sum came from the People's Postcode Lottery, a reminder, were one needed, how costly it can be to maintain a 200 years old network of waterways. The breach effectively closed the Four Counties Ring as a circular route for the best part of a year, making life particularly difficult for the hire fleets who rely on the Middlewich Arm as a strategic link between the Shropshire Union/Llangollen and Trent & Mersey canals. The Canal & River Trust suspected boater misuse, vandalism, and even badgers, as the cause, though on reflection it's likely that embankment failure was the real explanation. Had he been offered a sound-bite, Hamlet would doubtless have quipped about maintenance being 'more honoured in the breach than the observance'.

The Middlewich Arm's approach to the old salt making town from which it gained its name is innocuously suburban. At Wardle Lock Britain's 'shortest' canal is encountered. Rather than permitting a potential competitor to form a direct junction with its own canal, the Trent & Mersey - always concerned about the loss of trade and tolls - insisted on building its own short branch to meet the newcomer, thereby being in a stronger position to charge tolls. A similar phenomenon is to be found at Hall Green (Map 53) where the Trent & Mersey meets the Macclesfield Canal.

Four Counties Ringers turn right onto the Trent & Mersey (or left onto the Middlewich Arm if they're going anti-clockwise), so their acquaintance with the town proves perfunctory to say the least, and they're soon slewing off its redbrick terraces for pastures new. The fluctuating fortunes of industry create conservational gambits. Given that the majority of the district's many salt works have disappeared, it's reassuring to come upon one still very much in business, albeit that British Salt are now owned by the Indian conglomerate, Tata. Somewhat less resilient was the canalside sanitaryware works by Bridge 166, closed in 2013, its former location now devoted to waste recycling. Similarly vanished is the works, latterly operated by Rank Hovis McDougall, which made Bisto Gravy, it closed in 2008. By Booth Lane Locks stood Murgatroyd's, latterly owned by Hays Chemicals. Part of the site remains in industrial use by a German owned company, Brenntag, the rest has been redeveloped as housing. Clinging on for life in the heart of the new estate is Yew Tree Farmhouse, a 17th century half-timbered building which Murgatroyd's used as their social club for many years. It now resembles a Cavalier surrounded by hostile Roundheads.

Key
A sites of salt works
B site of gas works
C site of sanitaryware works
D site of Bisto gravy factory
E site of Murgatroyd's works
F former Moston Mill

'Passengers No More'
1: Middlewich - closed 4.1.60

*figures refer to Four Counties Ring

Middlewich
Maps 14/34

'Not an attractive town' in Pevsner's estimation, though he probably encountered it at its most salty, an activity undertaken here since the days of the Roman occupation. Middlewich's most interesting buildings (apart from the disconsolate wharf house) are arguably the parish church of St Michael (whose tower remains visibly wounded by missiles unleashed during the Civil War) and the former Technical School on Lewin Street embellished with low relief figurines. June's 'Folk & Boat' Festival continues to grow in popularity.

Eating & Drinking
BIG LOCK - Webb's Lane (Lock 75). Tel: 01606 836983. Open from noon daily, food served throughout; plus breakfasts Sat/Sun from 9am. Adjoining coffee shop open 9am-5pm daily. CW10 9DN
IL PADRINO - Wheelock Street. Tel: 01606 837888. Italian restaurant ('The Godfather') with a sister branch in Holmes Chapel. Open from 5pm Tue-Sat and from 2pm Sun. CW10 9AG
KINGS LOCK INN - Booth Lane (Lock 71). Tel: 01606 836894. Popular canalside pub built on two levels to provide stabling for boat horses beneath the bar. Food Thur-Sat from 5pm. CW10 0JJ
WHITE BEAR - Wheelock Street. Tel: 01606 837666. Good Beer Guide listed pub/restaurant. CW10 9AG

Shopping
There are Lidl and Morrisons supermarkets. A small market is held every Tuesday. Dave's, on Lewin Street, is an 'angling supercentre'. Broad's Bakery & Pottery lies just off Lewin Street by Bridge 169.

Connections
BUSES - D&G service 37 links Middlewich with Northwich (via Winsford Rly Sta) and Sandbach hourly (ex Sun). D&G service 42 runs to/from Congleton and Crewe, hourly Mon-Fri, bi-hourly Sat.

1 Andersen Boats
2 Middlewich Wharf/ Floating Holidays
3 Middlewich Canal Centre/ Kings Lock Chandlery

Sandbach
Maps 15/33

A likeable town, chiefly famous for its ancient Saxon crosses, Sandbach lies about a mile east of the canal at Ettily Heath, though there is easy access to the railway station from Bridge 160 and buses run frequently from Wheelock. The Town Hall - which houses the covered market, open Thur & Sat - is of decidedly Flemish appearance. More salubrious than neighbouring Middlewich (it has, after all, a Waitrose!), some excellent shops and pubs render Sandbach worth a detour. Godfrey C. Williams (Tel: 01270 762817) is a 'specialist grocer and cheese connoisseur' located on the cobbled market square. The Beer Emporium (Tel: 01270 760113) on Welles Street is a micropub and bottled beer outlet, whilst Old Hall (Tel: 01270 758170) on High Street is a classic Brunning & Price pub.

Connections
BUSES - D&G service 37 as Middlewich.
TRAINS - stopping services between Crewe and Manchester Airport and Manchester.

Wheelock
Maps 15/32

By-passed by the A534, Wheelock still endures more than its fair share of traffic - a culture shock after the peace of the canal. Nevertheless, it's a useful pitstop, and a launch pad for Sandbach. A substantial Methodist chapel overlooks the river.

Eating & Drinking
BARCHETTA - Bridge 154. Tel: 01270 314183. Italian restaurant housed in warehouse conversion, the name roughly translates as 'little boat'. CW11 3RL
CHESHIRE CHEESE - Crewe Road (adjacent Bridge 154. Tel: 01270 346600. Refurbished Hydes pub serving food daily from noon until 8pm. CW11 3R
MALKINS BANK - Bridge 150. Tel: 01270 765931. Canalside golf course cafe bar. CW11 4XN
SHAMPAAN - Crewe Road. Tel: 01270 753528. Indian restaurant open from 5pm (4pm Sun). CW11 3RL

Shopping
Small convenience store, and H J Lea Oakes pet shop.

Things to Do
WHEELOCK HALL - Crewe Road. Tel: 01270 764230. Family run farm shop, tea room (home cooked chips from their own potatoes!) garden centre and play area approximately ten minutes walk south of Bridge 154. 9am-6.30pm daily. CW11 4RE

Connections
BUSES - D&G service 37 as Middlewich.

Hassall Green
Maps 15/32

Isolated community somewhat impinged upon by the M6. Downhill, past the St Philip's shocking pink 'tin tabernacle', the old North Staffordshire Railway has been repurposed as the 'Salt Line' bridleway.

Connections
BUSES - D&G service 317 operates Mon-Fri to/from Rode Heath and Alsager and Sandbach.

15 TRENT & MERSEY CANAL Wheelock 5mls/12lks/4hrs

LOCKS proliferate, and are potentially habit-forming, as the Trent & Mersey ascends from (or descends to) the Cheshire Plain. There are twenty-six chambers to negotiate in only seven miles between Wheelock and Hardings Wood, and "Heartbreak Hill" - as this section has been known to generations of boaters - seems an all too appropriate nickname by the time you have reached the top or bottom; two hundred and fifty feet up or down.

With the exception of the Pierpoint pair, all the locks were 'duplicated' in the 19th century, paddles between adjoining chambers enabling one lock to act as a mini-reservoir to its neighbour. These side paddles were taken out of use when commercial traffic ceased towards the end of the 1960s, but the duplicated locks still ease delays today, though an increasing number appear 'temporarily' out of use; which perhaps suggests that the Canal & River Trust's maintenance budget is being stretched tighter and tighter.

The locks may, or may not, make life hard for the boater, but the canal itself is illuminated by a succession of small communities with interesting pasts. At Ettily Heath the quadrupled, electrified tracks of the Crewe to Manchester railway cross the canal at the site of a transhipment basin provided to facilitate traffic with the Potteries. Hereabouts the canal, concrete-banked and steel-piled, tends to be deeper than is normal on account of subsidence caused by salt-mining in the past.

The River Wheelock rises in the vicinity of Little Moreton Hall (Map 53) and gives its name to a former wharfingering community situated where the Crewe-Sandbach road crossed the canal. Malkin's Bank was home to the families of boatmen engaged in comparatively short-haul traffics connected with the salt and chemical industries. They lived cheek-by-jowl with employees at the huge Brunner Mond (later ICI) alkali works now buried beneath the greens and fairways of a golf course. Between locks 62 and 63, a side bridge carries the towpath over an old arm (now used by a boatbuilder) which once went into the works. Don't be deceived by the sign on the off-side below Lock 59 advertising the Romping Donkey public house, many years have elapsed since the last pint was served!

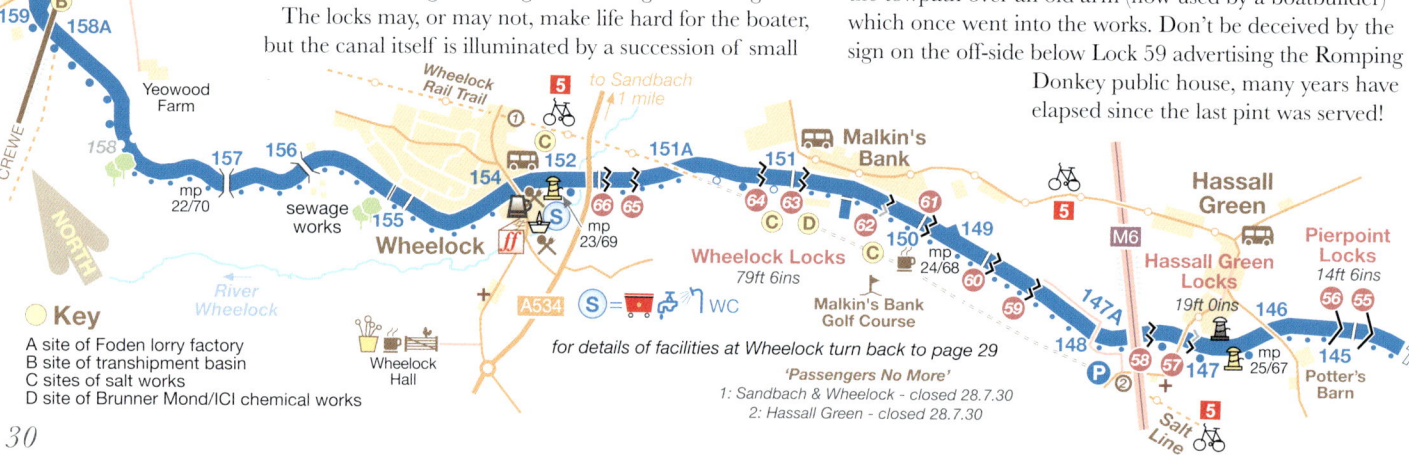

Key
A site of Foden lorry factory
B site of transhipment basin
C sites of salt works
D site of Brunner Mond/ICI chemical works

for details of facilities at Wheelock turn back to page 29

'Passengers No More'
1: Sandbach & Wheelock - closed 28.7.30
2: Hassall Green - closed 28.7.30

16 TRENT & MERSEY CANAL Rode Heath & Red Bull 4mls/13lks/3hrs

THERE'S roughly a mile of breathing space between Pierpoint 'Upper" and Thurlwood 'Lower'. A pretty interlude ensues as the canal curves past Chells Hill Farm and crosses the B5078 on a brick-built aqueduct. Proposals for a marina here have not, as yet, come to fruition. Sadly, for boaters who like to carry miniature versions of Kew Gardens around on their cabin roofs, A. P. Matthews' canalside nursery operates on a wholesale basis only.

Thurlwood Upper Lock (No.53) features only one chamber these days, but its long vanished counterpart once sported a most unusual contraption. Subsidence from the adjacent salt works had brought the lock to the brink of collapse, so a new chamber was designed in the form of a steel tank supported by a series of piers which could be raised should further subsidence occur. Entry was through guillotine gates. In practice this steel lock took longer to operate and was both disliked and mistrusted by boatmen. Consequently, it had seen little use before demolition took place in 1987.

Another structure of significance was lost to the canalscape at Rode Heath where a large warehouse with arched loading bay stood beside the waterway until being controversially demolished in 1981. Hearing that the mill, a local landmark, was to be demolished, the Trent & Mersey Canal Society successfully applied for the building to be given listed status. In response the mill's owners took the matter up with their local MP who managed to have protected status overturned. "After further consideration," quoted the DoE "we came to the conclusion that the building was not as interesting as at first thought."

Bridge 138A carries the A50 across the canal, whereas previously it passed beneath the neighbouring aqueduct. The road, as originally numbered, linked Hockliffe in Bedfordshire (near Leighton Buzzard) with Warrington, encountering a fair few canals en route. The countryside dips and sweeps away from the canal in folds and creases like a carelessly discarded garment. Lawton Treble Locks are Rennie's

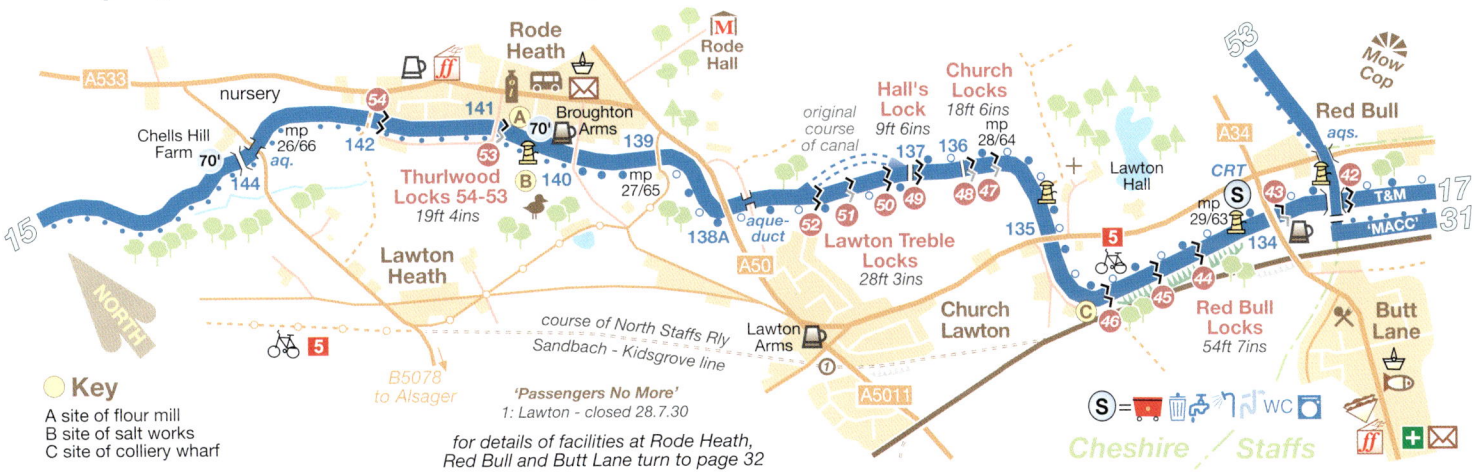

Key
A site of flour mill
B site of salt works
C site of colliery wharf

for details of facilities at Rode Heath, Red Bull and Butt Lane turn to page 32

31

work and replaced a Brindley staircase which was both time consuming and wasteful of water. Beyond Church Locks there is a brief respite from the locks and the welcoming sight of All Saints church across fields of maize. The doorway is Norman, but the nave early 19th century. Apparently the parish register contains the names of many boatmen and lock-keepers. When much of the nave was destroyed by fire in 1798, timber to rebuild it was brought down by canal from Liverpool Docks.

Mow Cop (pronounced to rhyme with 'cow') overlooks this delightful landscape from its high ridge, an appropriate platform for the sober, yet lofty ambitions of the Primitive Methodists who held their first open air meeting on its summit in 1807. The ruin on its ridge, typical of 18th century romantic landscaping, is known as Wilbraham's Folly after the local landowner who had it erected as an 'eyecatcher'.

Lawton Hall is a substantial and much rebuilt 17th century mansion, broken up into apartments now. A memorial in the grounds commemorates 'Bullie', a pet bullfinch who would reputedly sing the National Anthem when encouraged.

Red Bull Locks - once individually known as Townfield, Kent's and Yewtree in order of ascent - are probably the most visually satisfying on the whole of 'Heartbreak Hill'. There was once a wharf at the tail of Lock 46 where coal was brought down by tramway from a coal mine at nearby Talke called Bunkers Hill, a name derived from the first significant battle in the American War of Independence. Further up this hugely photogenic flight, an old whitewashed warehouse, once used for the storage of perishable goods, is now a base for the Canal & River Trust, with a well equipped facility centre catering for most boaters' needs. By sheer coincidence, Bridge 134 carries the A34 across the canal, one of England's most significant trunk roads before the motorway era, it connected Manchester with Winchester.

Pool Lock Aqueduct seems weighed down by the responsibility of carrying the Macclesfield Canal over the Trent & Mersey. It is not an elegant work of engineering, but it's stood here for the best part of two hundred years and is doubtless good for a few more. Neither is the upper canal technically the 'Macclesfield', because it was the T&M themselves who built the Hall Green Branch, the Macclesfield Canal proper beginning at Hall Green stop lock one mile to the north beyond a second bridge, the Red Bull Aqueduct, which carries the canal over the A50 trunk road. The Macclesfield Canal is part of the popular "Cheshire Ring" canal circuit of which more between pages 81 and 146. Southbound travellers along the Trent & Mersey, mystified by the Macclesfield's motive for crossing the T&M at this point, should turn to Map 17 for the denouement.

Rode Heath Maps 16/31
Sizeable modern village at junction of A533 and A50.
Eating & Drinking
BROUGHTON ARMS - Sandbach Road (adjacent Bridge 140). Tel: 01270 883203. Comfortable canalside Marston's pub open from noon daily. ST7 3RU.
JADE GARDEN - Sandbach Road (accessible from Bridge 141). Tel: 01270 873391. Chinese take-away open from 5pm daily ex Mon. ST7 3RW.
Shopping
Well stocked post office stores adjacent Broughton Arms, and Bargain Booze near Bridge 141.

Things to Do
RODE HALL - 18th century country house and gardens. Tel: 01270 873237. Open to the public on Wednesday and Bank Holiday afternoons throughout the summer. Refreshments. Farmer's Market first Saturday morning of each month. ST7 3QP
Connections
BUSES - D&G service 317 operates Monday to Friday to/from Sandbach and Alsager.

Red Bull/Butt Lane Maps 16/31
Just past the fish & chip shop, a blue plaque adorns the wall of the house where Reginald Mitchell, designer of the Spitfire fighter, was born in 1895, though the family moved to Longton soon after.
Eating & Drinking
MASOOMS MASSALA - Congleton Road (quarter of a mile south of Bridge 134). Tel: 01782 788444. Indian restaurant open from 5.30pm daily. ST7 1NE
RED BULL - Congleton Road (overlooking Lock 43). Tel: 01782 782600. Whitewashed without, cosy and welcoming inside, this southern outpost of Robinsons Brewery of Stockport offers a good choice of food lunchtimes and evenings. ST7 3AJ

17 TRENT & MERSEY CANAL Harecastle & Longport 4mls/11k/2hrs

HARECASTLE may not be the longest navigable tunnel currently in use on the canal network (it's a lowly fifth) but it's the only one controlled by keepers at either end, which undoubtedly adds to its mystique. These days the Canal & River Trust encourage boaters to pre-book their passage, though, somewhat confusingly, non-booked access to the tunnel is available on an ad hoc basis in the mornings - see separate panel below.

What is not in doubt, is that to boat through it is - to shamelessly purloin the title of a Beryl Bainbridge novel - 'An Awfully Big Adventure', whilst the orange water, which characterises the approach at either end, brings to mind the chocolate river in *Willy Wonka & the Chocolate Factory*.

> Access to Harecastle Tunnel is under the control of keepers at either end. Summer (Mar-Oct) and winter timetables operate and we recommend prospective boaters visit www.canalrivertrust.org.uk or telephone 0303 040 4040 to ascertain current operating times. At the time of writing pre-booked slots operate in the afternoons between 2pm and 4pm, whilst un-booked slots are available (subject to demand) in the mornings between 8am and noon. Winter passages *must* be booked in advance and the tunnel is only open Mon, Wed, Fri & Sat.

What makes Harecastle unique, is the system of 'forced' ventilation it employs, fumes being quite literally sucked out at the south end by a gigantic fan which would give your bathroom at home a run for its money. The affable keepers count you in and out - it would be embarrassing to mislay a boat in the middle - and gingerly you point your bow into the looming portal. Gradually all sense of light is lost. Nostalgically you look back over your shoulder at the retreating half-moon of daylight. Suddenly, with a shuddering clang, the doors at the southern end close and the fume extractor begins to suck with a muted roar. For the next three-quarters of an hour or so you are buried beneath Harecastle Hill with one small niggle at the back of your mind - will you, or won't you come face to face with the 'Kidsgrove Boggart', a headless ghost reputed to haunt the tunnel.

Nowadays it's easy to overlook that there were *two* Harecastle Tunnels; *five* if you count the railways ones as well. The original canal tunnel was designed by James Brindley. It took eleven years to build, was one and three-quarter miles long, and opened in 1775, three years after Brindley's death. A series of connecting tunnels led from the main bore to serve

adjacent coal faces, intersecting with several underground springs which provided additional, and much welcome water supplies to the canal's comparatively short summit level. These are the source of the ironstone particles which colour the water so peculiarly.

For half a century a team of 'leggers' propelled boats through Brindley's towpath-less tunnel, lying on their backs at right-angles to the boat and literally 'walking' from one end to the other, a feat of endurance which typically would last between two or three hours. Unsurprisingly, Harecastle became a serious bottleneck. Reluctantly, being well aware of the costs and difficulties involved, the canal proprietors commissioned a second bore with Thomas Telford as the consultant engineer. Some idea of the advances in technology gained in the interim can be gauged from the fact that the new tunnel, equipped with a towpath, was completed in less than three years, opening in 1827.

Until the early years of the 20th century, the two tunnels were used in unison: Brindley's taking southbound boats, Telford's north. Neighbouring mining activity had, however, caused concerns with regard to subsidence, particularly in respect of the newer tunnel. When the North Staffordshire Railway - owners of the canal since 1847 - proposed closing Telford's tunnel for half a year to effect repairs, boat operators and North Staffordshire industrialists called for a deviation canal to be cut to the west through Bathpool. Recoiling at the cost of such a notion, the NSR undertook much swifter repairs and, in 1914, electric tugs began to haul strings of boats through Telford's tunnel; Brindley's being abandoned around the end of

Harecastle South

the First World War.

These tugs were decidedly curious machines. They dragged themselves along a steel cable laid on the canal bed, collecting power through a tram-like pole from an overhead wire. L. T. C. Rolt described being hauled through the tunnel by one in 1939 in *Narrow Boat*. The tugs successfully solved Harecastle's traffic flow problems until the 1950s, by which time the number of boats using the tunnel had dwindled to a point whereby they were deemed unviable. In 1954 forced ventilation was introduced, enabling powered boats to pass through. Further subsidence concerns caused closure of the tunnel between 1973-77, but a good deal of money was spent on its rehabilitation and it is now in comparatively good condition, albeit with progressively lower headroom as you progress towards the middle, restrictions highlighted somewhat unnervingly by ghostly luminous arches.

Refurbishment of the tunnel involved removal of the towpath. Walkers are thus faced with the option of catching a local train between the handily placed railway stations at Kidsgrove and Longport, or following Boathorse Road across the top, encountering an arcane, crumpled and pock-marked landscape rising to some seven hundred feet above sea level, resplendent with views encompassing Jodrell Bank to the north, the Wedgwood (no, not *that* Wedgwood) monument to the west, and Wolfgang Buttress's 'Golden' sculpture adorning the site of Goldenhill Iron Works. Zig-zagging across the tunnel in the neighbourhood of Ravenscliffe, walkers come upon a travellers' camp where once stood terraced workers' cottages evocatively known as the 'Line Houses'.

In the 1840s, when the railway was faced with the challenge of passing under Harecastle Hill, it necessitated the construction of no less than three tunnels. Two of them were subsequently abandoned when the line was electrified and diverted in 1966, an event which inspired Peter Terson's celebrated television play of 1969, *The Last Train Through the Harecastle Tunnel*.

Between Harecastle's southern portal and Longport, the canal traverses its 408ft summit at the foot of a ridge supporting Tunstall, northernmost of the six Potteries towns. Once upon a time the canal served iron works, earthenware manufactures and chemical plants. Nowadays there are business parks and a giant distribution hub; served, needlessly to say, by neither the canal nor the railway. Nevertheless, there are abundant clues to the past. Look for the ruined edge of the side bridge which spanned an arm that tunnelled beneath the railway to a dock serving Chatterley Coal & Iron Works. At Copp Lane there's a pair of canal workers' cottages, as remote from any other habitation as in some lonely moorland setting. Juggernaut lorries creep cautiously over Bridge 129A, a far cry from the working narrowboats which once sailed beneath it. Keep your eyes peeled for the stubs of old arms which once splayed out from the off-side of the canal to serve numerous, long vanished works. Tradition has it that Josiah Wedgwood cut the canal's ceremonial 'first sod' by Bridge 128.

Created as a pleasure resort in the 1890s, Westport Lake is enhanced by a visitor centre cared for by the Staffordshire Wildlife Trust, an establishment whose cafe offers such enticing views across the water that you can fantasise it's Lake Como or Maggiore. The North Staffordshire Railway's Tunstall (or Pinnox) branch crossed the canal on Bridge 127A.

At Longport, some traditional aspects of North Staffordshire make their presence felt. Keep your eyes peeled for Canal St.! An 'unshaven' bottle kiln looms over the canal by Bridge 126. It belonged to Price Bros., famous teapot manufacturers. Local butcher and entrepreneur, Wayne Walker, aspires to transform the hitherto derelict site into 'a destination'.

The boatyard at Longport Wharf was a London & North Western Railway 'boatage' depot, as evidenced in faded sign-writing on the gable end of its main building. Steelite, manufacturers of bespoke crockery and glassware, present the contemporary face of Potteries industry.

Kidsgrove   Map 17

A former colliery town, on the wrong side of Harecastle Hill to ever qualify as a member of that exclusive hellfire club: The Potteries.

Eating & Drinking
BLUE BELL - Hardingswood (adjacent Lock 41). Tel: 01782 774052. Unspoilt pub prized for an absence of extraneous noise and half a dozen handpumps of ever changing microbrewery ales. Closed Mon. ST7 1EG

Shopping
Tesco, Lidl and Aldi supermarkets. Launderette (on Market Street). Make it your goal to find Kidsgrove Oatcakes on King Street (open from 7.30am) where you can watch oatcakes and pikelets being made on the griddle, and have your oatcakes crammed with a choice of nourishing fillings. Wrights pie shop next door.

Connections
TRAINS - services to/from Longport and Stoke useful for towpath/tunnel top walkers and/or boaters of a claustrophobic disposition.

Longport   Map 17

All the 'ports' - Long, Middle, West and New - lie down in the valley beside the canal and the origin of their names is obvious, forming as they do, a necklace of wharfingering communities where the import and export of cargoes of The Potteries were handled. There's an oatcake outlet on Station Street (open Wed-Sun from 8am) if you're peckish, and the petrol station hosts a Costa coffee shop, Greggs and Spar. Carnivores make a bee-line for Wayne Walker's Quality Meats outlet on Davenport Street - enterprisingly open from 7am daily.

35

Heading 'Up Shroppie' (Map 1)

Descending Audlem Locks (Map 9)

Fuel boat *Halsall* at Lock 71, Middlewich, Trent & Mersey Canal (Maps 14/34)

Middleport, Trent & Mersey Canal (Map 18)

Salt Bridge (No.82), Trent & Mersey Canal (Map 22)

Staffs & Worcs Bridge 105 (Map 24)

Motorway or Waterway? (Map 26)

Pendeford 'Rockin' (Map 27)

Surviving Bottle Kilns on the Caldon (Map 18)

Upstream on the River Churnet (Map 30)

18 TRENT & MERSEY Etruria & Stoke 4mls/5lks/3hrs*

THIS is the district which, Arnold Bennett amusingly averred, could never be described adequately, because Dante had lived too soon. Bennett was being uncharacteristically modest, for his 'Five Towns' novels and short stories evoke a vivid picture of North Staffordshire in the late 19th and early 20th century heyday of heavy industry. A smoke drenched landscape of pot banks, steel works and coal mines hard to equate with the equivocal Vodafones and bet365s of the present day. Bennett - better known now for his fishy omelette than his prose - is an author out of fashion, who needs a block-buster film or prime-time TV drama to revive his fortunes. If Amazon are to be believed, his books sell less than ours - a travesty!

In common with many other post-industrial heartlands, The Potteries have passed through a period of transition, and come blandly out the other side. Here, though, the pace of change has been less remorseless. From time to time you come upon examples of the area's most potent symbol, the bottle kiln. There was a time, before the Clean Air Act, when visitors could purchase postcards depicting The Potteries' skyline blackened by the combined emissions from serried ranks of these ovens.

Key 1 Goodwin's foundry

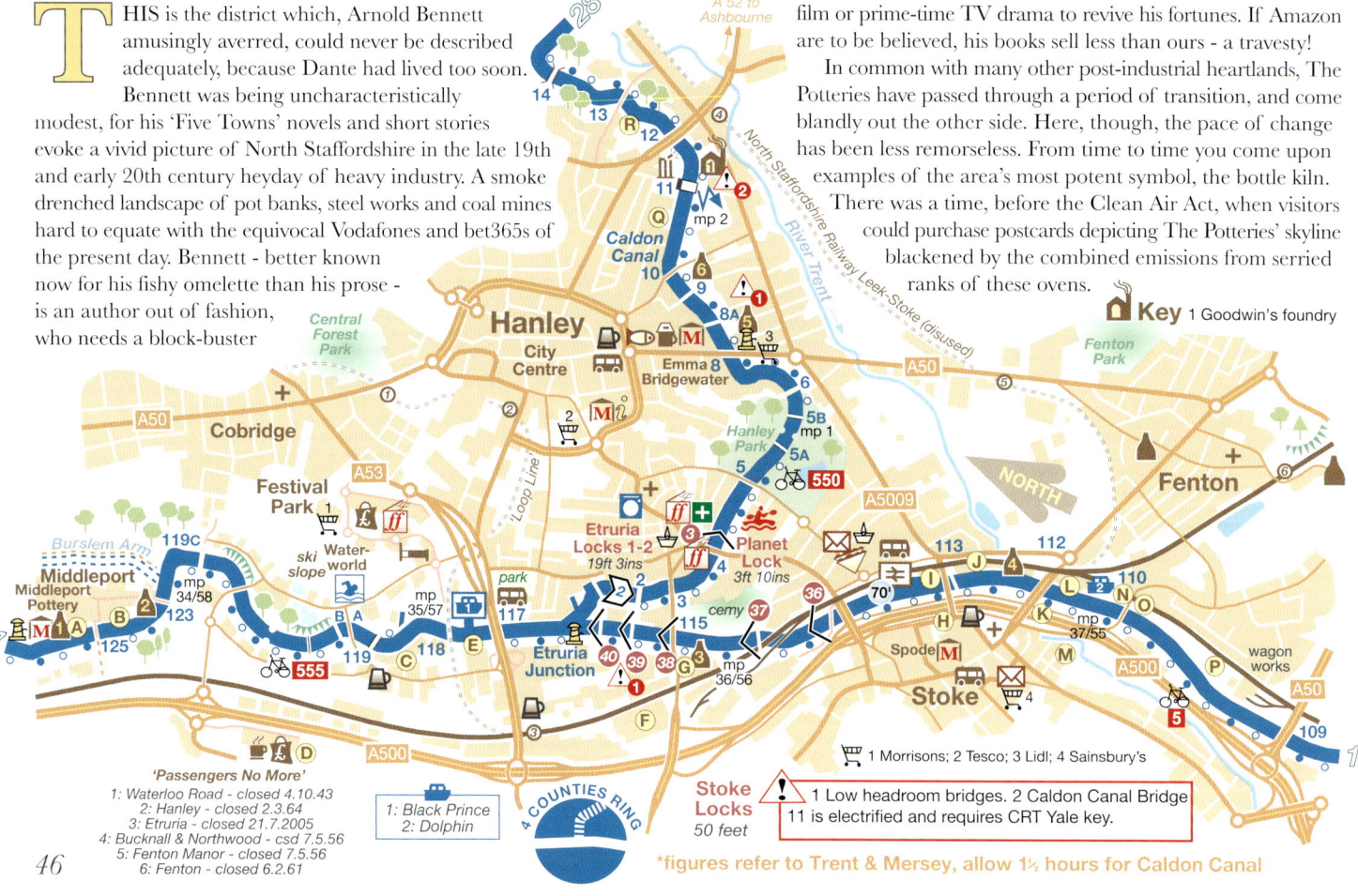

'Passengers No More'
1: Waterloo Road - closed 4.10.43
2: Hanley - closed 2.3.64
3: Etruria - closed 21.7.2005
4: Bucknall & Northwood - csd 7.5.56
5: Fenton Manor - closed 7.5.56
6: Fenton - closed 6.2.61

1: Black Prince
2: Dolphin

Stoke Locks 50 feet

1 Low headroom bridges. 2 Caldon Canal Bridge 11 is electrified and requires CRT Yale key.

1 Morrisons; 2 Tesco; 3 Lidl; 4 Sainsbury's

*figures refer to Trent & Mersey, allow 1½ hours for Caldon Canal

Key

A former Anderton Boat Co.
B site of Newport Pottery
C site of 'Shelton Bar'
D site of Wolstanton Colliery
E site of original Wedgwood Pottery
F site of Phoenix Engineering Works
G remains of Twyford's Cliffe Vale Pottery
H site of Shropshire Union Co. wharf (and junction of Newcastle Canal)
I site of NSR goods yard
J former Dolbey's Flint Mill
K site of Stoke Wharf
L remains of NSR railway works
M site of Victoria Ground (Stoke City FC)
N site of Stoke Basin
O site of Colonial Pottery
P site of Kerr Stuart railway works
Q site of Eagle Pottery
R site of Northwood Colliery basin

Key

1 Middleport Pottery
2 former flint mill
3 Cliffe Valley Pottery
4 Dolbey's flint mill
5 Imperial Pottery
6 Trent Sanitary Works

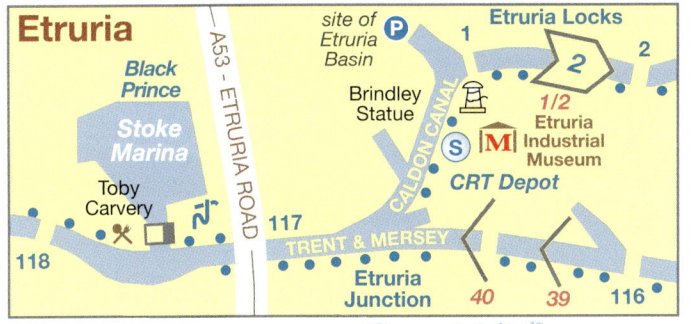

Between Middleport and Etruria the canal twists and turns frequently, following the contours of the valley of the Fowlea Brook, a tributary of the Trent much abused in the industrial past. You feel as if you are exploring a lost civilisation, and in many respects you are. The canal can be likened to a palimpsest, embued with a fresh, leisure inspired narrative. Prominent on the western horizon, beyond the railway and the A500, St Margaret's church pokes its lofty spire above the tree-line. Between it and the dual-carriagewayed Queensway stood Wolstanton Colliery, a post-war 'super-pit'. It closed in 1986, and its giant concrete-enclosed winding-gear was spectacularly demolished a couple of years later: folk cheered witlessly; as at a public execution.

Middleport Pottery evokes all the hallmarks of a traditional pottery, though its bottle kiln is the sole survivor of seven which once stood shoulder to shoulder on the site. This is where Burleigh's time-honoured china is manufactured, and off-side moorings are provided for visitors. Built locally in 1947, the Mersey-Weaver narrowboat *Dane* is usually exhibited alongside, echoing scenes from the canal's more busy working past. Next door stands the terracotta gabled end of the Anderton Boat Company's former warehouse, a well known carrier in the district whose boats were nicknamed 'knobsticks'. A little further on, the skeletal remains of a flour mill loom despondently over the canal.

Near Bridge 125, on a site now occupied by modern housing, stood Newport Pottery, famous for its connections with Clarice Cliff, the celebrated creator of 'Bizarre' and other Art Deco ceramics and pottery designs. By Bridge 123 an arm once led to Burslem Wharf, scene of the pantechnicon's immersion in Bennett's hilarious novel *The Card*. The arm was abandoned in 1961 after a breach, but proposals exist for it to be reinstated for moorings, and work parties have begun to clear debris. Until 1978 the canal penetrated the torrid core of Shelton Bar steelworks, scene of H. G. Wells' terrifying short story *The Cone*, in which the works manager murders his wife's would-be lover by pushing him into a furnace. For a couple of decades thereafter, a rolling mill remained, and boaters were required to pass through the subfusc gloom of two overhanging fabrication sheds, waving at the diminishing workforce: fellow travellers into an uncertain future.

The derelict acres left behind after demolition, hosted the National Garden Festival in 1986, one of five post-industrial regeneration schemes (along with Liverpool, Glasgow, Gateshead and Ebbw Vale) attributed to the Conservative Secretary for the Environment, Michael Heseltine, in the early 1980s. The festival site east of the canal was subsequently developed into a hackneyed mix of leisure, retail and commercial facilities; that to the west has only recently become populated again, by the ubiquitous and ever so slightly anonymous distribution hubs of the 21st century.

The ebb and flow of land use is not without bathos. Centrepiece of

Etruscan Bone Mill

Festival Park is an hotel converted from Josiah Wedgwood's original Etruria Hall, built on a greenfield site contemporary with the canal. Intriguingly, an image of it adorned one of the Frog Service dishes Wedgwood made for Catherine the Great of Russia in 1774. Subsequently, the steelworks encroached on the mansion, gradually engulfing its landscaped grounds. Ironically, the developments of the 1980s returned the neighbourhood to its origins.

Here and there, midst the present's innocuous wooded glades, are clues to a more purposeful past: a high girder bridge which carried an elevated railway into Shelton Bar; a boat dock beneath a roving bridge; and another bridge (118) where the 'Loop Line' railway once weaved its way from one Six Towns community to the next. Paul Johnson devoted a nostalgically appreciative chapter to this much mourned railway in his homage to a 1930s Potteries childhood *The Vanished Landscape*.

A timber, windlass-operated lift bridge frames entry to Festival Park Marina where secure moorings are available for an overnight stop, and there's the opportunity to indulge in all the spurious activities modern life offers: supermarkets, ski slopes, swimming pools with wave machines, ten pin bowling alleys, fast food outlets and cinemas; everything, in fact, that you took to the water to avoid. Wedgwood's pottery stood opposite before subsidence and pollution forced the company to move to Barlaston (Map 19). All that remains is an enigmatic roundhouse, fronting the premises of bet365. Galling to reflect that the CEO of this family run concern earns more annually than CRT's combined turnover.

Etruria Junction boasts all the ingredients of a compelling canalscape: well, *most* of them. Echoing Barbridge (Map 11) the top lock was attractively roofed over until the 1960s, a significant loss. Fortunately, the resonantly named Etruscan Bone Mill survives, standing alongside a small arm issuing from the tail of the second lock down. The bone mill now houses an industrial museum, the entrance to which is beside the Caldon Canal and overlooked by a statue of Brindley, appearing rather more svelte, it must be said, than he does at Coventry Basin: who ate all the Wright's pies, James? Etruria's busy basin did not always deal solely in goods. In the 1840s, during a recession in the pottery trade, large numbers of emigrants began a long, life-changing journey aboard narrowboats from this wharf, destined for Wisconsin in North America, where a township named Pottersville was established.

Southwards from Etruria, the Trent & Mersey negotiates Stoke Locks. A cemetery creates an oasis. Two old bottle ovens (pictured on page 2) are engulfed by modern housing. If you've time to spare, nip over the low wall on the off-side at Lock 38 and go and admire the frontage of Cliff Vale Pottery, once the domain of Twyfords, pioneers of the toilet pedestal. The bottom lock in the flight, deep and concrete lined, is a rebuilding dating from construction of Queensway in the 1960s. Barnam & Bailey's 'Circus Train' (of decidedly American appearance) used to be stabled at the Phoenix Engineering Works between tours.

Squeezed between rail and road, the canal keeps itself moodily to itself, much encroached by vegetation on the off-side. Redevelopment is in the air, its promoters promising to 'turn an unloved industrial site into a vibrant urban quarter'; they'll have their work cut out. Myriad wharves once stood along this length of canal. By Bridge 113 was the former Newcastle-under-Lyme Canal's egress. Opened in 1798, it ran in a V shape for 4 miles to the nearby borough of that name which, curiously, already had a canal. The Sir Nigel (no, not *that* one) Gresley Canal, a three mile private waterway unconnected with any other canals, had opened in 1775 to carry coal from outlying collieries belonging to the Gresley family into Newcastle itself. The Newcastle Junction Canal was subsequently built to link the two canals, but an inclined plane, planned to bridge the disparity in height between the two 'Newcastle' canals, was never constructed.

A solitary bottle kiln looms over the canal between bridges 113 and 112. This belonged to Dolbey's Flint Mill where cargoes of feldspar were delivered by boat until as late as 1969. Blink and you'll miss the canal's crossing of the stripling Trent, churning through man-made channels just beyond the bottle kiln; symptomatic of the way we treat our rivers.

The single-deck cars of the Potteries Electric Traction Co used to zip across Bridge 112, but were replaced by motor buses in the late 1920s. The hotch-potch of business premises on the off-side occupy remnants of the former North Staffordshire Railway Locomotive, Carriage & Wagon Works. Production ceased in 1928, five years after 'The Knotty' had been gobbled up by the LMS. Serendipitously, many of its skilled workforce were able to find employment with Michelin Tyres.

Colonial Pottery stood off-side south of Bridge 110. Sanitaryware was a speciality, so it seems likely that this was where Tom and Angela Rolt were amused to spot 'a warehouse full of chamber pots' as they entered Stoke from the south in 1939, as described so vividly in *Narrow Boat*. Scant evidence remains of Kerr Stuart's locomotive works where Rolt served an apprenticeship for three years from 1928. He writes vividly about his days in Stoke in *Landscape With Machines*, his first volume of autobiography.

The site of Stoke City's Victoria Ground lies buried beneath housing: at least the streets are named after former players and managers. The canal appears, disconcertingly, as if it's about to be engorged by Stoke's 'energy from waste' plant. Relax, the canal dips its shoulder, like Stanley Matthews in his baggy shorts of yore, to emerge unscathed on Map 19.

Caldon Canal

The Caldon Canal departs somewhat unpropitiously from Etruria, ascending a pair of 'staircase' locks which can cause queues to form at busy times. Dipping through an overbridge, it runs beside a stone wall over which peeps a typical northern terrace, a simple throwback emphasising, eloquently enough, the inherent pathos of The Potteries. Planet Lock is a latecomer, dating from 1909, inserted in response to subsidence, it is both slightly longer and wider than the norm.

Hanley Park is spanned by a pair of suitably ornamental bridges. From a balcony embellished with terracotta, steps climb past a bandstand to a clock-towered pavilion from which you half expect Edwin Clayhanger or Hilda Lessways to emerge at any moment. Then ensues a zone of redevelopment, where pottery works have been replaced by housing, some of it quite appealing, it must be acknowledged. The towpath is pavemented as far as Bridge 11, and liberally provided with mooring rings beyond Bridge 8; the latter affording access to Emma Bridgewater's pottery and Lidl's supermarket. Between the 1960s and the 1980s, a trio of purpose-built narrowboats (*Milton Maid*, *Princess* and *Queen*) carried finished pottery out to a warehouse at Milton. Time was money and they didn't hang about. Encounters were invariably presaged by a tidal bow wave. Finally, don't be duped by the mileposts, Uttoxeter hasn't been accessible by canal since 1848. Froghall, seventeen miles away, is as far as you'll get - stoppages permitting!

Bedford Street 'Bottom'

Etruria (aka Bedford Street) Locks are a 'staircase' pair, but differ from most of their type in that an overflow weir permits the top chamber to be emptied even when the lower chamber is full.

49

Hanley
Map 18

Arnold Bennett sits nonchalantly outside the Potteries Museum & Art Gallery reading a copy of *The Card*, arguably his most approachable novel. Bennett called his 'Hanbridge' the Chicago of the Five Towns, which was his way of clarifying the confusing situation whereby it is Hanley that is the commercial heart of Stoke-on-Trent. Stoke is just one of the six communities, along with Tunstall, Burslem, Hanley itself, Longton and Fenton, that were merged to form Britain's fourteenth largest city in 1910. In any case the people of The Potteries have never been enamoured with the concept of belonging to an amorphous whole, preferring to shelter within the proudly individual characters of the six constituent towns. Hanley has suffered most from the pressures of the Consumer Age, and development has exorcised a good deal of the previously entrenched atmosphere of dignified northern provincialism. Heavens above, there is even a 'Cultural Quarter' now, something that would have Bennett choking on his Parisian cocktail.

Eating & Drinking
COACHMAKERS ARMS - Lichfield Street (up from Bridge 8 on the Caldon Canal, opposite bus station). Tel: 0787 614 4818. Unspoilt throwback. ST1 3EA
HOLY INADEQUATE - Etruria Old Road (west of Bridge 118). Tel: 0777 135 8238. Real ale and locally sourced pork pies. *Good Beer Guide* entry. ST1 5PL
MIRCHI - Snow Hill, Shelton (just up from Bridge 4 on the Caldon Canal). Tel: 01782 284368. Warmly regarded Indian restaurant and take-away open from 5pm daily (noon Sat & Sun). ST1 4LY
PORTOFINO - Marsh Street. Tel: 01782 209444. Italian restaurant open for lunch and dinner (5.30pm). ST1 1JD

Shopping
The centre of Hanley is about 15 minutes walk from the Trent & Mersey Canal at Etruria, but less distant from the Caldon Canal at Bridges 4 or 8. Frequent buses run from stops on Bridge 117. The Market Hall provides an outlet for local retailing. North Staffordshire staples include 'oatcakes' and 'pikelets'; whilst Wrights have a number of shops and stalls selling their popular meat pies etc. Should you need a supermarket, Morrisons are located in Festival Park, Sainsbury's can be found in Hanley and Stoke, and Tesco reasonably close to the canal in Etruria.

Things to Do
TOURIST INFORMATION CENTRE - Museum & Art Gallery, Bethesda Street. Tel: 01782 236000. ST1 3DW
EMMA BRIDGEWATER - Lichfield Street. Tel: 01782 201328. Tours, shop & cafe. Mooring rings on the towpath above Bridge 8 on the Caldon Canal. ST1 3EJ
ETRURIA INDUSTRIAL MUSEUM - canalside Bridge 116 (entrance beside the Caldon Canal). Admission charge. Tel: 0790 026 7711. Cafe/shop. The Etruscan Bone Mill is of exceptional interest, dating from 1857 and built to grind animal bones for use in 'bone' china. Open 'most' Fridays and selected weekends. ST1 4RB
MIDDLEPORT POTTERY - Port Street, Burslem (between bridges 125 & 126). Tel: 01782 499766. Manufacturers of Burleigh ware. Tours, museum, shop & cafe. Open 10am-4pm. Visitor Moorings. ST6 3PE
POTTERIES MUSEUM & ART GALLERY - Bethesda Street, Hanley. Tel: 01782 232323. Open 10am-5pm (11am-4pm Sun), admission free. Features the Staffordshire Hoard, ceramics, a section devoted to local man Reginald Mitchell's Spitfire fighter plane, and a rich collection of drawings, paintings and prints. ST1 3DW

Connections
TAXIS - City Cabs. Tel: 01782 844444/888888.

Stoke
Map 18

Known as 'Knype' in Arnold Bennett's stories, Stoke was, and remains, The Potteries railhead. Here, his Five Towns characters waited for Loop Line trains to convey them to 'Hanbridge' (Hanley), 'Bleakridge' (Cobridge) and 'Bursley' (Burslem). The station (east of the canal) is disguised as a Jacobean mansion with platforms where you might intuitively expect to find the croquet lawn. Neighbouring Winton Square is being redeveloped (a snip at £29m!) and Josiah Wedgwood's statue will be moved across the road. West of the canal the town itself is somewhat lacklustre, only the Classical Town Hall and Minster Church of St Peter ad Vincula make any architectural impact, though the tombs of Wedgwood and Spode lie in the latter's capacious and arboreal churchyard.

Things to Do
SPODE MUSEUM - Elenora Street, Stoke. Tel: 01782 411421. Open Wed-Sun, 10.30am-4pm. ST4 1QQ

Connections
TRAINS - major railhead near Bridge 113. Local trains to Longport, Kidsgrove, Stone etc.

Barlaston
Map 19

Suburban enclave with a useful row of shops west of the canal and a convenience store/PO to the east.

Eating & Drinking
PLUME OF FEATHERS - Station Rd. (Bridge 103). Tel: 01782 373100. Open daily from 11am, this congenial pub is owned by the actor Neil Morrissey. ST12 9DH

Things to Do
WORLD OF WEDGWOOD - Wedgwood Drive (adjacent Bridge 104). Tel: 01782 282986. Tours, museum, shop, and refreshments served on Wedgwood china. 10am-5pm daily. Set in 240 acre estate grounds. ST12 9ER
TRENTHAM ESTATE - Stone Road (a mile west of Bridge 106) Tel: 01782 646646. Hugeley popular regeneration of the old Sutherland estate. Gardens, woodlands, shopping, eating, monkeys. ST4 8JG

19 TRENT & MERSEY CANAL Hem Heath & Barlaston 4mls/11k/1½ hrs

HAVING adroitly escaped being recycled as waste energy, and notwithstanding the off-stage presence of numerous distribution hubs, the canal appears to move rapidly out into open country. Even Stoke City's stadium lies beyond the canal travellers field of vision, though enterprisingly a boat selling scrumptiously-filled oatcakes often appears as if by magic on match days. Yummy!

Bridge 108A once carried a railway connecting Michelin's tyre factory with the main line. A dramatic photograph in *Bylines* (Vol: 16 Issue 12) showed a heavy Claughton 4-6-0 locomotive testing the newly built bridge's strength in 1927. Coal from Florence Colliery at Longton - southernmost of the Six Towns - was loaded onto boats on the off-side at Sideway until the 1960s. Hem Heath (aka Trentham) Colliery was the penultimate of the North Staffordshire pits to close in 1997. Only Silverdale Colliery - west of Newcastle-under-Lyme - lasted another year.

Another long lost railway, marked now by blue-brick abutments where it crossed the canal, conveyed hordes of North Staffordshire day-trippers to the gardens of Trentham Hall. Trentham had been the seat of the Dukes of Sutherland, the most recent property having been completed in 1842 to the designs of Sir Charles Barry, architect of the Houses of Parliament. By all accounts it had been a most beautiful house set in the loveliest of landscaped parklands and Italian gardens. However, the Trent ran through these gorgeous grounds and, as the river grew more and more polluted by the combined effluents of The Potteries, life for the Duke, his household and visitors - which often included royalty - became less and less idyllic. Eventually he was forced to quit Trentham for another of the family seats, and the hall was demolished just before the Great War. Rather patronisingly he left the grounds to the people of The Potteries and, as more sophisticated methods of sewage control were developed, Trentham Gardens became a celebrated resort for the residents of North Staffordshire. After a lengthy period in limbo, Trentham has been regenerated at considerable expense, and now once again features spectacular Italian Gardens. A tall monument commemorating the second Duke of Sutherland may be seen rising above woodlands to the west of Trentham Lock; as does one above the small coastal town of Golspie in Sutherland.

Re-gated in 2021, Trentham Lock boasts a deep chamber with a pronounced undertow when filling. The foundations of its erstwhile keeper's cottage are readily apparent. Nearby stands the famous pottery works of Wedgwood. The company moved to Barlaston from their original site at Etruria in 1940. At one time there was a busy boatbuilding yard at Barlaston. A row of cottages occupied by its workforce - now highly desirable properties indeed - may be observed on the offside south of Bridge 103.

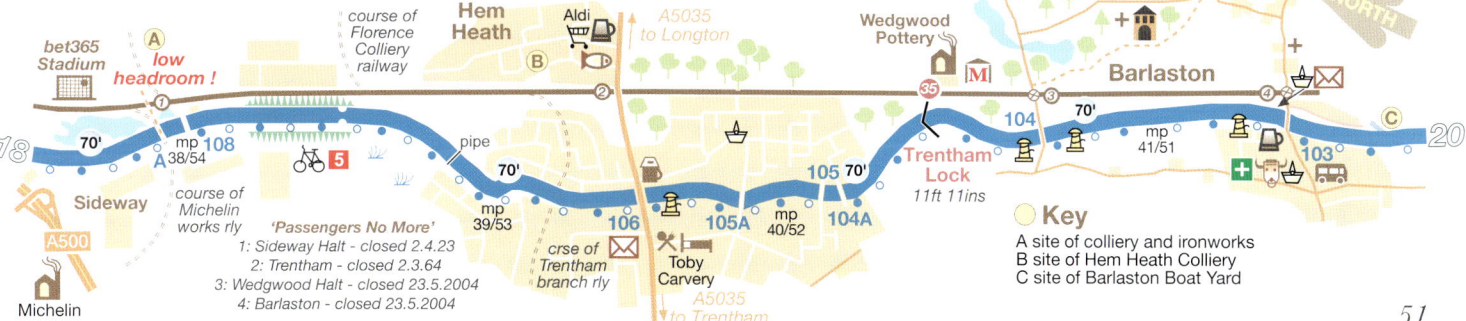

51

20 TRENT & MERSEY CANAL Meaford & Stone 4mls/8lks/3hrs

MEAFORD Power Station's five sentinel cooling towers were demolished in 1991. 'Gigantic' (and) 'strangely beautiful' John Hillaby found them, early one morning on his *Journey Through Britain* (Constable, 1968), an epic and engrossing walk from Land's End to John O' Groats inexplicably no longer in print. The generating plant had been the first to be commissioned by a post-war exhausted Britain, being somewhat inauspiciously opened by Manny Shinwell in 1947, two weeks after his sacking as Minister of Fuel and Power. Once the highest upstream of many which drew their cooling waters from the Trent - as indigenous to that river as castles to the Rhine and chateaux to the Loire we used to say - its site is slowly being redeveloped as a business park; as indeed is much of the UK.

There are four locks in the Meaford flight. Originally three of them were combined as a 'staircase'. Traces of the original course are vaguely apparent just west of the present layout. Meaford Locks form an attractive group, and they are bordered by a country lane with stone walling; one of the first signs that the north is beginning to give way to the midlands, or vice versa. Should you fall into conversation with any locals, it is disconcerting to hear them pronounce the place 'Method'.

Meaford Hall is a pale shadow of its heyday, for much of it was demolished in the 1940s. It was the birthplace of Admiral Jervis, feted for his victory at the Battle of Cape Saint Vincent in 1797 during the Anglo-Spanish War. The hall remained in the Jervis family until 1943, thereafter experiencing a chequered existence, not least ownership by a businessman subsequently imprisoned for a giant VAT fraud.

East of the canal lies Common Plot, 75 breezy acres of public open space administered by a group of elected trustees. Government forces were stationed here during the Jacobite uprising of 1745, deeming it more hospitable than the bleak uplands of the Peak District where they expected to encounter Bonnie Prince Charlie's forces marching south. Nowadays it's an invigorating spot to stretch lock-weary limbs.

Making its way through the upper valley of the River Trent, the canal arrives at the market town of Stone, original headquarters of

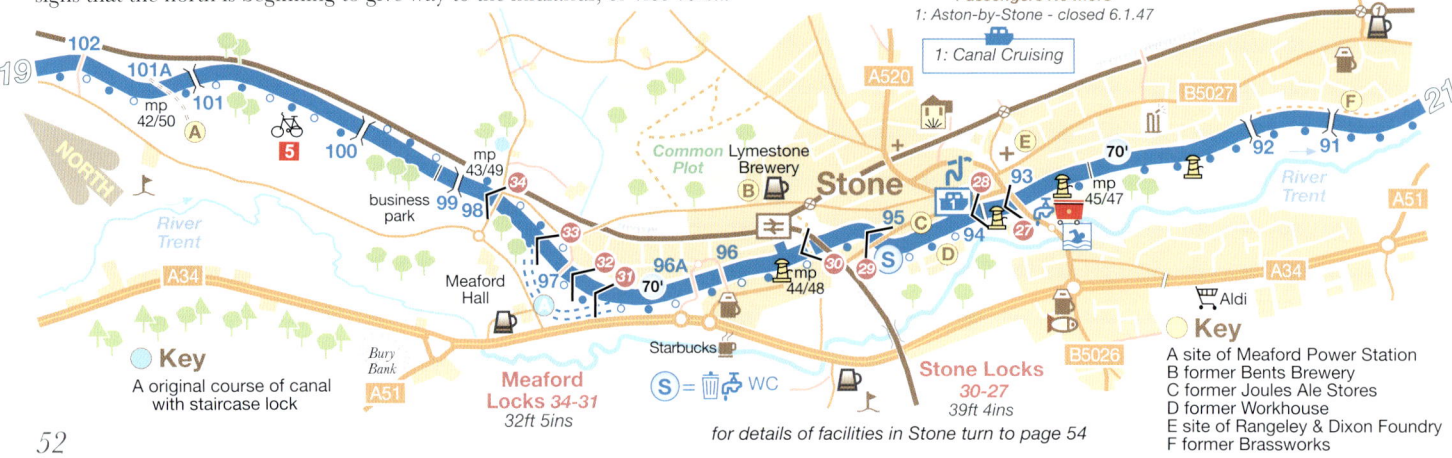

for details of facilities in Stone turn to page 54

the Trent & Mersey Canal Company, which probably explains why the rather obscure local foundry of Rangeley & Dixon won the contract to cast the T&M's distinctive mileposts, not that it made their fortune, for they ceased trading in 1829. Or perhaps they just 'took the money and ran'. Incidentally, the milepost which measures 44 miles from Preston Brook and 48 from Shardlow stands opposite Fuller's boatyard, enhanced by a narrow gauge railway with a sprinkling of attendant semaphore signals.

Stone lost its role as the administrative centre for the canal when it was bought out by the North Staffordshire Railway in 1846, but retained an extensive dockyard for maintenance purposes. Naturally, these days the emphasis is on leisure use, though there is still much to see as you chug through the four locks of the Stone flight. Lock 29 is overlooked by the large convent school of St Dominic's which was designed by Joseph Hansom, the man who invented the Hansom cab. A former pupil, the writer, A. N. Wilson, lived at Stonefield Cottage, the first house after the railway bridge below Lock 30. His father was managing director at Wedgwood and, indeed, had been influential in the firm's move from Etruria to Barlaston. Wilson's *The Potter's Hand* is a thoroughly readable novel with a Wedgwood theme.

A boat horse tunnel leads beneath Newcastle Street. Still quaintly signwritten, the former ale stores of the original Joule's Brewery border the canal before it widens by a fascinating spread of docks: covered and uncovered; wet and dry. These belong to the Canal Cruising Company, a pioneer of boating holidays on the canals, having been founded in 1948. It was here that L. T. C. Rolt's boat *Cressy*, of *Narrow Boat* immortality, met its untimely end, being broken up and cremated after failing a survey in 1951.

Crown Wharf has been redeveloped and features a flagship Joule's pub with the promises of a theatre and heritage centre to follow. On the other side of the canal the town's former hospital - once a workhouse - has, rather ironically, been converted into prestige accommodation. By Bridge 94, an enigmatic female sculpture commemorates Christina Collins, who perished on the Trent & Mersey Canal in 1839. She had boarded the Pickford's flyboat *Staffordshire Knot* at Preston Brook in order to join her husband, a Liverpudlian who had gone to London to find work. The railway network was in its infancy and most people still undertook lengthy journeys by stage coach, though travel by canal was a cheaper, if rather insalubrious option. By any stretch of the imagination, it cannot have been a pleasant experience for an unaccompanied woman to travel with a crew of three working boatmen and a boy. At both Stoke and Stone, Christina complained about the crew's behaviour towards her and their excessive drinking. She was concerned, in the euphemistic language of the era, that they would 'meddle' with her, to which an official at Stone responded fatuously by advising her to report any 'meddling' when she reached London. Christina was last seen alive around midnight on the second day of her journey by the lock-keeper at Hoo Mill (Map 22) and her body was later discovered in the canal near Rugeley.

Apprehended at Fazeley, the crew initially claimed their passenger had drowned herself, but subsequently began accusing each other of murder. Following further investigation, the cabin boy was set free, but the rest of the crew were tried for both rape and murder. Two trials ensued, and at the second the jury returned a unanimous verdict of guilty. All three were sentenced to death, though as they were receiving the sacrament from the chaplain at Stafford Gaol one had his sentence reduced to transportation to Australia. The other two were hanged publically on 11th April 1840. Their victim's gravestone can be found in St Augustine's churchyard, Rugeley (Map 23A).

Stone's gas works overlooked Lock 27. At one time the top of its gasometer was adorned with Joule's trademark red cross ... for the benefit of passing aviators one assumes. The Star public house predates the canal by some two hundred years. Across the road stood Westbridge House, headquarters of the T&M. A former warehouse, on the off-side beyond Bridge 93, has been converted into retirement flats.

With suburbs on one side and meadowlands on the other, the canal steels innocuously out of Stone. By and large the houses are unexceptional, apart from a handsome, three-storey Georgian edifice adjacent Bridge 91. In the first half of the 19th century there was a brass works here, and this was the manager's house.

Stone   Map 20

Self-billed 'Canal Town', Stone is a lively market town of some twelve thousand souls who display much affection for the canal on their doorstep. Conscious of their heritage, the local civic society have erected plaques on walls recalling that Peter de Wint, the landscape watercolourist, was born here; that the Duke of Cumberland came here to do battle; that the Star Inn has long attended to the thirst of passers-by; and that Henry Holland designed the bow-fronted Crown Inn in 1780. Stone has a history of brewing, Joule's and Bents being well-regarded far beyond the town's hinterland. Joule's - reinvented now - began brewing in the town in 1758 and, with the advent of the canal, and the possibilities of export it brought, their ales became fashionable in Europe and the Americas. Once they operated a pair of boats to bring in coal for firing the steam plant. In 1970, however, they were absorbed into the Bass Charrington conglomerate and, hardly surprisingly, brewing ceased four years later; though the canalside ale stores remain intact. Bents, the town's other brewers, closed in the early 1960s, though bits of their brewery survive in industrial use, notably the micro-brewers Lymestone.

Eating & Drinking
BEAR - High Street. Tel: 01785 819053. Stylish cafe/bar open 8am-5pm plus evenings Fri & Sat. ST15 8AH
BOREHOLE - Mount Road. Tel: 01785 813581. Lymestone's award-winning brewery tap. Open from noon. Home made food served until 8pm. ST15 8LL
CROWN WHARF - Crown Street. Tel: 01785 550450. Joules flagship brewery tap. ST15 8QW
GRANVILLES - Granville Square. Tel: 01785 816658. Brasserie and jazz bar. ST15 8AB
PASTA DI PIAZZA - High Street. Tel: 01785 813214. Refurbished Italian restaurant. 12-3/5-10pm Mon-Sat and from noon throughout Sun. ST15 8AW

POSTE OF STONE - Granville Square. Tel: 01785 827920. Wetherspoons housed in former post office. Wide range of real ales and inexpensive meals with breakfasts being served from 8am. ST15 8AB
PRIORY FISH BAR - Lichfield Street. Tel: 01785 819992. Excellent fish & chip shop. ST15 8NA
ROYAL EXCHANGE - Radford Street. Tel: 01785 812685. *Good Beer Guide* listed Titanic town pub featuring up to a dozen real ales on tap. ST15 8DA
SMOKE & RYE - Stafford Street. Tel: 01785 501254. American inspired bar & restaurant. ST15 8QW
THE STAR - canalside Bridge 93. Tel: 01785 813896. Lockside Marston's pub. ST15 8QW
SWAN INN - Lichfield Street (adjacent Bridge 93). Tel: 01785 815570. *Good Beer Guide* listed town centre local. Coach House ales from Warrington. ST15 8QW

Shopping
Stone is a good shopping centre with the advantage of being so close to the canal that you can easily carry bulky carrier-bags back to the boat. The annual Food & Drink Festival takes place in October. Fine stoneware and bone china from Dunoon on High Street. Griffins butchers on Adies Alley off High Street. Morrisons and Aldi supermarkets; M&S Foodhall south-west of Bridge 93. Market on Tuesdays, Fridays & Saturdays. Farmers Market on the 1st Saturday of each month. Tim Toft Violins is a marvellous string instrument shop at the town end of Station Road.

Connections
BUSES - First Potteries service 101 to/from Stafford and Hanley runs half-hourly Mon-Sat. D&G provide a bi-hourly service on Sundays.
TRAINS - London & Northwestern services connect Stone's handsome Jacobean station hourly with Stoke, Kidsgrove and Crewe in one direction and Stafford, Wolverhampton and Birmingham in the other.
TAXIS - Smart Cars. Tel: 01785 288999.

Aston-by-Stone   Map 21
NO.26 - Lichfield Road. Tel: 01785 819702. Marina restaurant serving breakfasts at weekends from 10am; lunch Mon-Sat 12-5pm, and dinner 5-9pm; on Suns meals are served throughout from noon. ST15 8QU

Burston   Map 21
THE GREYHOUND - Poolside. Tel: 01889 508263. Country inn owned by three generations of the Jordan family. Closed Mon: lunches and dinners (from 6pm) Tue-Fri; food throughout Sat & Sun. ST18 0DR

Sandon   Map 21
DOG & DOUBLET - Sandon Road. Tel: 01889 508331. 'Arts & Crafts' style pub owned by the Lewis partnership who also operate the Moat House at Acton Trussell. Food and accommodation. ST18 0DJ

Salt   Map 22
HOLLYBUSH INN - Willowmore Banks. Tel: 01889 508404. Historic inn highly regarded for its food. Open from noon weekdays, 9am weekends. ST18 0BX

Weston   Map 22
SARACEN'S HEAD - Stafford Road (Bridge 80). Tel: 01889 270286. Village pub with pet llamas. Open daily from 7.30am: breakfast served until 10.30am, thereafter food from noon. Accommodation. ST18 0HT
THE WOOLPACK - The Green. Tel: 01889 270238. Marston's pub overlooking the village green. ST18 0JH
WESTON HALL - Weston Bank. Tel: 01889 271082. Impressive 17th century mansion now used for functions. Cellar Restaurant, afternoon teas. ST18 0HS
AMERTON FARM - Stowe-by-Chartley. Tel: 01889 270294. Just over a mile east of the canal on the A518. An eclectic mix of food and craft outlets with a tea room and narrow gauge railway (weekends only). Chaserider bus service 841 runs to/from Uttoxeter and Stafford hourly Mon-Sat.

21 TRENT & MERSEY CANAL Aston & Sandon 4mls/2lks/1½ hrs

TAKING apparent pleasure in each other's company, canal and river, road and railway make their undemonstrative way through a shallow valley, skirting, but scarcely encountering, a succession of small settlements, barely in the category of villages. With no great dramas to catch the eye, the canal traveller is thrown back on their own resources. They can pass the time wrestling with the great conundrums of life or anticipate the slow drawing of a foaming pint in the convivial bars of the Greyhound at Burston or the Dog & Doublet at Sandon.

Aston Lock marks the half-way point of the Trent & Mersey's route from Preston Brook to Shardlow; names which mean nothing now but were once as well known as Spaghetti Junction and Watford Gap. One of the distinctive cast iron mileposts, originally made in Stone by Rangeley & Dixon, quotes 46 miles in either direction. Flat-decked, Bridge 88 breaks the monotony of its hump-backed neighbours.

Burston is a well-kept secret, a beautiful small community idyllically grouped about a pond. The tiny church of St Rufin's can trace its origins back to medieval times. An axle from Burston's former watermill is displayed on the green, recalling an era when communities like this worked rather than slumbered.

Between Aston and Burston a nature trail runs parallel to the canal, crossing farmland owned by Severn Trent water authority and chosen for experiments in biodiversity. When we last passed they appeared to be 'experimenting' with Belted Galloways, a black and white breed of cattle indigenous to south-west Scotland.

It's but a short stroll from Sandon Lock to the picturesque village of the same name, albeit one where you have to keep one eye on the B5066's unaccommodating motorists. Sandon Hall, home of the Harrowbys, is a Victorian house in Jacobean style, well hidden from the world in rolling parkland. Above the tree-line peeps a slender urn-topped column commemorating William Pitt. Another Prime Minister, the assassinated Spencer Perceval, is recalled by a nearby shrine.

Unfortunately the house and its grounds are only occasionally open to the public, but you can continue eastwards and upwards along a foxglove jostled lane which initially does an impression of Devon, but which by the time it has plateaued out - some four hundred feet above sea level - thinks it's somewhere in the Scottish borders. Pheasants roam about, waiting to be shot, whilst from the churchyard of All Saints distant views of The Wrekin provide consolation for an interior - reputedly blessed with myriad tombs and monuments - invariably locked. Other points of interest include the war memorial, the 'arts & crafts' style village hall and matching pub, and the ornate former station house, notable for the *porte-cochere*, built to accommodate the carriage from Sandon Hall.

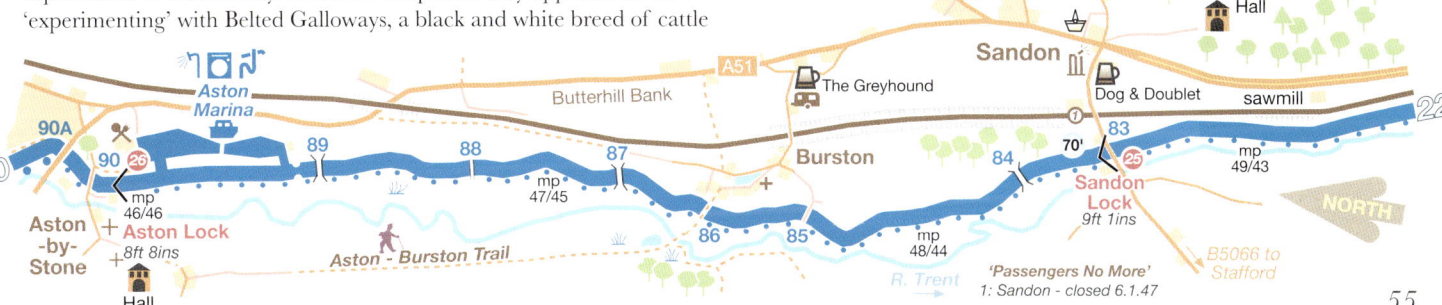

22 TRENT & MERSEY CANAL Salt & Weston 4mls/2lks/1½ hrs

RECOGNIZING a little slice of Arcady when they saw one, several wealthy families put down grandiose roots in the upper valley of the Trent. Built of brick and stone for the benefit of Sandon's gentry, Bridge 82 evokes the high aesthetic values of the 18th century. To pass beneath it is akin to entering a church.

Any scar tissue wrought by the advent of the canal must have been healed by the time the railways arrived. The North Staffordshire Railway followed the course of the Trent & Mersey (which it was soon to acquire) down the valley to Colwich and became part of a main line of some importance as a through route between Manchester and London via The Potteries. Another line arrived in the landscape, was absorbed into the Great Northern Railway, and became a far-flung outpost of the LNER at the grouping of the railway companies in 1923. Passenger traffic was never significant - how could it be in these rural haunts? - but the milk of the Trent Valley's cows was creamy enough for the scheduling of a daily milk train to the capital. One activity in this otherwise rural area that the canal did help to prosper was the making of salt. The Trentside village of that name has associations with the trade going back to Medieval times; perhaps even Roman. But at both Shirleywich and Weston brine pumping developed significantly in the 18th century because the canal was used to bring in coal to fuel evaporation and to carry away the finished product. Agriculture and industry combined to corner the market in salted beef for the Royal Navy, conveyed in barrels by narrow boat. When brine extraction ceased, around the end of the 19th century, the works at Weston was taken over by a firm specialising in the manufacture of alabaster bowls.

West of the canal (though frustratingly inaccessible *legally* from Bridge 78) stands Ingestre Hall, a 17th century mansion in the Jacobean style built at the behest of the Chetwynds who morphed with the Talbots and became the Earls of Shrewsbury. The accompanying church is said to have been designed by Sir Christopher Wren (though it's unlikely that he attended its construction) and John Nash added later parts. The hall was sold in 1960 - to West Bromwich Borough Council of all people - and has been used as a residential centre for the arts ever since. A pavilion in the grounds can be booked for holiday accommodation through the Landmark Trust.

Pasturefields Saltmarsh is an extremely rare - if not unique - example of an inland saltmarsh and provides an environment in which a number of halophytic, or salt tolerant, plants can thrive, amongst which are the charmingly named lesser sea-spurrey and saltmarsh rue. Snipe, redshank and lapwing nest here too.

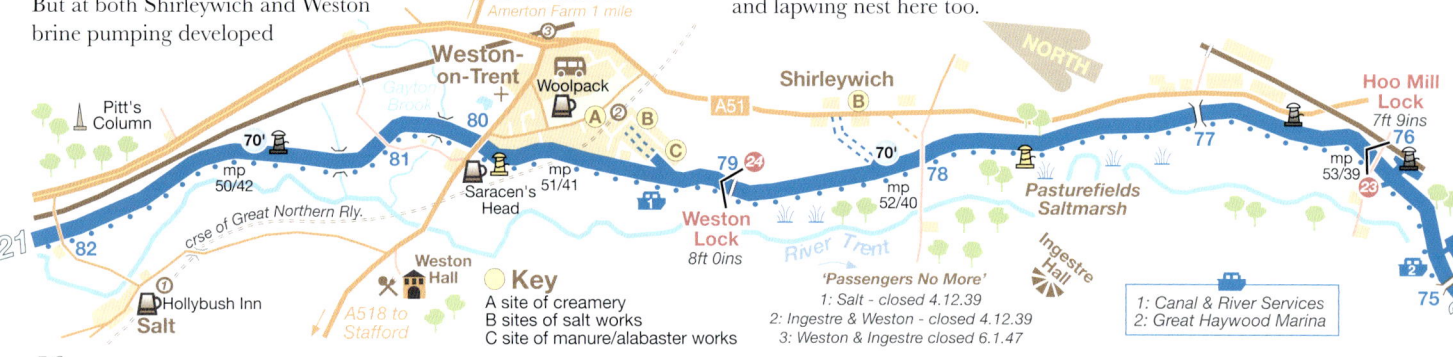

Key
A site of creamery
B sites of salt works
C site of manure/alabaster works

'Passengers No More'
1: Salt - closed 4.12.39
2: Ingestre & Weston - closed 4.12.39
3: Weston & Ingestre closed 6.1.47

1: Canal & River Services
2: Great Haywood Marina

23 TRENT & MERSEY CANAL Great Haywood 4mls/11k/2hrs*

BRINDLEY invariably found it simpler to follow river valleys, and Great Haywood was an obvious choice of location for a canal junction designed to establish his scheme for a 'Grand Cross' of man made waterways linking the four great English estuaries: Humber, Thames, Severn and Mersey. With the completion of the Staffordshire & Worcestershire Canal in 1772, and the Trent & Mersey five years later, Haywood became a canal junction of major importance, as significant to transport in the 18th century as any motorway interchange today. One is only left to marvel at the simplicity of it all - two quiet ribbons of water meeting beneath a bridge of exquisite beauty - and compare it wistfully with transport interchanges of the 21st century, acres of concrete, noise and pollution. Where did we go wrong?

History may have taken some wrong turnings, but there is little chance for the canal traveller to make a mistake, for a prominent fingerpost directs one concisely enough to "Wolverhampton", "The Trent", or "The Potteries". The Trent & Mersey (covered in this guide as far as Fradley Junction (Map 23C) is at its most memorably beautiful as it skirts the boundary of Shugborough. On one bank beechwoods tumble down to the water's edge. On the other, across the river, there are glimpses of the statues, antiquities and follies which pepper the grounds of this famous home of the Anson family. Colwich Lock lies in an attractive setting between the village church, a picturesque farm, and a bend in the Trent. From Bridge 72 you can walk to Seven Springs,

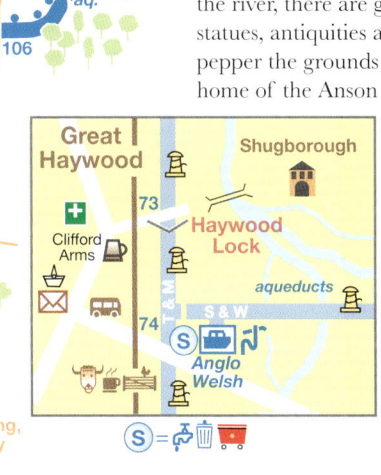

a wonderful springboard for exploring Cannock Chase. Hidden from the canal, but visible from passing trains, St Mary's Abbey was occupied by an order of Benedictine nuns who could trace their origins back to 17th century France and an English order based in Cambrai. Sadly, however, the abbey closed in 2020, due to diminishing numbers.

Staffordshire & Worcestershire Canal

Through the arch of Bridge 109 - an 18th century fusion of functional engineering and enduring loveliness - the Staffordshire & Worcestershire Canal commences its 46 mile journey down to the Severn at Stourport. Two aqueducts carry it across the Trent and a millstream. A couple of miles further on it crosses the Sow. Between these river crossings the canal suddenly casts off its inhibitions and widens into a broad lake of quite un-canal-like proportions, bordered by thick reedbeds inhabited by a gorgeous array of wildfowl. Boaters may find their craft looping the loop out of sheer exuberance. This is Tixall Wide or Broadwater and there are two theories for its surprising existence. Some maintain that the canal was widened into an artificial lake to placate the owner of Tixall Hall. Others that the expanse of water predates the canal, that it was naturally formed, and that Izaak Walton learnt to fish here. Whichever explanation suits you, don't miss the extraordinary Elizabethan gatehouse which overlooks The Wide. The hall itself, where Mary Queen of Scots was imprisoned for a fortnight in 1586, was demolished long ago. The gatehouse is let for holidays by the Landmark Trust who specialise in restoring and holiday-letting properties worth saving.

West of Tixall's solitary lock the canal meanders enchantingly through the valley of the Sow. A plethora of trees adds lustre to the landscape. Towpath walkers can hear southbound trains being gobbled up by the decorated portal of Shugborough Tunnel. Those of a railway bent may be intrigued to learn that Francis William Webb, the great locomotive engineer of the London & North Western Railway, hailed from Tixall, where his father was Rector for over half a century. Sir Nigel Gresley, of *Flying Scotsman* and *Mallard* fame, also famously had a man of the cloth for a father.

The Haywoods   Map 23

The villages of Great and Little Haywood are separated by a long, high 'make-work' wall. Dormitory housing has inevitably expanded both populations, but the centres remain peaceful and largely unspoilt; especially so in the charming lane leading from Great Haywood, under the railway and over the canal, to the Essex Bridge, one of the finest examples of a packhorse bridge imaginable. Tolkien convalesced in Great Haywood after catching trench fever during the Battle of the Somme, and it is thinly disguised as 'Tavrobel' in *The Tale of The Sun and The Moon*. It is further suggested that the rivers Gruir and Afros were inspired by the Trent and Sow.

Eating & Drinking

CANALSIDE CAFE - Mill Lane (Bridge 74). Tel: 01889 881747. Open 9am-5pm daily. Nicely furnished and airy waterside premises. ST18 0RQ

CLIFFORD ARMS - Main Road. Tel: 01889 881321. Open daily from noon. Bar food lunchtimes and evenings from 6pm. ST18 0SR.

Two pubs in Little Haywood: Lamb & Flag (Tel: 01889 359789) and Red Lion (Tel: 01889 881314).

Shopping

Great Haywood has a Spar convenience store with Post Office, a pharmacy, and a superbly-stocked farm shop, with butchery alongside the junction.

Things to Do

SHUGBOROUGH ESTATE - access via Haywood Lock and Essex Bridge. Tel: 01889 880160. National Trust estate with many attractions. Open daily throughout year though some restrictions to house. ST17 0XB

Connections

BUSES - Chaserider service 828 operates hourly Mon-Sat between Stafford and Lichfield via Rugeley.

Milford   Map 23

Public access via a bridge beneath the railway just west of Bridge 105 (Map 24) has been rescinded, so the only practical way to reach this Cannock Chase-side village legally is by Holdiford Road from Bridge 106, which is provided with a pavement beyond the river. Milford's pride is its vast village green, part of which is given over to parking. Milford Hall Cricket Club won the Village Cup at Lords in 2023.

Facilities include: a mountain bike hire facility (Run & Ride - Tel: 01785 662769. ST17 0UR); the Barley Mow (a Greene King 'Eating-Inn' - Tel: 01785 665230. ST17 0UW); and The Viceroy (an Indian restaurant - Tel: 01785 663239. ST17 0UH); and what is reputedly Britain's most long-lived Wimpy fast food outlet. Chaserider bus 826 links Milford hourly (ex Sun) with Stafford, Rugeley and Lichfield.

23A TRENT & MERSEY CANAL Colwich & Rugeley 4mls/0lks/1½ hrs

SEVERAL big houses were built by prosperous landowners in this enchanting countryside. Bishton Hall overlooks the canal and is now a showroom for Hansons Auctioneers. You may have seen its ebullient owner, Charles Hanson, on one or other of the popular television antiques programmes. Intriguingly, the hall once featured a Grecian boathouse on the banks of the Trent, the remains of which can be found amidst the undergrowth on the riverbank by a spill-weir. Another mansion, Wolseley Hall, stood opposite on the far bank of the river. It was demolished long ago, but the grounds have been incorporated into the Staffordshire Wildlife Trust's Wolseley Centre. Wolseley Bridge has graced the Trent here since 1800. It was designed by John Rennie, best known in canal circles for his work on the Kennet & Avon.

At Brindley Bank the canal suddenly stops running parallel with the Trent and turns sharply to cross it. Once there was a transhipment wharf here where flint was swapped between canal and river vessels for the short run down to Colton Mill by Trent Valley railway station. A handsome pumping station overlooks this crossing of water over water, though the aqueduct itself is of little aesthetic appeal. By Bridge 68 a short, reedy arm adjacent to the railway provides a useful turning point for lengthy craft. This may have been used as a transshipment basin in the fledgling days of the railway.

The towpath plays host to a pair of walking routes: the Staffordshire Way (Mow Cop to Kinver) and Millennium Way (Newport to Burton-on-Trent). Rugeley usually gets a bad press from guidebooks, but we have always had a soft spot for this down to earth little town, once home to the notorious Victorian poisoner, William Palmer and also remembered as the scene, in 1839, of the canal murder of Christina Collins. In years gone by Rugeley was the site of a malodorous tannery where flats have been built at Bridge 66. Demolished in 2021, Rugeley Power Station's site is being redeveloped as a low carbon community.

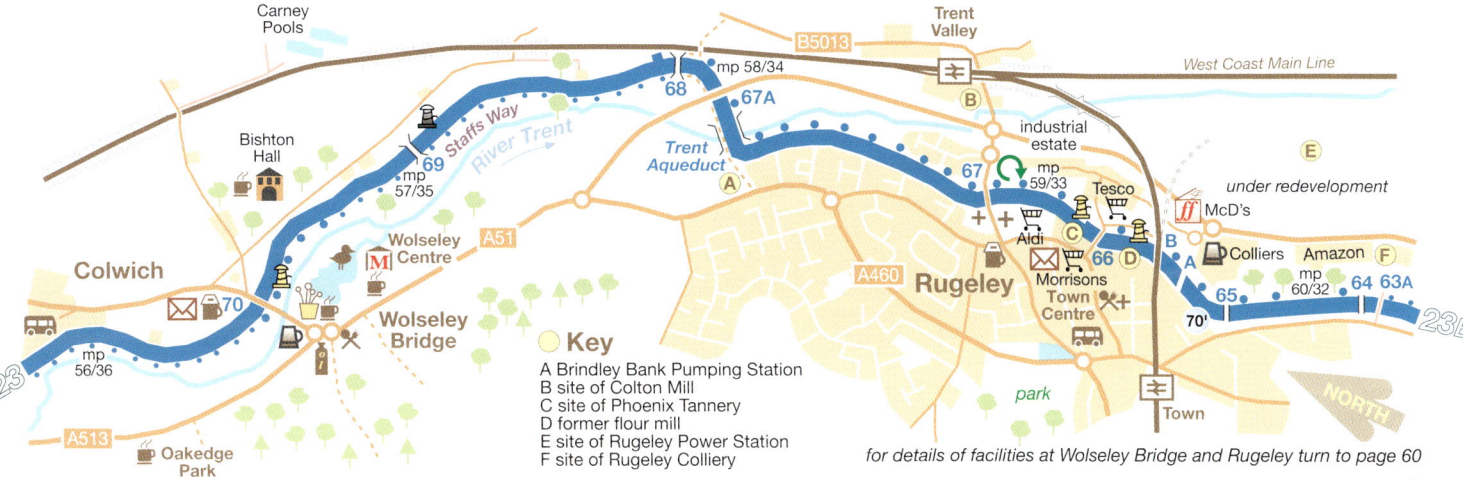

Key
A Brindley Bank Pumping Station
B site of Colton Mill
C site of Phoenix Tannery
D former flour mill
E site of Rugeley Power Station
F site of Rugeley Colliery

for details of facilities at Wolseley Bridge and Rugeley turn to page 60

59

Wolseley Bridge   Map 23A

Pleasantly wooded visitor moorings to the east of Bridge 70 make this a popular stopover. Moreover, it's an eclectic community with plenty of places to seek refreshment. A reconstructed barn houses an antiques outlet and there's a cluster of other rescued buildings and artefacts: dovecot, RAC patrolman's hut, and a William Foster threshing machine bearing the Lincoln agricultural machinery firm's WW1 tank trademark.

Eating & Drinking
SHIMLA PALACE - far side of river bridge by roundabout. Tel: 01889 881325. Indian restaurant, eat in or takeaway. ST17 0XS

WOLSELEY ARMS - far side of river bridge. Tel: 01889 883179. Vintage Inns establishment, once the meeting place for the canal's promoters. ST17 0XS

Shopping
Wolseley Bridge Garden Centre (Tel: 01889 574884 - ST17 0YA) (with cafe) is easily accessed from Bridge 70. Wolseley Wine Loft (ST17 OXS) is open Thur-Sat from 1pm. Other craft outlets too, but exercise care crossing the busy roundabouts.

Things to Do
BISHTON HALL - Wolseley Bridge. Tel: 01889 882397. Splendid Georgian mansion now an antiques venue. Auctions and valuation days. Tea room open daily 10am-4pm. Courtyard with deli and craft shops. Well worth an excursion ashore, if only to absorb the hall's imposing architecture. ST17 0XN

THE WOLSELEY CENTRE - Wolseley Bridge (far side of river bridge beyond roundabout). Tel: 01889 880100. Staffordshire Wildlife Trust HQ set in revitalised 26 acre garden park. Kingfisher Cafe & gift shop. Open 9am-5pm daily. ST17 0WT

Connections
BUSES - Chaserider 826/8 as per Rugeley.

Rugeley   Map 23A

Sculpted figures of miners on a traffic island recall that this was a coal mining town up until 1990. It is difficult to escape the impression that life here is lived 'on the cheap' - though not without a certain deadpan dignity. Here in the tight-knit streets, and on the old Coal Board estates, one finds thrift and graft and a perverse civic pride, whilst a consoling beauty is to be found up on the nearby Chase. In the churchyard of St Augustine's (adjacent Bridge 67) an isolated gravestone remembers Christina Collins, noting that 'having been most barbarously treated was found dead in the Canal in this parish on 17th June 1839'. The story of her misadventure (see page 53) inspired Colin Dexter's novel *The Wench is Dead*.

Eating & Drinking
THE COLLIERS - Power Station Road (adjacent Bridge 66A). Tel: 01889 503951. Table Table bar/restaurant open for breakfast from 6.30am (7am weekends); main meals from noon 'til late. WS15 1LX

PLAZA - Horsefair. Tel: 01889 586831. Wetherspoons characterfully housed in former cinema. Open from 8am daily. WS15 2EJ

TERRAZZA - Lichfield Street. Tel: 01889 570630. Charming, family run Italian which has been in Rugeley since 1996. Open Tue-Sat from 6pm. WS15 2EH

VINE INN - Sheep Fair. Tel: 01889 574443. Unselfconsciously old-fashioned pub - in a quiet corner of the town opposite Elmore Park - which brews its own beer. Fish & Chip Fridays from 5pm. WS15 2AT

Shopping
Morrisons, Tesco and Aldi supermarkets. Sadly, the indoor market has been 'mothballed'.

Connections
BUSES - Chaserider 826/8 provide a half-hourly Mon-Sat service linking Rugeley with Stafford and Lichfield.

TRAINS - useful hourly London Northwestern service along the Trent Valley and half hourly West Midlands from Town or Trent Valley stations to Cannock (a pretty quarter of an hour's ride away up over the flanks of the Chase), Walsall and B'ham.

TAXIS - Chase Cars. Tel: 01889 584545.

Armitage   Map 23B

Offside moorings provide access via an alleyway to a goodly number of shops on the main road.

Eating & Drinking
ASH TREE - canalside Bridge 62. Tel: 01889 578314. Marston's 'Two for One'. WS15 1PF

PLUM PUDDING - canalside Bridge 61A. Tel: 01543 490330. Revitalised canalside pub open from noon daily. WS15 4AZ

Shopping
Butcher/baker, post office, pharmacy, convenience store.

Connections
BUSES - Chaserider 826/8 as per Rugeley.

Handsacre   Map 23B

The High Bridge spanning the Trent to the north of Bridge 58 rewards a visit. Its graceful cast-iron arch was made at Coalbrookdale in 1830, though a livelier colour scheme might do it more justice.

Eating & Drinking
THE CROWN - canalside Bridge 58. Tel: 01543 318164. Canalside pub. WS15 4DT

MICHAEL'S - The Green. Tel: 01543 491314. Queues testify to quality fish & chips. WS15 4DT
Another pub called The Old Peculiar (Tel: 01543 491891) plus a cafe at Tuppenhurst Farm (Tel: 01543 491955).

Shopping
Convenience store tucked away on Tuppenhurst Lane.

Connections
BUSES - Chaserider 826/8 as per Rugeley.

23B TRENT & MERSEY CANAL Armitage & Handsacre 4mls/0lks/1½ hrs

WHILST by no means a length of canal likely to endear itself to connoisseurs of the picturesque, this stretch of the Trent & Mersey is never actually overwhelmed by industry, and there are a number of invigorating views over the Trent Valley or up on to the flanks of Cannock Chase.

The characteristic Trent & Mersey mileposts measure your progress, more relevant perhaps to the perspiring towpath walker than the languorous boater, laid-back on their tiller. They were put in place originally to facilitate the calculation of tolls, but at the outset of the Second World War - in common with most of Britain's road and railway signs - they were removed to befuddle invaders. Remarkably, following a commendable campaign by the Trent & Mersey Canal Society in the 1970s, they have all been returned to their rightful places. The originals are inscribed 'R&D Stone 1819', the replicas cast to replace those which had 'disappeared' during the interim, are inscribed 'T&MCS 1977'.

Connections are apparent with a famous earthenware firm at Spode House and Hawkesyard Priory. Josiah Spode, a member of the North Staffordshire pottery family, left his house to a Dominican Order in 1893 and the monks proceeded to build a priory in the grounds, completing the work just prior to the First World War. The priory is now a day spa and retreat whilst the grounds have become a golf course.

Passing beneath the A513, the canal narrows and negotiates a rocky cutting. One-way working is the order of the day. This was formerly the site of Armitage (or "Plum Pudding") Tunnel, a dramatic unlined bore through the rock face. Subsidence, induced by coal mining, necessitated opening out of the tunnel, and concrete lining of the canal banks.

Armitage's church is perched above a sandstone bluff by Bridge 61. Though much rebuilt by the Victorians, it retains its highly decorated Norman font. A path worth taking leads beneath the railway and over the Trent to the isolated settlement of Mavesyn Ridware which also has an interesting church.

Armitage and Shanks are synonymous with toilet plumbing. Their trade marks are emblazoned on public conveniences throughout the world. Once they were separate firms, merging in 1969, but the site alongside the canal at Armitage dates back to 1817. Sanitaryware became a speciality in the 19th century under the management of Edward Johns - the origin of the Americanism "Going to the John". Today the factory, towering over a narrow stretch of canal spanned by the West Coast Main Line railway, is huge and convincingly prosperous, and Ideal Standard - as they are now somewhat less resonantly known - are a public limited company flushed with success.

Handsacre will be the point where the truncated HS2 railway joins the WCML, resulting in a 'bottleneck' critics insist.

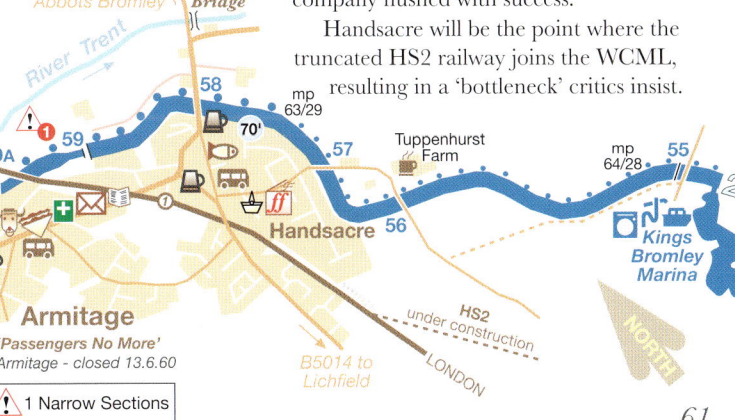

61

23C TRENT & MERSEY CANAL Fradley Junction 2½ mls/3lks/1½ hrs

A BEND in the canal south of Woodend Lock, and glimpses of the three spires of Lichfield Cathedral, tell you that you and the Trent & Mersey have travelled as far south as you are ever going to get in the canal's arc-like journey between Preston Brook and Shardlow. Ravenshaw Woods are a riot of rhododendron colour in early summer. The works by Bridge 54 was once the smelly 'milk factory' referred to by L. T. C. Rolt in *Narrow Boat*.

What would Tom Rolt have made of HS2? A traditionalist at heart, he would probably have recoiled at the despoliation wrought on the countryside neighbouring the new route. But then didn't 18th century observers feel the same about construction of the Trent & Mersey Canal? Besides, Rolt loved railways too, as evinced by his books *Railway Adventure*, *Lines of Character*, and *The Making of a Railway*. So his likely response is open to conjecture, and something for you to mull over too as you make your way to Fradley Junction, passing evidence of the project's construction en route. HS2 was to bifurcate at Fradley, with a chord linking to the West Coast Main Line at Handsacre, whilst the main route advanced north to Crewe and Manchester. But while we were putting this guide together, the Government announced that they would no longer proceed with the Manchester leg of the line. So the projected route, earmarked to cross the canal in woodland above Shade House Lock may never come to fruition, leaving the upgraded towpath as the multi-billion pound scheme's sole legacy in the neighbourhood.

A couple of locks lead down to the Trent & Mersey's assignation with the Coventry Canal. On hot summer days the junction is hugely popular with sightseers, but on winter afternoons it isn't difficult to imagine how it must have looked in the latter days of cargo carrying. Listening posts offer entertaining insights into Fradley's heritage. A popular cafe occupies part of the T&M's maintenance yard. On the opposite bank, woodland masks Fradley Pool, which has been opened out as a visitor attraction with bird hides and facilities for pond dipping. The Trent & Mersey constructed a channel from above Middle Lock to feed the reservoir, ensuring that their valuable supplies weren't diverted into the Coventry Canal.

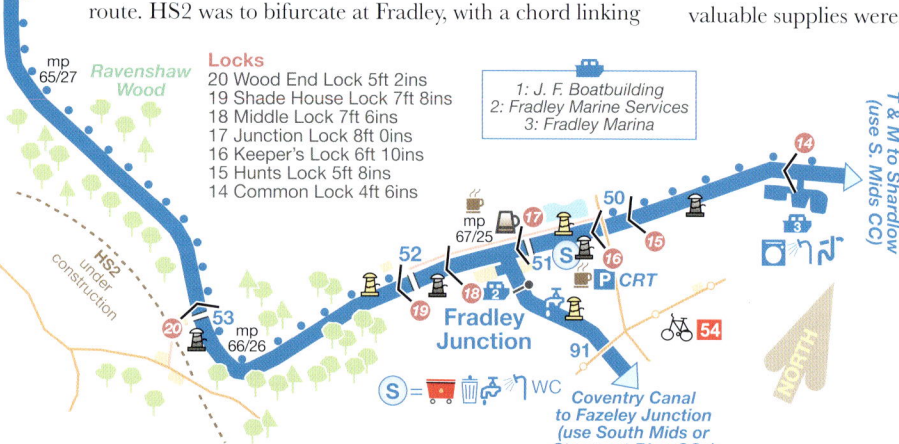

Locks
20 Wood End Lock 5ft 2ins
19 Shade House Lock 7ft 8ins
18 Middle Lock 7ft 6ins
17 Junction Lock 8ft 0ins
16 Keeper's Lock 6ft 10ins
15 Hunts Lock 5ft 8ins
14 Common Lock 4ft 6ins

1: J. F. Boatbuilding
2: Fradley Marine Services
3: Fradley Marina

Fradley Junction

Quintessential canal junction, perennially popular with motorists and boaters alike.

Eating & Drinking
THE SWAN - canalside, Fradley Junction. Tel: 01283 790330. Everard's pub. Food lunchtime and evening (from 5.30pm) daily; noon to 6pm Sun. DE13 7DN
LAUGHING DUCK - Tel: 01283 792508. Cafe located in part of the former maintenance yard buildings. Outdoor waterside tables too. DE13 7DN
KINGFISHER CAFE - cafe connected to holiday park. Tel: 01283 790407. DE13 7DN

Connections
TAXIS - Alrewas Direct Cars. Tel: 01283 790373.

24 STAFFS & WORCS CANAL Stafford 4mls/11k/1½hrs

THE canal cold-shoulders the county town. Nothing personal, it would have incurred a great deal of extra work on Brindley's part to take the canal across the marshy valleys of the Sow and Penk. But later - in 1816, to be precise - the Sow was made navigable into the centre of Stafford, and remained so up until the 1920s. J. Ian Langford, in *Towpath Guide No.1*, recalls that Ernie Thomas, a renowned boatman, carried a cargo of swedes and mangels down the branch just before the Great War. A group known as the Stafford Riverway Link are actively promoting restoration of navigability into the centre of town, a thoroughly worthwhile cause. Meanwhile you can walk there (half an hour at a brisk pace) along the riverbank past the cleared site of English Electric's engineering works in the process of being redeveloped as housing.

Baswich church stands aloof above housing estates like a shy vicar impelled to attend a noisy children's party. Note the spelling of the village's name with a 'k' on Bridge 100. There was a substantial wharf by Radford Bridge, but its site is now somewhat less interestingly occupied by a car showroom following demolition of the original warehouses in the philistine seventies.

Stafford Boat Club - with their impressive club house and warm welcome to visiting boaters - occupy a former brickworks arm near Hazelstrine Bridge. Most of the works' output was despatched by canal. Bridge 97 has disappeared completely, there being not even any tell-tale narrowing in the canal's channel where it once must have stood.

Radford Meadows form part of the River Penk's floodplain and are now administered by the Staffordshire Wildlife Trust as a nature reserve. Public access is restricted to special events, but the towpath offers fine views and interpretive boards.

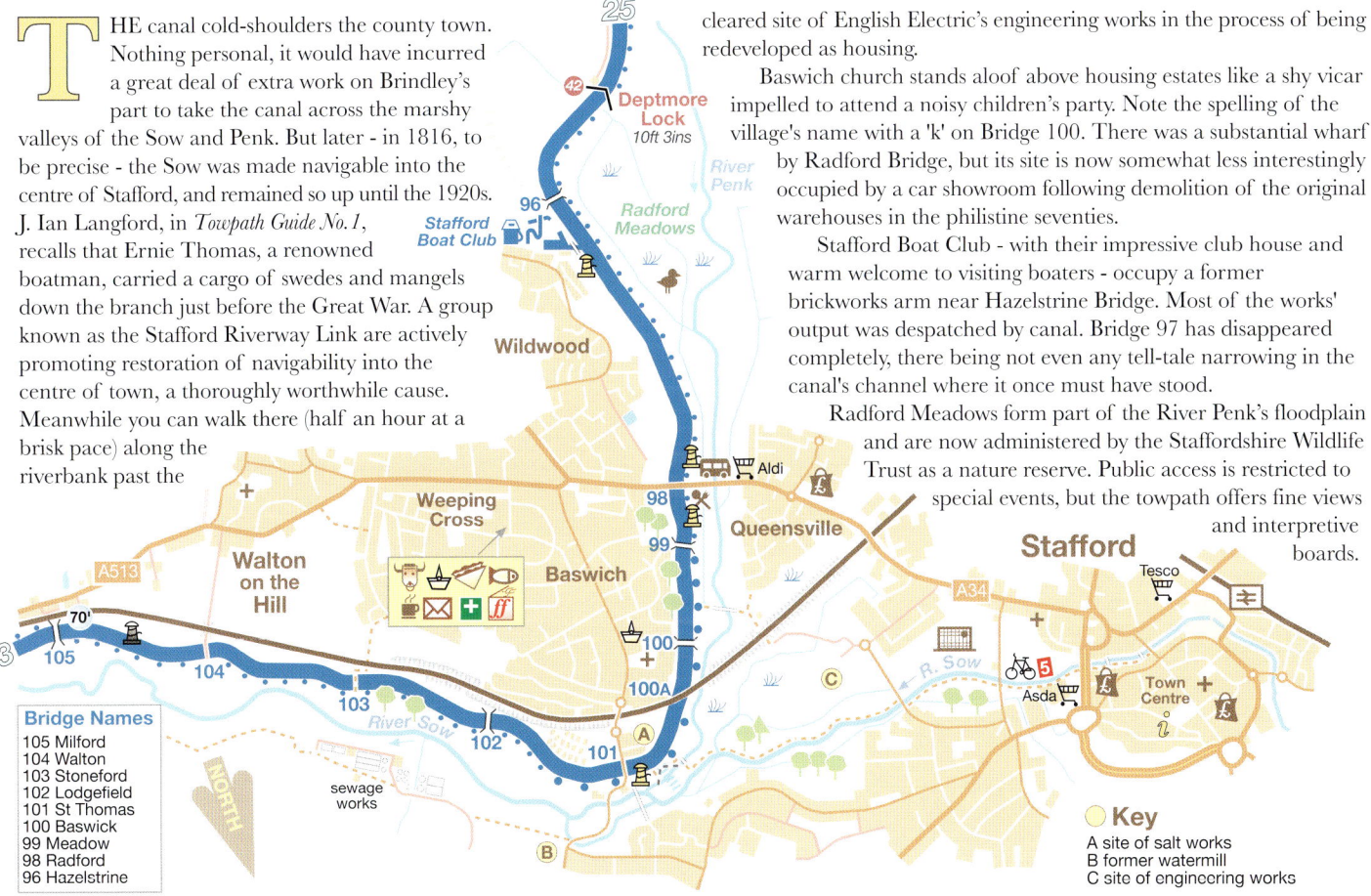

Bridge Names
105 Milford
104 Walton
103 Stoneford
102 Lodgefield
101 St Thomas
100 Baswick
99 Meadow
98 Radford
96 Hazelstrine

Key
A site of salt works
B former watermill
C site of engineering works

63

Stafford   Map 24

Frustratingly for canal folk, the centre lies over a mile from Radford Bridge. But there are frequent buses, and those with time at their disposal will find Stafford a rewarding place to visit. First stop should be the Ancient High House in Greengate Street. Dating from 1595, it is thought to be the largest timber-framed town house remaining in England. Inside there's a heritage exhibition tracing Stafford's history since 913 when Ethelfleda, daughter of Alfred the Great, fortified the settlement against marauding Danish invaders. King Charles I stayed at High House in 1642, and in later years Izaak Walton visited relatives who owned it. An alleyway beguiles you off Greengate Street to discover the town's large parish church of St Mary, much restored by Gilbert Scott in the 1840s and containing a bust of Izaak Walton. Another delightful church worth visiting is St Chad's on Greengate Street.

Eating & Drinking
RADFORD BANK - canalside Bridge 98. Tel: 01785 242825. Stonehouse pizza and carvery restaurant open from 9am daily. ST17 4PG
THE SOUP KITCHEN - Church Lane. Tel: 01785 254775. Open 9.30am-4pm Mon-Sat. Quaint, sprawling eatery with attentive staff serving coffees, lunches and teas. Rooftop garden. ST16 2AW

Shopping
Comprehensive shopping centre featuring all the well known 'high street' names plus many attractive individual shops tucked away down twisting side streets. Large Asda and Tesco supermarkets. Indoor market (Earl Street) Tue, Thur, Fri & Sat. Farmers' Market on the second Saturday in the month. Aldi 5 minutes west of Bridge 98. Good range of suburban shops on Bodmin Avenue in Baswich about 15 minutes walk east of Bridge 99.

Things to Do
TOURIST INFORMATION - Gatehouse Theatre, Market Street. Tel: 01785 619619. ST16 2LT
ANCIENT HIGH HOUSE - Greengate Street. Tel: 01785 619131. Local history and gifts. ST16 2JA
STAFFORD CASTLE - Tel: 01785 257698. Preserved Norman remains on western outskirts. ST16 1DJ

Connections
BUSES - Chaserider services 74/826 run from Radford (Bridge 98) to town centre. Select services 877/8 operate from the town centre to Wolverhampton via Brewood and Coven (878 serves Gailey).
TRAINS - Important railhead with wide variety of services. Useful links with Penkridge and Rugeley for clued-up towpath walkers.
TAXIS - Stafford Taxis. Tel: 01785 500123.

Acton Trussell   Map 25
THE MOAT HOUSE - canalside Bridge 92. Tel: 01785 712217. Four star hotel in former moated farmhouse: restaurant and bars, lovely gardens. Lunches and dinners (from 6.30pm weekdays, 7pm Sat). Food served noon-5.30pm on Sundays. ST17 0RG

Penkridge   Map 25
A congenial little town in which to break your journey. Five minutes walk from the wharf will take you to the narrow main street, a pleasant spot to shop and saunter. At its foot, across the A449, stands St Michael's, an impressive sandstone church.

Eating & Drinking
BOAT INN - Cannock Road (Bridge 86). Tel: 01785 715170. Canalside pub open from noon. ST19 5DT
CROSS KEYS - Filance Lane (Bridge 84). Tel: 0781 008 0668. A once isolated pub, described by Rolt in *Narrow Boat*, but now surrounded by a housing estate. Opens 11am. ST19 5HJ
FLAMES - Mill Street. Tel: 01785 712955. Contemporary Eastern cuisine housed in one of Penkridge's most historic buildings. ST19 5AY
HORSE & JOCKEY - Market Street. Tel: 01785 716299. Cosy Black Country Ales pub. ST19 5DH

Shopping
Convenience shops near bridges 84 and 86. The town centre features a (relocated) Co-op/PO, pharmacy, Jasper's Bakery, and Adams butchers and game dealer. Down by the river, the outdoor market operates on Wednesdays and Saturdays 8am-3pm.

Connections
BUSES - Select 878 runs to from Stafford (via Acton Trussell) and Wolverhampton (via Gailey).
TRAINS - twice-hourly London Northwestern services to/from Wolverhampton and Stafford.
TAXIS - Corkys. Tel: 01543 505058.

Gailey   Map 26
Handy facilities (strung out along the pavemented A5, but beware traffic) include a filling station with Londis convenience store and Greggs fast food outlet; Piper's Garden Centre (est. 1947) with tea room; a charming pottery housed in a former church; a Marston's pub called the Spread Eagle; and Dobbies Garden World.

Coven   Maps 26/27
Coven's village centre is less than ten minutes walk from Bridge 71, but do take care crossing the A449.

Eating & Drinking
ANCHOR INN - canalside north of Bridge 71. Tel: 01902 798786. Vintage Inns establishment offering food throughout from 11am daily. WV10 7PW
Fish & chip shop, and another pub in the village centre.

Shopping
Co-op convenience store, butcher (on the road in), pharmacy, and post office.

25 STAFFS & WORCS CANAL Penkridge 4mls/5lks/2½hrs

CLIMBING steadily towards its summit, the Staffs & Worcs for the most part sustains its inherent rurality, which even the proximity of the M6 motorway can't impair. Acton Trussell - which you'd expect with such a name to be a picture book English village - fails to live up to expectations with its banal 1960s architecture. The solitary building on the towpath side used to be a boatmen's pub. Present day boaters, however, slake their thirst in the old moated house by Bridge 92, now well-established as a bar, restaurant and hotel set in charming grounds. It is said that Brindley actually used the old house's moat for a few yards when building the canal: anything to save a few bob. The towpath between bridges 90 and 86 is 'hijacked' by the "Staffordshire Way" which seems forever to be bumping into canals and appropriating towpaths in the course of its 92 mile journey from Mow Cop to Kinver Edge. Its route has come down off The Chase and crossed Teddesley Park. Teddesley Hall was the seat of Sir Edward Littleton, one of the chief promoters of the Staffordshire & Worcestershire Canal. Indeed, the family remained involved with the canal company until its nationalisation in 1947. The hall itself was demolished by the army in the mid Fifties (having been used as a prison camp for German officers during the Second World War) but the estate farm remains, hidden from the canal by some woodland known as Wellington Belt in commemoration of a visit to the hall by the Iron Duke. Bridge 89 once had ornate balustrades commensurate with its importance as the gateway to the hall, but, irresponsibly and unforgivably, these have been infilled by ugly brickwork. Penkridge's built-up outskirts can counter-intuitively come as a bit of a relief after all that open countryside. Trees are alright in their place, but nothing beats a good bungalow when you feel like being nosey.

Bridge Names
94 Roseford
93 Acton
92 Acton Moat
91 Shutt Hill
90 Park Gate
89 Teddesley Park
88 Longford
87A Woodbank Lane
87 Broom
86 Penkridge
85 Princefield
84 Filance
83A Cross Keys

Locks
41 Shutt Hill Lock 6ft 0ins
40 Park Gate Lock 7ft 6ins
39 Longford Lock 10ft 0ins
38 Penkridge Lock 9ft 3ins
37 Filance Lock 10ft 3ins

26 STAFFS & WORCS CANAL Gailey & Hatherton 6mls/5lks/3hrs

REACHING its summit - 340ft 6ins above sea level - at Gailey, the S&W has climbed a hundred feet from its junction with the T&M at Great Haywood: understandably, ordnance datum achieves more significance when travelling by canal than other modes of transport; if you've been doing the locks, every inch is personal!

The heron-grey girders of Bridge 80A carried the colliery railway to Littleton pit across the canal. In the early years of the Canal Companions it was still in use. But the mine closed in 1993, the last in the Cannock coalfield. As a nostalgic gesture a pair of steam saddle tanks, *Whiston* and *Wimblebury*, were employed to haul loaded wagons from the pit head to the

Locks
36 Otherton Lock 10ft 3ins
35 Rodbaston Lock 8ft 6ins
34 Boggs Lock 8ft 6ins
33 Brick Kiln Lock 8ft 6ins
32 Gailey Lock 8ft 6ins

Bridge Names
83 Lynehill
82 Otherton
81 Otherton Lane
80A Littleton Colliery
80 Rodbaston
79 Gailey
78A Four Ashes
78 Gravelly Way
77 Calf Heath
76 Long Moll's
75 Deepmore
74 Moat House
73 The Laches
72 Slade Heath

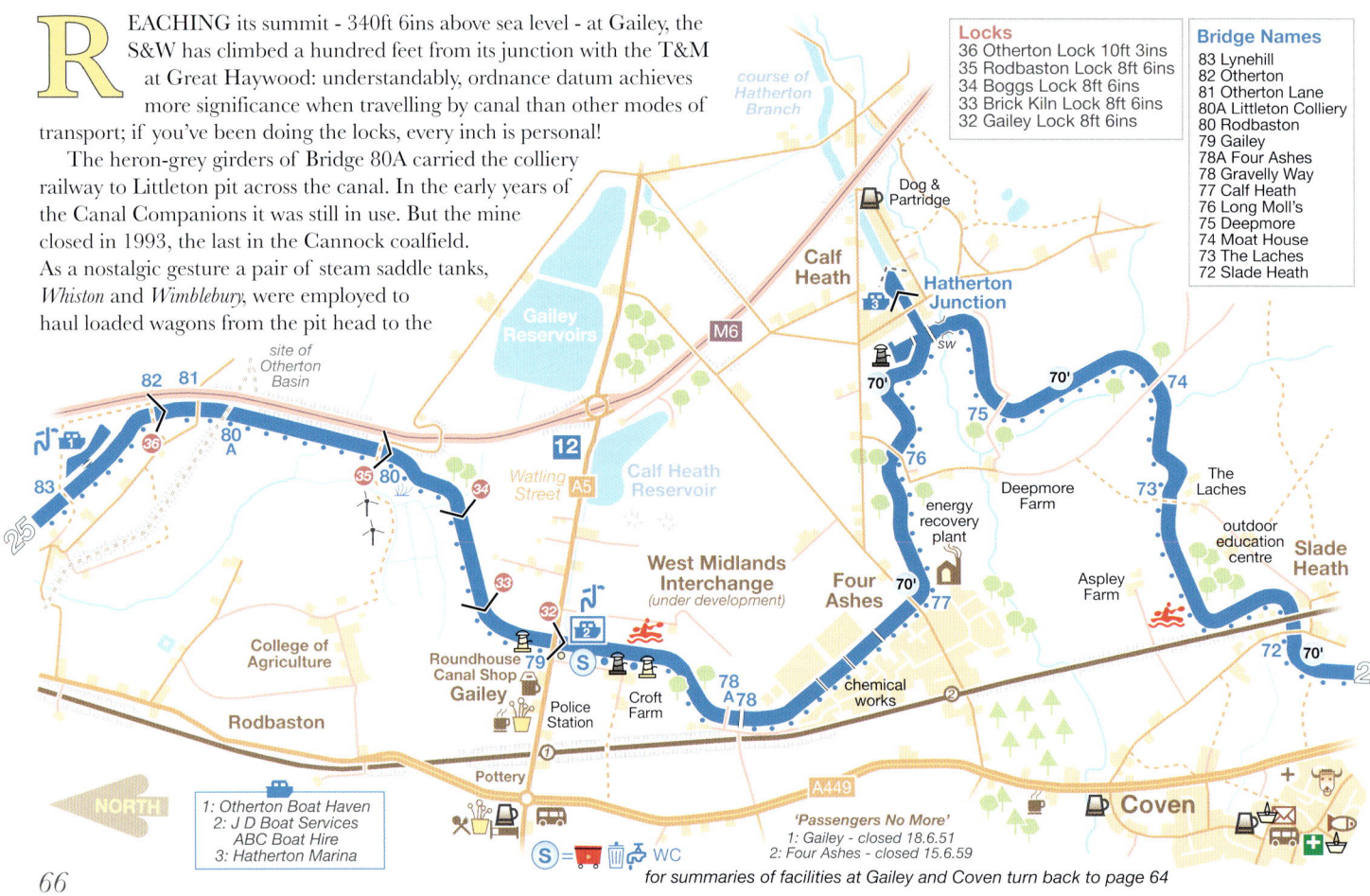

1: Otherton Boat Haven
2: J D Boat Services
   ABC Boat Hire
3: Hatherton Marina

'Passengers No More'
1: Gailey - closed 18.6.51
2: Four Ashes - closed 15.6.59

for summaries of facilities at Gailey and Coven turn back to page 64

exchange sidings on the main line. There was also a huge basin, long since covered by the motorway, where boats were loaded by gravity from a raised pier. The chief traffic flow for Littleton coal in later years was to Stourport Power Station. Littleton featured in Chris Arnot's beautifully illustrated book *Britain's Lost Mines*, a bittersweet paean to lost endeavours, as were his companion volumes covering breweries and cricket grounds.

Rodbaston Lock boasted a keeper until the noise from the newly constructed motorway drove him out. With no one mad enough to live there, the cottage was subsequently demolished. West of the canal, pinpointed by twin wind turbines, stands Rodbaston Hall. The house dates from 1834 and once belonged to a Wolverhampton ironmaster. It's a wedding venue now, of course - isn't everywhere - but the extensive grounds play host to South Staffordshire College's agricultural and horticutural campus. A feeder from Gailey Reservoirs enters the canal at the tail of Boggs Lock. Divided by a dam, the upper pool is fished, the lower sailed; both are birdwatched.

Conquest of the summit comes at Gailey where the A5 - or, for those of a more romantic disposition, Watling Street - crosses the canal. By our calculations - yours may differ - the A5 crossed nineteen canal bridges on its way from London's Marble Arch to Holyhead on Anglesey. When the road at Gailey was widened in the 1930s it brought about the demise of a canalside pub called The Plough. Gailey's Victorian church (now a pottery) was designed by George Thomas Robinson, also responsible for Burslem's angel-topped Town Hall.

A notable landmark for canallers and motorists alike, Gailey Roundhouse dates from the year of Trafalgar and may well have been inspired by the

Gailey Roundhouse

Martello towers of the Napoleonic wars. For many years it has been run as a delightful little canal shop by mother and daughter team Eileen and Karen Lester. To our deep regret, for she had always been a staunch supporter of the Canal Companions, Eileen passed away in 2022. It goes without saying that she will be missed greatly, but thankfully Karen has kept the shop going. Pop in and say 'hello'; particularly if, like her (and Tom Hanks) you're an avid 'Villan'. A busy hire base adds to Gailey Wharf's purposeful air, and canoeing takes place on the summit pound to boot.

It only seems five minutes ago that you were lolling about in the lush farmland of the upper Penk valley ... now you're traversing a strangely isolated tract of country known as Calf Heath, pancake flat and reminiscent of the sullen potato fields Van Gogh used to paint before he was blinded by the light of Arles.

Change, however, is on the horizon, for a vast logistics hub is being developed here. West Midlands Interchange has potential to provide 'up to 8 million square feet' of warehousing space. Strategically placed between the M6 motorway and the Stafford to Wolverhampton railway, it will boast great transport links. Though naturally, and somewhat sadly, these will not involve the canal.

In 1841 a branch was opened from Hatherton Junction to tap the fruits of the Cannock coalfield. At Churchbridge (one of those nineteen canal crossings of the A5) a flight of thirteen locks connected with the Cannock Extension of the Wyrley & Essington Canal. The Lichfield & Hatherton Canals Trust have ambitions to reconnect the two, though a different route will need to be dug in the process. Meanwhile, the bottom lock at Hatherton survives, providing access to moorings.

27 STAFFS & WORCS CANAL Autherley & Aldersley 3½ mls/0lks/1½ hrs

VISITOR moorings, either side of the Anchor Inn at Cross Green, make this a popular point to moor overnight. Coven's shops (and fish & chips) lie less than ten minutes walk to the north-west, but take care crossing the A449, the road connects Newport in South Wales with Stafford, and many of its users seem determined to get there as quickly as possible.

Boaters tend not to pay much heed to fishing beat signage any more than motorists do manhole covers, but often the societies involved evoke lost industries and enterprises. Hereabouts one is reminded of Goodyear, the tyre makers, who once had a massive plant on the northern outskirts of Wolverhampton.

If it's your nose that's afflicted by the fruity aromas which emanate from the sewage works by Bridge 69, it's your ears which take the brunt of the M54, opened between the M6 and Telford in 1983. As you pass beneath the motorway you are crossing the county boundary between Staffordshire and something, invented by Ted Heath in 1974, inspirationally known as West Midlands.

i54 ('driving jobs, attracting business') is a 240 acre technology-based business park amongst whose blue-chip occupants Jaguar Land Rover are probably the best known. Employees use the towpath as a short cut to Morrisons for their take-away lunches. South of the motorway bridge on the towpath side there's access to a marshy nature reserve by way of a beguiling boardwalk.

In the vicinity of bridges 68 and 67, Pendeford 'Rockin' is the old boatmen's name for a shallow, but tellingly narrow cutting hewn by Brindley's navvies through a solid belt of sandstone which breaks through the clay strata at this point. There are, however, one or two passing places - as on a single lane road - where oncoming boats can be successfully negotiated without losing one's temper. Autherley and Aldersley junctions are often confused. The former provides access to the Shropshire Union Canal; the latter the inimitable BCN a mysterious labyrinth of canals enthusiastically charted in our Stourport Ring Canal Companion.

Bridge Names
71 Cross Green
70 Brinsford
69 Coven Heath
68A M54
68 Forster
67 Marsh Lane
66 Blaydon Road
65 Oxley Moor

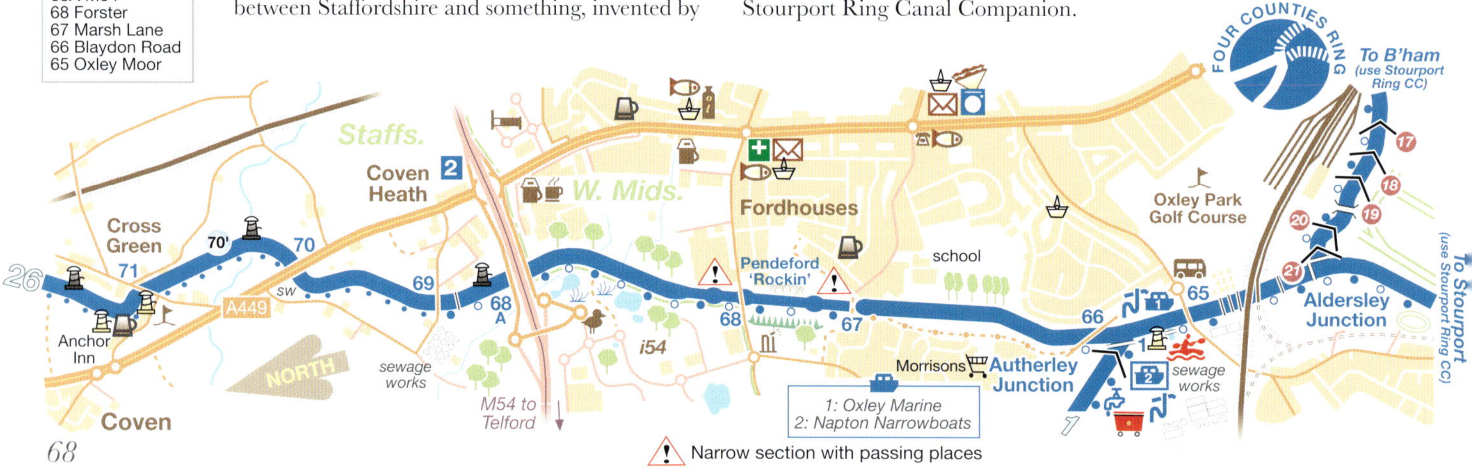

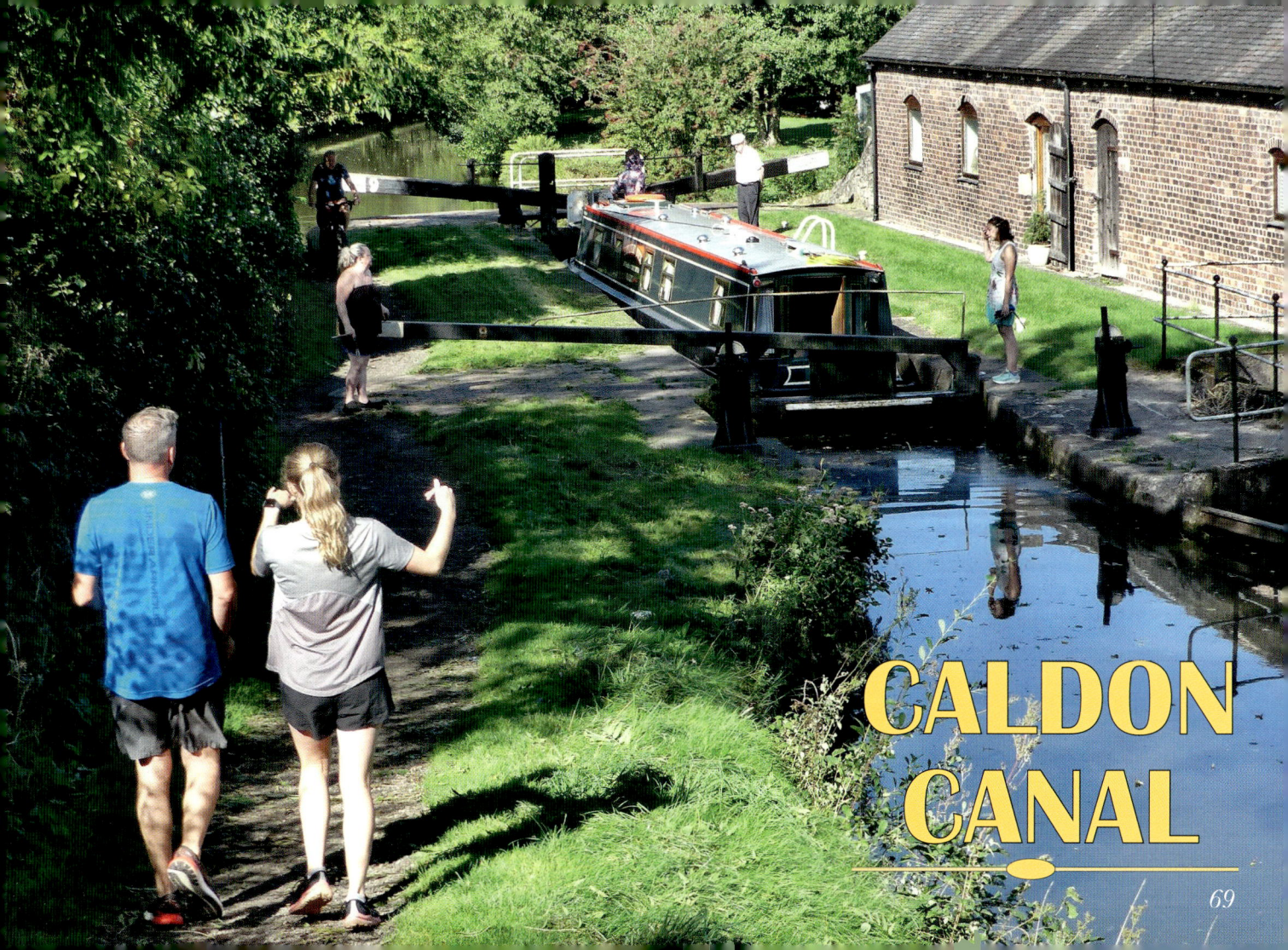

RAMPANT vegetation ameliorates the continued presence of Stoke's sprawling suburbs. All those houses are there, yet you hardly see them. Opposite Milepost 3, a reedy swamp anecdotally conceals the hulks of long submerged working boats. Roads in the vicinity bear the names of illustrious British composers; Delius, Elgar, Holst and Tallis. Thirty-nine voices short, Lock-wheeler spiritedly did his best to do justice to *Spem in Alium*. Your taste may lead you along alternative musical avenues.

Dogs are 'exercised' (as, indeed, are their owners' vocal chords) along the old Biddulph Valley railway line crossing Bridge 14A. Not since the late 1980s have the rails been burnished by sand trains from Oakamoor or limestone from Cauldon (sic) Low with passing goods trains, but they remain in place, pierced by saplings well on their way to becoming trees.

The canal runs south to north through the upper valley of the Trent. 'Scummy and ocherous' was how Tom Fort described the Caldon in his 2008 book *Downstream*. He was following the Trent and had to wait until Trentham before he could get aboard his boat *Otter*, which he would row all the way to Cromwell.

The suburb of Abbey Hulton developed in the 1920s as part of a programme of slum clearance. It gained its name from the remnants of a Cistercian monastery dissolved by Henry VIII in 1535. A Scheduled Monument, its scant remnants are open to the public. The remains of a decapitated male were found in the grounds in the 1970s. They were transported to the University of Reading where, three decades later (time being of no consequence in archaeological circles) identified as the hung, drawn and quartered body parts of a 14th century nobleman, Hugh Despenser the Younger, a favourite of Edward II. By all accounts a thoroughly bad lot - even by the standards of his time - he was horrifically executed for treason at Hereford in 1326. Several artefacts from the abbey can be found at the Potteries Museum & Art Gallery.

By Bridge 15 lies Drayton Beaumont Park, home of Abbey Hulton United FC formed in 1947. They ply their trade in the First Division South of the North West Counties Football League, shoulder-barging the likes of Stockport Georgians, Cheadle Heath Nomads and Cammell Laird 1907. From this point northwards the old railway becomes a cyclepath appropriately known as the Biddulph Valley Way, followable all the way to Congleton if you fancy 'playing trains' for a bit. Somewhat less onerously, it provides access to Ford Green Hall, an enchanting 17th century timber framed farmhouse, open to the public Thursday to Sunday afternoons. Some of the bridges from 15 upwards bear their numbers carved in stone.

On the offside beyond Bridge 16A stood the British Aluminium Works, merely a wasteground now, ripe for a housing development one imagines. Apparently it was targeted by enemy bombers during the Second World War, though with native wit, locals avowed that bomber pilots would take one look at the industrially ravaged landscape beneath them and conclude that it had already been successfully attacked. Latterly, Johnson Brothers pottery had a packing department here, served by the craft alluded to on page 49. Note the off-side's masonry bank where they berthed.

Suddenly the canal turns sharp right, at which point a branch canal led via a single lock to Ford Green Ironworks and Norton Colliery. Narrows hint at the presence of a former swing-bridge. Milton is a popular overnight mooring point (rings to the south of Bridge 18, grassy bank to the north) with useful shopping and eating & drinking opportunities easily accessed. Whilst here you may care to enrol at the canalside Hardman Football Development Centre, an organisation seemingly determined to correct a worrying trend towards the softening up of what was once regarded as a contact sport. The name actually recalls John Hardman, philanthropic owner of a local chemical works established in 1864.

Bridge 19 carries the A53 across the canal, a road linking Shrewsbury with Buxton. Housing occupies the site of Bullers electrical porcelain works, specialists in the manufacture of insulators for telegraph poles. Industry survives in the shape of a works processing animal parts for use in the pottery industry.

At last the landscape becomes rural, albeit shaggy and unkempt, as though this were a war-torn no-man's land between true countryside and town. Engine Lock recalls the existence of a pumping engine in the

28 CALDON CANAL Milton & Stockton Brook 5mls/6lks/3hrs

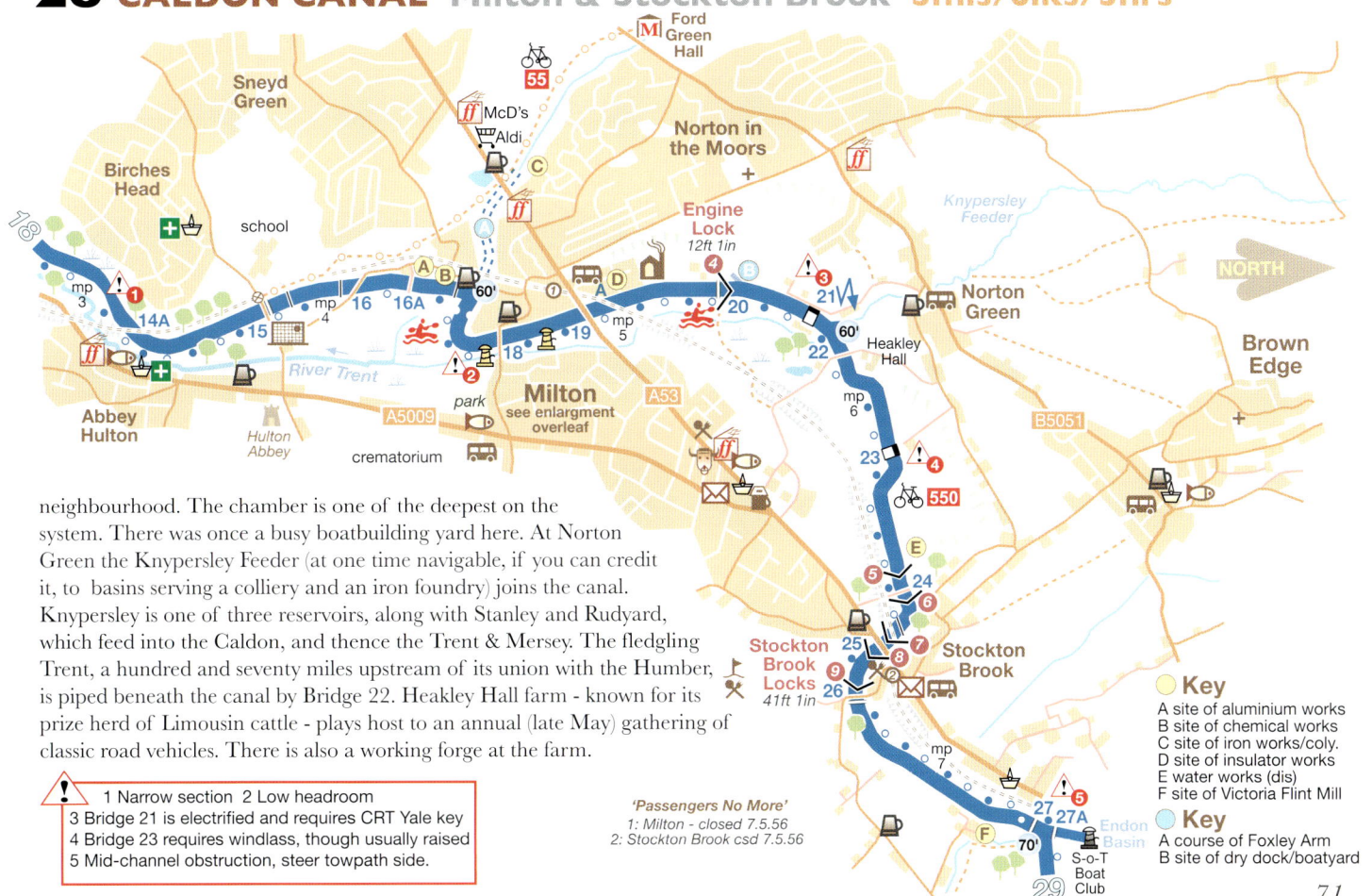

neighbourhood. The chamber is one of the deepest on the system. There was once a busy boatbuilding yard here. At Norton Green the Knypersley Feeder (at one time navigable, if you can credit it, to basins serving a colliery and an iron foundry) joins the canal. Knypersley is one of three reservoirs, along with Stanley and Rudyard, which feed into the Caldon, and thence the Trent & Mersey. The fledgling Trent, a hundred and seventy miles upstream of its union with the Humber, is piped beneath the canal by Bridge 22. Heakley Hall farm - known for its prize herd of Limousin cattle - plays host to an annual (late May) gathering of classic road vehicles. There is also a working forge at the farm.

! 1 Narrow section 2 Low headroom
3 Bridge 21 is electrified and requires CRT Yale key
4 Bridge 23 requires windlass, though usually raised
5 Mid-channel obstruction, steer towpath side.

'Passengers No More'
1: Milton - closed 7.5.56
2: Stockton Brook csd 7.5.56

Key
A site of aluminium works
B site of chemical works
C site of iron works/coly.
D site of insulator works
E water works (dis)
F site of Victoria Flint Mill

Key
A course of Foxley Arm
B site of dry dock/boatyard

Reflections at Foxley Turn

the centre of the channel, marking the site of a swing-bridge which carried a standard gauge railway line into Victoria Mill, which manufactured ceramic colours and glazes. They operated a cute little battery operated shunting engine called *Nina*.

Endon Basin was once used as a transhipment point from rail to canal for Cauldon Lowe limestone. A substantial tippler - built at the North Staffordshire Railway's Stoke workshops - speeded up this otherwise laborious process. The basin is now occupied by Stoke-on-Trent Boat Club whose members were strong advocates for the retention of the Caldon Canal when it was threatened with abandonment in the 1960s. From Bridge 27 a footpath can be followed to Stanley Pool, half a mile or so to the south. Interestingly, mileposts along the A53 bear more than a passing resemblance to those on the canal.

The Stockton Brook flight carries the canal forty feet up to its summit level of 486ft. The disused waterworks at the foot of the flight was built by the Staffordshire Potteries Water Co. in 1884 and once contained a pair of horizontal compound tandem 'Davey' differential steam engines.

Attractive ceramic sculptures adorn locks 6 and 7. They are the work of Anthony Lysycia who has also provided canalside artworks at Hatton, Trevor and Llanymynech. 'The Knotty's' Stoke to Leek line crosses the canal between the second and third lock. Disused since the 1990s, attempts to resuscitate it as a link to the quarries at Cauldon Lowe and the theme park at Alton Towers regrettably appear to have failed. A more successful initiative has been Staffordshire County Council's upgrading of the towpath between Stockton Brook and Leek and Cheddleton. It's part of the Pedal Peak cycle route, and a very good job they've made of it too, with a firm 'all weather surface' of compacted stone.

Stone walls and small holdings begin to create a Pennine sense of obduracy. Before Bridge 27 an unusual circular metal platform obstructs

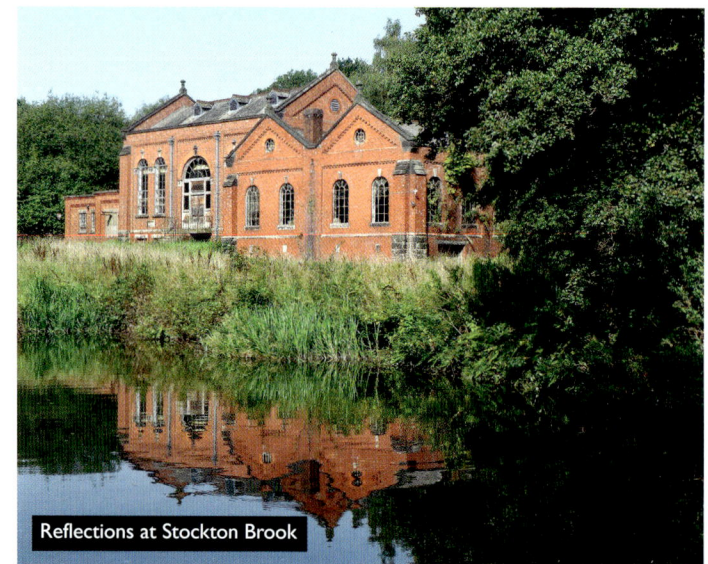

Reflections at Stockton Brook

Abbey Hulton
Map 28

Densely built-up suburb. There are shops and take-aways on the A5009, though not as easily accessed as Milton. The former abbey grounds are open to the public.

Milton
Map 28

Milton is a lively little frontier post, a last chance for human contact and meaningful shopping until you reach Leek - always assuming you're going that way - and its facilities become even more significant if you're heading off into the sequestered folds of the Churnet Valley. Traditionally, the community is divided into 'up-enders' and 'down-enders'. Miners from the North-east and South Wales brought new blood to the area. Just west of Bridge 18 an interpretive board celebrates the pottery designer Susie Cooper (1902-1995).

Eating & Drinking
FOXLEY HOTEL - Foxley Lane. Tel: 01782 535684. Canalside pub with offside moorings but no direct access from the towpath. ST2 7EH
MILLRACE - Maunders Road. Tel: 01782 926757. Friendly Marston's local near Bridge 18. Sandwiches. ST2 7DU
MILTON FRYER - Leek Road. Tel: 01782 214897. Chippy which has been 'frying' since 1947. ST1 6HD

Shopping
There are two butchers, a bakery, deli, pharmacy, One-Stop (PO) and Co-op with a cash machine. Abacas (Tel: 01782 543005) is a splendid secondhand bookshop with a wide-ranging stock, plus new North Staffordshire publications.

Connections
BUSES - D&G service 43 runs hourly (ex Sun) to/from Hanley.

Norton Green
Map 28

Self-styled (with justification) as 'the first village on the River Trent'. Hugh Bourne (1772-1852), co-founder of the Primitive Methodists, lived at nearby Bemersley Green.

Eating & Drinking
THE FOAMING QUART - Tel: 01782 911171. Quaint Marston's pub (8 mins walk from Br. 21) which Eric Bristow represented when winning the World Darts Championship in 1983. Open from noon. ST6 8PD

Connections
BUSES - D&G service 8A runs hourly (ex Sun) to/from Hanley.

Stockton Brook
Map 28

Wayside community on the main road between Hanley and Leek. The former timber-built station building houses a firm specialising in fitted kitchens and bathrooms. The station was euphoniously known as 'Stockton Brook for Brown Edge'.

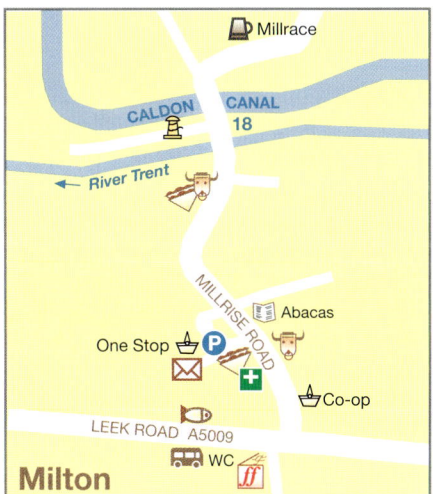

Eating & Drinking
THE SPORTSMAN - Tel: 01782 505307. Stone-built Marston's local adjoining Bridge 25. ST9 9NT
THE HOLLYBUSH - Tel: 01782 502116. Ego Mediterranean restaurant & bar. ST9 9NL

Shopping
Post office: also sells bread, milk and newspapers etc.

Connections
BUSES - First service 18 runs hourly Mon-Sat to/from Hanley and Leek. Sparse Sunday service by D&G.

Endon
Map 29

Suburbanised village chiefly known for its Spring Bank Holiday well-dressing festival. St Luke's church features a memorial window to the First World War poet T. E. Hulme, killed by a direct hit from a shell at Oostduinkerke, West Flanders in 1917.

Eating & Drinking
RAILWAY TEAROOM - Station Road. Tel: 01 782 503512. Open Thur-Sun 9am-2pm. ST9 9DR
TOBY CARVERY - Leek Road. Tel: 01782 502115. 11.30am Mon-Thur and from 9am Fri-Sun. ST9 9BE

Shopping
Convenience store and pharmacy.

Connections
BUSES - as Stockton Brook, plus D&G service 8A to/from Hanley via Brown Edge and Norton Green.

Denford
Map 29

THE HOLLY BUSH - Denford Road (Bridge 38). Tel: 01538 371819. Something of an institution with locals, boaters and walkers alike, this comfortable and beautifully situated canalside pub is owned by Thwaites of Lancaster. Food served lunch and evenings (from 5.30pm) weekdays and from noon throughout at weekends. ST13 7JT
In the farm adjoining Bridge 38 is Thumper's Kitchen, an artisan bakery - Tel: 0792 332 0765.

29 CALDON CANAL Hazelhurst, Cheddleton & Leek 5mls/6lks/3hrs*

SKIRTING Endon - a cricket club and an ostrich farm - the canal comes to Park Lane Wharf where comprehensive boater facilities are laid on by CRT. Use them judiciously: there are none on the Leek Branch; and, if your boat can't get through Froghall Tunnel (Map 30) only a water tap at Consall Forge to fill up from.

We have venerated Hazelhurst Junction for the best part of half a century, but felt it was looking a bit sorry for itself on the occasion of our most recent visit. Two million pounds - we had it on good authority - had been spent on rebuilding Bridge 37. And a very good job had been made of it too - as the accompanying photograph illustrates - but why so much for a modest hump-back?

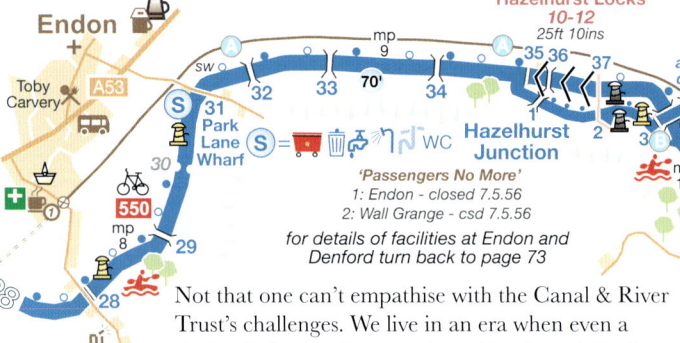

Not that one can't empathise with the Canal & River Trust's challenges. We live in an era when even a single platform railway station with a 'bus shelter' can cost in excess of £18m to construct (yes, Soham, that's you!) and when solely the most basic of new homes are deemed 'affordable': the rest, by implication, being completely 'unaffordable'.

But back to Hazelhurst. Originally the Caldon descended to the valley floor from Endon. Then, with construction of the Leek Branch, the new line we use today was built, with a staircase lock forming an abrupt descent adjacent to Bridge 3 at Denford. But the staircase was a bottleneck for the heavy traffic of limestone boats from Froghall, and so in 1841 the present layout was arrived at, with three single chambers taking the main line down under a new aqueduct, which carried the Leek branch and Rudyard feeder; ensuring that the latter joined the main canal, of necessity, at its summit level.

*figures refer to main line, allow 1 hour to cruise Leek Branch (one way).

Bridge 37

were also limekilns, silk and paper mills and a brewery here. The tall-chimnied silk mill still stands prominently alongside the canal by Bridge 42. Brittain's paper mill dated from the late 18th century. In its heyday over a thousand people were employed. Vera Brittain, the celebrated writer and feminist, was a family member. Products ranged from transfers for the pottery industry to thin but durable paper used in bibles. Manufacture ceased in the 1990s, and the site has become a business park.

Dropping through a pair of locks, the canalscape is full of appeal. A plaque by the upper lock marks the re-opening of the Caldon Canal in 1974 after it had fallen into dereliction in the early 1960s. No one should pass this point without mouthing a silent 'thank you' to the waterway enthusiasts and local authorities who 'engineered' this magical canal's restoration. One just prays that the Caldon Canal doesn't become a victim of financial stringencies and have to be restored all over again.

The Leek Branch

Now commences two and three quarter canal miles of surpassing loveliness as the Leek Branch curves away from the main line, which locks down to pass beneath it. Two overbridges precede a sharp turn at the site of the old staircase locks before the branch then crosses the main line on an imposing brick aqueduct dated 1841. A lesser aqueduct over the old railway follows before the branch settles down on the opposite hillside for the delightful journey to Leek.

Genuflecting in and out of overbridges, and passing some appropriately heavenly waterside properties, one's progress afloat is slowed by both the slenderness of the channel and lines of moored boats, not that there's the slightest imperative to hurry in any case. Masked by woodland down in the valley beyond Bridge 7 stand the remains of the Staffordshire Potteries Water Works Co.'s Wall Grange Pumping Station of 1849. A pair of lofty engine houses originally contained beam engines manufactured by Sandys Vivian of Hayle, Cornwall. Old photographs depict a decidedly handsome couple. One of the engines was called 'Stafford', its neighbour 'Davenport'. Inevitably, they were replaced by diesel engines in 1933, and subsequently

Ten miles out from Etruria, the Caldon reaches Denford, chiefly known for the Holly Bush inn and its associations with the championship-winning Norton Tug of War Team. Interestingly, the adjoining row of cottages don't appear on Ordnance Survey mapping until the 1920s.

Beyond Denford the Caldon's Main Line passes through the glorious environment of Deep Hayes Country Park. Glorious now, but once the extensive premises of Wall Grange Brick Works lined Park Lane as it ascended the ridge leading to Cheddleton. The company was active between the 1890s and 1950s, and at one time operated a fleet of Foden steam lorries, though one suspects the canal and adjoining railway also provided transport.

Heavily wooded, the canal veers south-eastwards, entering the Churnet Valley. Enclosed by high ridges, it reaches Cheddleton where a delightful flint mill, powered by twin waterwheels, graces the scene. In the past there

the engine house containing 'Davenport' was demolished, though happily 'Stafford's' remains intact, converted into a remarkable private dwelling.

The canal traverses a gorgeous belt of woodland, full of bluebells in spring, where jays screech jocularly amongst the tree tops and brackeny banks spill down into the valley of the River Churnet. "Look out for the kingfisher," a passing walker exclaimed excitedly on our most recent reconnaissance trip. Presently the view ahead opens out towards the high flanks of The Morridge rising to 1,300ft in the east. The Leek Branch is like the 'big tune' in a symphony, and you wish it would go on much longer.

To the south a curious landmark forcibly catches your eye. It's the 135ft high octagonal tower of St Edward's Hospital, one of Staffordshire's three 'county' asylums, the others being at Burntwood near Lichfield, and Stafford itself. Work began on the 'self-contained' institution in 1895 and was completed four years later. Initially there were six hundred inmates, though this was subsequently extended to over a thousand, equally divided by gender. A curious electric railway connected the asylum to the Churnet Valley railway at Leekbrook. The hospital gained a positive reputation for advanced treatment techniques, patients being encouraged to undertake useful employment on site, brass tokens were issued as a form of wage. Closure occurred in 2002, and the site was somewhat ironically redeveloped as luxury housing with many of the original buildings being repurposed alongside new-builds. That intimidating tower is now an eight storey holiday let. What would the inmates have made of that!

Refocussing on the canal, you suddenly encounter a remote pool enclosed by low hills: cattle squelch gingerly down to drink or cool off in its reedy margins. Indisputably, this is one of the most idyllic mooring spots on the whole system. The canal builders had no alternative but to dig a tunnel in order to reach Leek. The confined 130 yard bore is fronted by an ornate portal of red sandstone. Walkers take the precipitous horsepath across the top and are rewarded by panoramic views over the town to The Roaches beyond.

Less than a mile of canal remains in water. The final full size winding hole is just beyond Bridge 9. On one occasion, we just managed to

Leek Tunnel Pool

navigate a 45ft boat to the shallow end of the canal and turned it with some difficulty, but essentially, the canal peters out as its feeder comes in from Rudyard, three miles to the north. A public footpath (part of the Staffordshire Way) follows the feeder to the reservoir which gave Kipling his Christian name. An aqueduct, dated 1801, once carried the canal across the Churnet to reach a terminal wharf nearer the town centre. The aqueduct stubbornly remains but is bereft of water, whilst the bed of the canal lies beneath an industrial estate whose occupants range from Bestwick's scrap yard to Ornua's 'state of the art' Kerrygold processing plant. Butter wouldn't melt in their collective mouths, but those responsible for denying the Leek Branch a fulfilling terminus back in the philistine 1950s deserve all the opprobrium we disinherited canallers can muster.

Leek
Map 29

Full of sudden architectural treats, Leek is tucked away from the outside world in deep folds of the Staffordshire Moorlands and is an entertaining and evocative place to explore. Canal travellers are thus entitled to mourn the disappearance of the old terminal arm and the resultant bleak trudge through an industrial estate to reach the town centre. Perseverance brings its rewards, however, and you'll soon find yourself warming to Leek, much as William Morris did on his frequent visits to Wardle's dyeworks. The Nicholson War Memorial is of poignant significance, a grieving father's tribute to a son lost in the First World War.

Eating & Drinking
DUCK GOOSE - St Edward Street. Tel: 01538 713008. Charming bistro, open daily ex Tue. ST13 5DS
FOXLOWE - Market Place. Tel: 01538 386112. Comfortable art centre cafe 10-4pm daily. ST13 6AD
LEEK BAR & GRILL - Getliffe Yard (off Derby Street). Tel: 01538 382812. Stylish restaurant/cafe/wine bar with alfresco eating opportunities on cobbled courtyard. Open daily ex Mon. ST13 6HU
LEEK OATCAKES - Haywood Street. Tel: 01538 387556. A mandatory pilgrimage for filled oatcakes. Open from the crack of dawn Wed-Sun. ST13 5JX
WHITE HART - Stockwell Street. Tel: 01538 372122. Tea room with sun-kissed courtyard. B&B. ST13 6DH

Shopping
An outdoor retail market is held on Wednesdays (flea market Sats) but the charming little indoor Butter Market additionally functions on Fridays and Saturdays. The delight of shopping in Leek lies in the proliferation of small shops offering individuality. There is a Farmers' Market on the third Saturday in the month. Good new/secondhand bookshop (closed Mon) on Stanley Street. Leek boasts a profusion of antiques outlets.

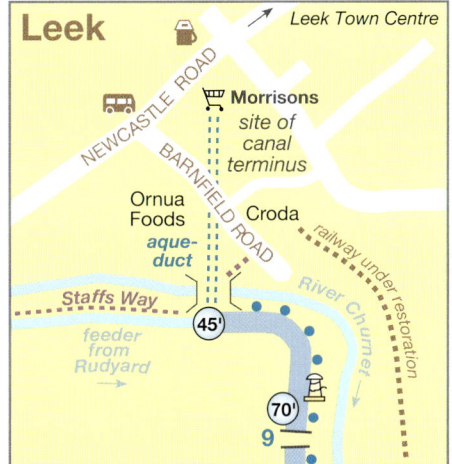

Things to Do
NICHOLSON MUSEUM & ART GALLERY - Stockwell Street. Tel: 01538 483741. Open Mon-Sat 10am-4pm, admission free. Local history and travelling exhibitions housed in building designed by the local Sugden architectural practice. Emphasis on Leek Embroidery School. Tourist Information. ST13 6DW
BRINDLEY MILL/MUSEUM - Mill Street. Small admission charge. Open Easter- September Sun & BH Mons 2-5pm. Ditto selected weekdays during school summer holidays. Restored water powered corn mill built by James Brindley in 1752. ST13 8FA

Connections
BUSES - First Potteries service 18 operates hourly daily to/from Hanley, and will whisk you up the hill to the town centre if you're not minded to walk. D&G service 16 provides a half-hourly link (ex Sun) with Hanley via Cheddleton, whilst Aimee's service 30 runs twice daily Mon-Fri to/from Cheadle via Froghall.
TAXIS - Malkins. Tel: 01538 386797.

Cheddleton
Map 29

Hilly village strung out along a busy A road. Thankfully tucked away from the latter's inherent cacophony, the parish church of St Edward the Confessor is something of a gem, dating back 800 years. The tower contains six bells, the oldest dating from 1632. There are stained glass windows by William Morris, Burne-Jones and Ford Madox Brown. The painted ceiling in the chancel depicts, amongst other local associations, a canal boat.

Eating & Drinking
BOAT INN - Basford Bridge Lane (Bridge 44). Tel: 01538 360521. Canalside Marston's pub. ST13 7EQ
OLD SCHOOL TEA ROOM - Hollow Lane. Tel: 01538 528942. Splendid tea room and gift shop (Wed-Sun, 10am-4pm) about quarter of an hour's walk up past the church.
THE FLINTLOCK - Cheadle Road (Bridge 42). Tel: 01538 361380. Canalside restaurant open for lunch Sat & Sun, and for dinner (from 5.30pm) Wed - Sat. ST13 7HN

Shopping
Off licence, convenience store, and fish & chips half a mile up a steepish hill from the canal.

Things to Do
CHEDDLETON FLINT MILL - one of the great little museums of England. Opening hours are dependent on the availability of volunteers, but Mon & Wed afternoons are your best bet. ST13 7HL
CHURNET VALLEY RAILWAY - Tel: 01538 360522. Preserved railway evoking much nostalgia plus an excellent way to facilitate a one-way towpath walk. Trains run between Froghall and Ipstones. ST13 7EE

Connections
BUSES - D&G service 16 as Leek.

30 CALDON CANAL Consall Forge & Froghall 4mls/2lks/2hrs

'AMAZONIAN', we used - somewhat fancifully - to term the Caldon's serene passage through the Churnet Valley. Now, it pains us to say, neglect is in danger of endorsing that view too literally. Nature, we sense, is slowly regaining the upper hand. Where once the canal appeared purposeful, now it seems diffident, unequal to the challenge of maintaining the status quo. Perish the thought that one day in the future this waterway would be solely the domain of Fenton and Cheadle's stoic anglers.

Briefly, the canal merges with the River Churnet at Oakmeadow Ford Lock, though there is little change of character, other than when heavy rainfall causes the river current to increase its normally sluggish pace - check the gauge at Bridge 48 to ensure that it is sensible to proceed.

You begin to wonder why on earth they ever bothered to build a canal in such an extraordinarily remote outpost of Staffordshire. But this is a countryside with plenty of skeletons in its closet. Haematite iron oxide and limestone were extensively mined in the area, and there were also several coal shafts and flint-grinding mills. At its zenith in the 1860s, an average of thirty boats a day were carrying ore out of the Churnet Valley.

The Caldon Canal was promoted for two main reasons: for the export of limestone from Cauldon (sic) Lowe; and to provide the summit of the Trent & Mersey with extra water. It opened in 1779, but was literally the death of James Brindley, who reputedly caught pneumonia on a surveying trip with fatal consequences for that genius of the early canal era. All but buried in balsam by the end of summer, Milepost 14 finds a strange echo on the neighbouring railway, whose own mileposts measure various increments of 14 miles from Uttoxeter. Once a picturesque byway of the North Staffordshire Railway, it is now a preserved line of considerable charm.

Inaccessible by public highway, Consall Forge revels in an enviable sense of isolation. The river disengages itself from the canal, disappearing over a weir to race ahead down the valley. The canal, on the other hand, squeezes under the railway, running beneath the cantilevered waiting room of Consall's beautifully restored station. The channel grows noticeably more slender, so that the passing of oncoming boats becomes a matter of discretion and a little 'give and take'. Canal, river and railway

○ Key
A site of ironstone shaft
B site of quarry
C limekilns
D site of Crowgutter Mill
E former flint mill
F remains of Thomas Bolton works

1 River Level Gauge
2 One-Way Working
3 Advance Tunnel Gauge
4 Restricted Tunnel

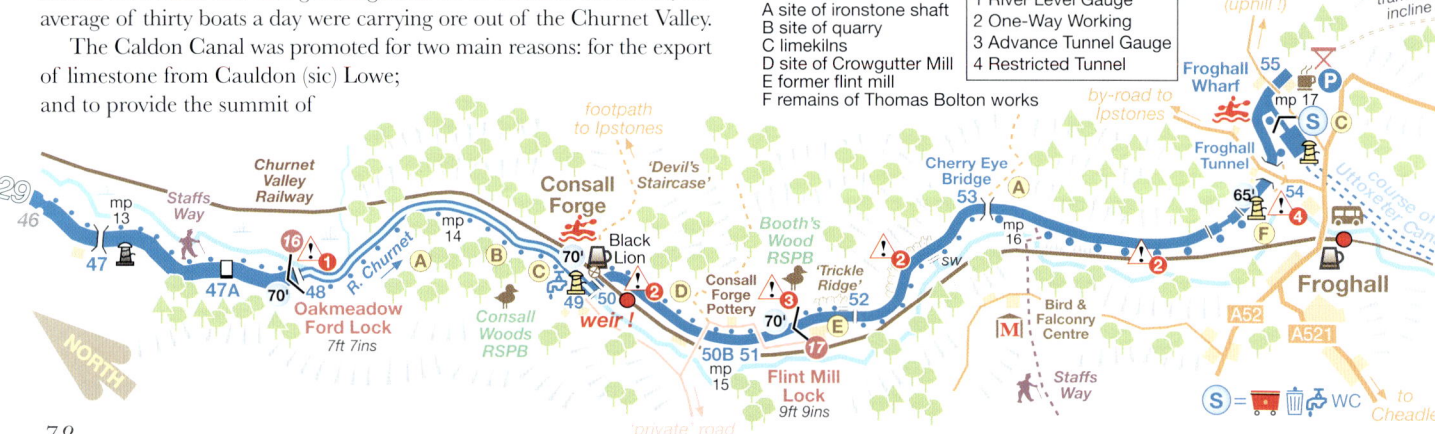

78

amiably share the precipitous valley's narrow floor. A row of redbrick railway workers houses appear incongruously suburban in so bucolic a setting. Bridge 50B additionally bears its LMS Railway number 39.

Milepost 15 appears to be on the wrong side of the canal, but apparently the towpath ran along the opposite bank before the railway was built. A lofty conifer stands guard over Flint Mill Lock, at which point the captains of craft over 65ft have to consider whether they are likely to be able to squeeze through Froghall Tunnel or not. The biblical metaphor concerning camels and eyes of needles springs to mind. Consall Mills, long retired from manual labour, are another reminder of the valley's past industry. Their origins can be traced back to the 17th century. Latterly they belonged to W. & A. J. Podmore, manufacturers and millers of materials for the pottery, glass, and enamel industries who operated their own fleet of narrowboats. Some, engaged in carrying flint in liquid 'slop' form, were quaintly referred to as 'buttermilk boats'.

A little curiosity catches the eye on the towpath side between the tail

Froghall Wharf

'Trickle Ridge'

of Flint Mill Lock and turnover Bridge 52. 'Trickle Ridge' is a layer of limestone created by liquid lime deposits running down the hillside over the centuries, the Churnet Valley's equivalent, perhaps, of Mother Shipton's Well at Knaresborough. A long abandoned boat on the opposite bank appears to be undergoing the same calcifying process. Cherry Eye Bridge recalls, it is said, the inflamed, bloodshot eyes of the neighbourhood's ironstone workers. Its Gothic pointed arch would not look out of place in the nave of a parish church. The Staffordshire Way leaves the canal in the vicinity of Milepost 16, duplicated by one of the original stone mileposts.

A concreted section of canal follows as an embanked length prone to breaching is negotiated. Woodland tumbles down to the water's edge on one side, whilst on the other, an equally steep descent leads to the Churnet. Suddenly a factory wall looms out of the trees, heralding the formerly vast copper wire works of Thomas Bolton & Sons. The factory dates from 1890 and once operated a small fleet of narrowboats named after female members of the family, though most of its transport needs were supplied by the railway. It was turned over to munitions during the war and apparently the Luftwaffe tried to bomb it but couldn't find it; which is not surprising when you take into account its position in this amphitheatre of heavily wooded hills. A company specialising in military hardware now occupies part of the site, but Bolton's lofty chimney remains, a haunting landmark of past endeavour. There are plans, as yet unrealised, to redevelop the site for housing, though a good deal of residual contamination would need to be dealt with first.

Frustratingly, many boats won't fit into Froghall Tunnel, so a 65ft winding hole is provided for boats to turn before encountering its diminutive western portal. If your boat conformed to the loading gauge (roughly five feet square above the water line) at Flint Mill Lock, however, you can proceed to the picturesque terminus which lies beyond. Furthermore, and rather irritatingly for boaters whose craft foul the gauge, this is where the water point, Elsan and rubbish disposal facilities are located. Old maps depict the presence of a pub called the Navigation Inn above the tunnel, but presumably its custom fell away as trade on the canal diminished, and what workers remained swapped their allegiance to the rival Railway Inn.

The peace and quiet of Froghall Basin today is hard to reconcile with the busy site where limestone, brought down by plate tramway from the quarries, was cut to size and loaded on to narrowboats. Here were sidings, great banks of limestone, smoking kilns, and, significantly, the top lock of the Uttoxeter extension, opened in 1811. The latter proved financially unviable, and when the North Staffordshire Railway acquired the Trent & Mersey system they quickly closed it down and built a railway over much of its thirteen mile course. Now, of course, the railway has gone the way of the canal, though it has been converted into a delightful bridleway between Oakamoor and Denstone.

A feasibility study has been published with a long term view to re-opening the Uttoxeter Canal, but in some respects it would be a shame to disturb this secret valley all over again. At Froghall, the top lock has been refurbished to provide access to a mooring basin. The best part of a century has elapsed since the wharf was abandoned commercially, and in the intervening period nature has reclaimed what she obviously regards as rightfully her own. Several fine walks are to be enjoyed in the vicinity, one taking you up an old tramway incline which rises 250 feet in 300 yards.

Consall Forge   Map 30

Peace and tranquility characterise Consall to such an extent now that it is hard to visualise the activity of the forges, furnaces and slitting mills which clustered here in the seventeenth and eighteenth centuries. Consall Forge Pottery (between bridges 50B and 51 - Tel: 01538 266625) produce domestic stoneware.

Eating & Drinking

BLACK LION - Consall Forge. Tel: 01782 550294. One of the most isolated pubs on the system, the delightful Black Lion has happily recovered from fire damage and is once again serving food. Open mic Sundays. ST9 0AJ

Froghall   Map 30

The Copper works' 328ft high chimney, threatened with demolition, has been saved as a landmark, for the time being at least. Incidentally, copper cable from Bolton's sister factory at nearby Oakamoor was laid across the ocean bed to form the first Transatlantic telegraph in 1866. It was heartening, on the occasion of our most recent visit, to see the wharf revitalised after a period of decay. The former stables have become a workshop for basket weaving. Self-catering holidays at Foxtwood Cottages - Tel: 0787 028 0907.

Eating & Drinking

HETTY'S - Froghall Wharf. Tel: 01538 266288. Marvellous tea room (correspondents recommend the oatcakes!) open daily (ex Tue & Wed) 10am-4pm. ST10 2HL
RAILWAY INN - Tel: 01538 750025. Open from noon daily. Food lunch and evening (from 6pm) weekdays and throughout at weekends. B&B. ST10 2HA

Things to Do

CHURNET VALLEY RAILWAY - as Cheddleton. Tea room and souvenir shop on Froghall station open on operating days. ST10 2HA
KINGSLEY BIRD & FALCONRY CENTRE - Sprinks Lane, Kingsley (access via Staffordshire Way from Cherry Eye Bridge). Tel: 01538 754784. Pre-booked visits only. ST10 2BX

Connections

BUSES - Aimee's service 30 offers a twice daily Mon-Sat service linking Froghall (stop by railway bridge) with Cheadle (a nice little town dominated by Pugin's ornate RC church) in one direction, and Leek in the other, and is thus ideal for expediting one-way towpath walks through this delightful valley. Tel: 01538 385050.

CHESHIRE RING

31 TRENT & MERSEY CANAL Kidsgrove & Rode Heath 5mls/14lks/4hrs

DON'T tell anyone, but we commence coverage of the Cheshire Ring in Staffordshire! Canals can be like that, wilfully anomalous. What could be more puzzling, for example, than the layout at Hardings Wood Junction, where ring-doers have to turn so counterintuitively in the opposite direction to what their gut is telling them? There'll be another indiscretion, when it gets to the outskirts of Manchester. But, for the most part, this 97 mile, 92 lock canal circuit stays in its eponymous county.

Authenticity is regained as the Trent & Mersey Canal passes beneath Pool Lock Aqueduct on the outskirts of Kidsgrove. To reach this ancient, and rather sagging aqueduct from Hardings Wood Junction - the Cheshire Ring's most southerly nodal point - you will have already descended through two locks. Relax, there's only another couple of dozen to go before you reach the bottom of what has been infamously known to generations of boaters as 'Heartbreak Hill'. With the exception of the Pierpoint pair near Hassall Green (Map 32), all the locks were 'duplicated' in the 19th century to speed up the passage of working boats. A further refinement was the provision of paddles between the parallel chambers, enabling one lock to act as a mini-reservoir for its neighbour. These water-saving side paddles fell out of use when commercial carrying petered out on the T&M in the 1960s, but most of the duplicated chambers remain ostensibly in use, though, with budget constraints, they seem to spend lengthy periods awaiting repair.

Twenty-six locks in seven miles between Hardings Wood and Wheelock is not as intimidating as it sounds. Boaters find themselves falling into a rhythm; though, of course, there is no imperative to do it all in one go. Besides, the constituent flights exude their own individual character, and there's scarcely a dull moment as the canal slips off the shackles of urbanisation and meanders through for the most part charming countryside. By Bridge 134, a former warehouse is employed as an out station for the Canal & River Trust. During the Second World War emergency rations of flour were secretly stored here

The three (out of six) Red Bull locks which follow are photogenically set against a wooded backdrop which masks the Stoke-Crewe railway and its clattering trains from view. Up until the railway grouping of 1923, this belonged to the North Staffordshire Railway - affectionately known as 'The Knotty' on account of its heraldic crest

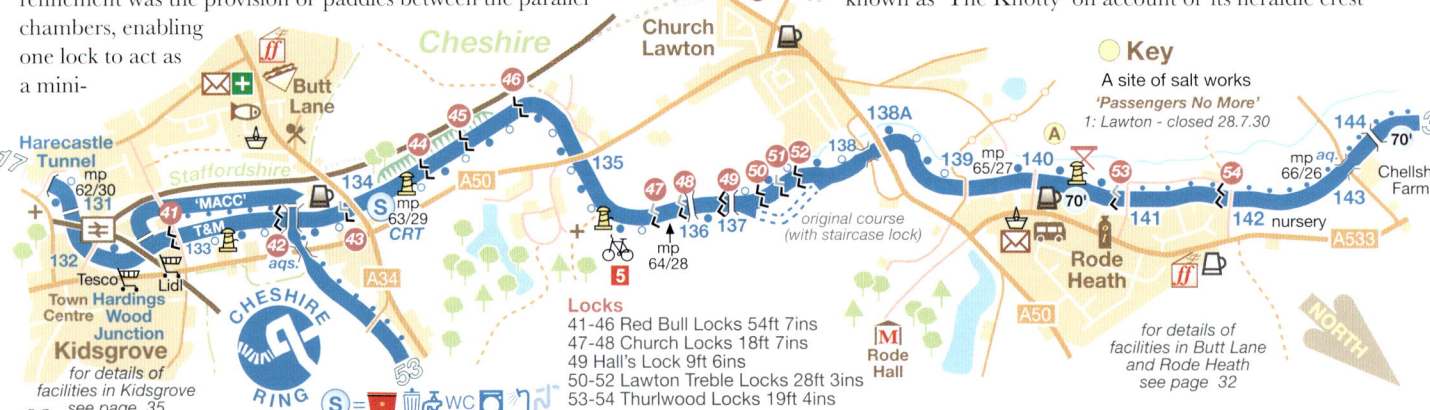

Key
● A site of salt works
'Passengers No More'
1: Lawton - closed 28.7.30

Locks
41-46 Red Bull Locks 54ft 7ins
47-48 Church Locks 18ft 7ins
49 Hall's Lock 9ft 6ins
50-52 Lawton Treble Locks 28ft 3ins
53-54 Thurlwood Locks 19ft 4ins

for details of facilities in Kidsgrove see page 35

for details of facilities in Butt Lane and Rode Heath see page 32

Pool Lock Aqueduct

incorporating the historic Staffordshire Knot - under whose ownership the canal had been absorbed in 1846. Unlike some railway companies, who purchased inland waterways in order to suppress them, the Knotty did its best to encourage trade, especially in raw materials between the Mersey ports and the Potteries. In the 1890s, Edwin B. Smith, the NSR's engineer, proposed an upgrade of the Trent & Mersey north of the Potteries to enable barges of 60 tons capacity or more to ply the canal. Locks would be widened, lengthened and deepened - the latter improvement resulting in a reduction in the number of chambers, 21 as opposed to 35 - but though the scheme was authorised by an Act of Parliament, solely some widening between Anderton and Middlewich ever took place. Viewed from the perspective of the leisure age, perhaps we should be grateful for this uncharacteristic example of late19th century inertia. Heaven forbid that the Trent & Mersey was still a working waterway replete with dirty barges, getting in the way of our pristine pleasure craft.

Lawton Treble Locks replaced a Brindley staircase which was both time consuming and wasteful of water. They date from a recommendation by John Rennie in 1801. He noted 'great detention and inconvenience to the boats' as they made their way slowly through the staircase. He also voiced concern at the 'many sharp turns' impairing the passage of boats. A realignment was dug to the south-west of the original line. Further information on this improvement, and much enlightening detail besides, can be found in Ray Shill's *The Trent and Mersey Canal*, published by the Crowood Press in 2021.

Bridge 138 (Snapes Aqueduct) carries the canal across the original route of the A50 road whose modern alignment goes over the canal on Bridge 138A. These old trunk roads have been largely rendered irrelevant in the Motorway Age, but they can reward exploration in their own right. This one once linked Northampton with Warrington; an odyssey of acquired taste where most topographical palates are concerned.

Chellshill Aqueduct conveys the canal across a B road to Alsager, an unusually named and curiously self-effacing town two miles to the south. Boaters can take a bit of a breather in the one and a half mile pound between Thurlwood and Pierpoint locks.

Duplicated Lock 42

32 TRENT & MERSEY CANAL Hassall Green/Wheelock 4mls/12lks/4hrs

HEAVING a self-congratulatory sigh, the northbound, clockwise boater comes to earth with a bump at the bottom of Wheelock Locks, and offers a wry smile to the upgoing boat crew waiting to replace him or her in the lock chamber: In the paraphrased spirit of the football cliche, they must take each 'Heartbreak Hill' lock as it comes. Not that there's much respite, mark you. Three miles ahead, the locks begin all over again, as the Trent & Mersey makes its way down through the salt-manufacturing town of Middlewich.

Salt? You should have seen this misleadingly bland landscape a hundred years ago! Brine extraction and chemical production had given it the appearance of a First World War battleground. A photograph held in the archives of the Cheshire Record Office depicts the vast Brunner Mond alkali plant which filled the land between the canal and the railway at Malkin's Bank. Brine was pumped from below the surface and converted into sodium carbonate. The works closed in 1930 and was demolished within a couple of years, its footprint now covered by a golf course.

Sections of the North Staffordshire Railway's Sandbach branch, have been converted into routes for walking and cycling: part of National Cycle Route 5 where the latter is concerned. Between locks 62 and 63, a side bridge carries the towpath over an old arm (now used by a boatbuilder specialising in the upkeep of traditional craft) which led into the works.

Hassall Green and Wheelock are both popular lay-over points for boaters. At the former, the proximity of the M6 motorway doesn't overly intrude, though perhaps that's because we're all too tired to notice. At the latter, boating facilities are laid on (including recycling) and access is afforded to the not uninteresting town of Sandbach. Several works and mills congregated alongside the canal at Wheelock Wharf and trade here (in corn, fustian, acid et al) was brisk in the heyday of the canal. A small aqueduct carries the canal across the River Wheelock, an insubstantial tributary of the Dane, which flows into the Weaver at Northwich. And the Weaver? Well that, of course, is subsumed into the Mersey somewhere out on Frodsham's lonely marshes - see page 148.

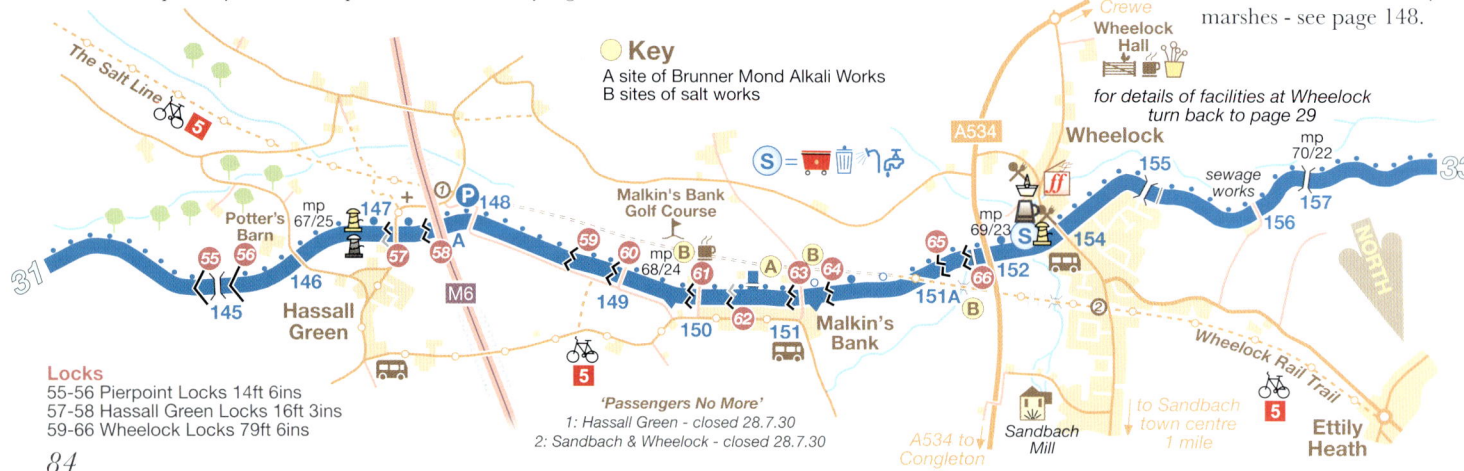

Locks
55-56 Pierpoint Locks 14ft 6ins
57-58 Hassall Green Locks 16ft 3ins
59-66 Wheelock Locks 79ft 6ins

84

33 TRENT & MERSEY CANAL Ettily Heath & Stud Green 4mls/4lks/2hrs

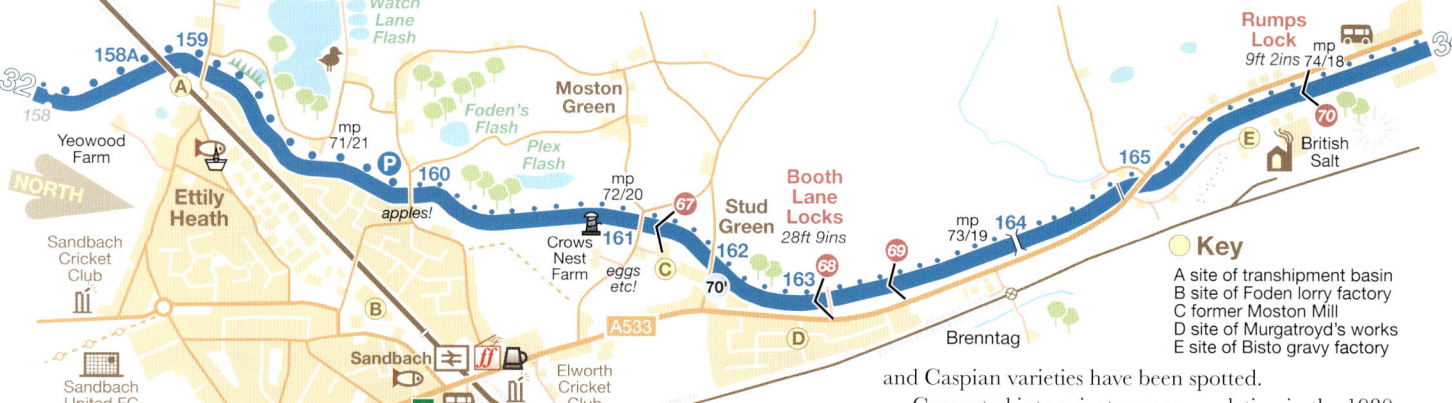

BRUSQUELY ignoring the blandishments of Sandbach and its Saxon Crosses (see page 29), the Trent & Mersey forges northwards, traversing an area ravaged by salt-mining subsidence. Concrete-banked, and steel-piled, the canal is deeper than usual, and your boat surges forward, relishing the novelty value of clear water beneath its counter.

Sandbach Flashes are expanses of water similarly brought about by salt extraction. They have become a bird-watcher's paradise, and almost a hundred and fifty species have been indentified. No matter that they are located well inland, the flashes are particularly rich in gulls, and even such esoteric species as Glaucous, Icelandic and Caspian varieties have been spotted.

Converted into private accommodation in the 1980s, the building alongside Booth Lane Top Lock (No.67) was formerly Moston Mill. It dated from around 1825 and was engaged in grinding corn until the mid-1950s. The other two Booth Lane locks stood alongside what was originally known as Murgatroyd's Salt & Chemical Co. who were in the business of transforming raw salt into various chemicals. Model railway enthusiasts of a certain age will recall that Triang produced an attractive bogie chlorine tank wagon in Murgatroyd's livery in the 1960s. The once extensive works have been replaced by a housing development, but a half-timbered farmhouse remains on the site. Dating from the 17th century, it had survived to become the works' sports and social club. Another vanished industry was the Bisto gravy factory. In contrast British Salt, source of over half the UK's domestic output, remains very much in business, albeit owned by the Indian conglomerate, Tata, now.

85

34 TRENT & MERSEY CANAL Middlewich 4mls/5lks/2hrs

IN the old days it was salt which brought so much traffic to Middlewich's canals: the salt boats, and, of course, the coal boats, without which, in the pre-electric age, no industry could function. Now, though, it is with pleasure boating that this small mid-Cheshire town is focussed; two hire fleets and a boatyard and chandlery adding to the often frenetically busy Trent & Mersey Canal which, south of Middlewich, accommodates the orbital traffic of both the Cheshire and Four Counties rings. Sometimes, it seems, there are so many boats wanting to cross your path that you begin to think the town would be more aptly known as *Muddle*wich.

Middlewich Locks form a dog-leg trio, all deep and tediously slow to use. Seddons salt works long ago having been demolished, the canal is rather drearily bounded by light industrial premises, though Middlewich Wharf and Floating Holidays' hire base, with its old canal manager's house and valanced canopy, strikes a welcome element of humanity and sense of purpose. The drydock, on the bend between locks 72 and 73, was once used to maintain Seddons' fleet of narrowboats.

The Town Wharf by Bridge 172 handled general cargoes. Its buildings stand embarrassingly derelict. In a more popular setting, one imagines, they'd have been snapped up for refurbishment long ago. Etched interpretive boards summarise Middlewich's history with the emphasis on its Roman origins. Parallel to the tiny River Croco, visitor moorings are provided between Bridge 172 and Big Lock which is named after its width rather than its depth. A ropewalk stood alongside for many years. Even further back on your time machine dial, the Romans had a fort/station called Salinae at the confluence of the Croco and Dane.

Croxton Aqueduct was rebuilt to broad-beam dimensions in 1891 so as to permit wide beam craft to work between Anderton and Middlewich. However, after being damaged by flooding in the 1930s, it reverted to its present narrow status. A flint grinding mill stood alongside. In the woods between bridges 176 and 177 the mangled remains of old wagon tipplers hint at the existence of clay or puddle pits. Note also how the bridges along this length are flat topped so that they could be relatively easily raised in the event of subsidence.

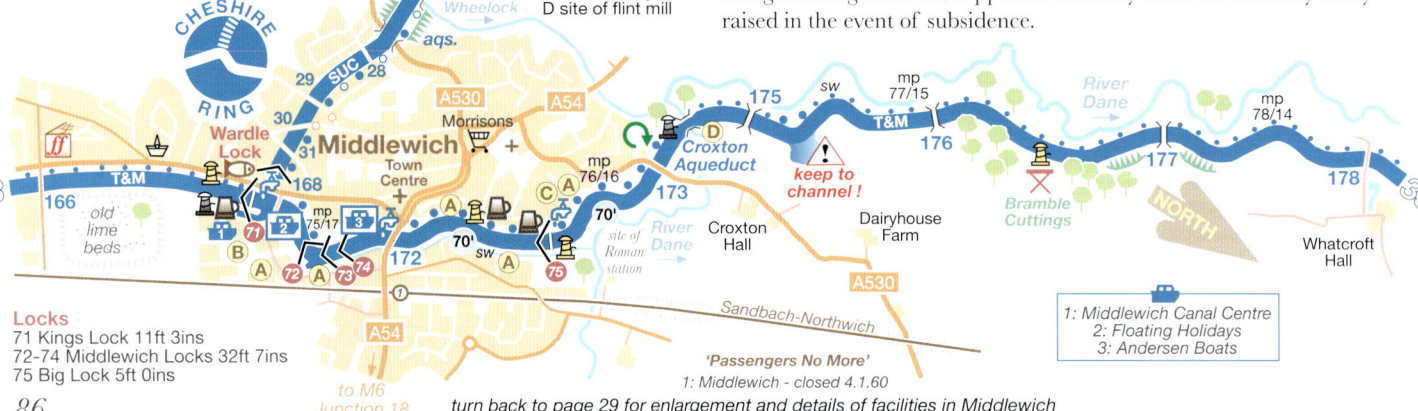

Locks
71 Kings Lock 11ft 3ins
72-74 Middlewich Locks 32ft 7ins
75 Big Lock 5ft 0ins

'Passengers No More'
1: Middlewich - closed 4.1.60

turn back to page 29 for enlargement and details of facilities in Middlewich

35 TRENT & MERSEY CANAL Rudheath & Wincham 4½ mls/0lks/1½ hrs

WOODLAND interludes and subsidence-induced flashes characterise the Trent & Mersey's serene passage through the Dane Valley. Hereabouts the river (having risen in the Derbyshire Peak District on the flank of Axe Edge - and having been crossed again by Cheshire Ring travellers at Bosley - Map 51) has grown sluggish with age, meandering about its level valley in a series of lazy loops; one moment it is hard by the canal, the next away across the pasturelands of milking herds. The soil here is soft and the Dane carves deep banks made shadowy by alder and willow. The canal shares the valley with a Roman Road known as King Street and a now lightly used railway which once sported a 'push & pull' service between Crewe and Northwich, affectionately known as 'The Dodger'. Bringing railway history bang up to date, HS2's Birmingham-Manchester leg, was due to cross the canal twice in the vicinity of Bridge 180A ... before Rishi pulled the plug on it.

The most curious feature of this section of the canal are the flashes bordering the main channel to the south of Bridge 181. That nearest the bridge was once filled with the submerged wrecks of abandoned narrowboats, an inland waterway equivalent of Scapa Flow. Many of the boats were brought here and sunk *en masse* during the Fifties in circumstances as controversial - in canal terms, that is - as the scuttling of the German Fleet after the First World War. In what was probably a book-keeping exercise, British Waterways rid themselves of surplus narrowboats in a number of watery graves throughout the system. In recent years the wrecks have been raised and taken off for restoration. You know how it works: one generation's cast-offs become the next's prized possessions.

Industry impinges: though some may welcome it as an antidote to all those soporific pasturelands encountered to the south. Steamy pipes span the canal between bridges 186 and 189. Inovyn extract and process brine; Tata, soda ash. The works, previously owned by Brunner Mond/ICI, retains a handsome brick-built, Dutch-gabled office block, but has lost the canal basin which once served it, the only remaining clue being a side bridge which lifts the towpath over its former entrance. The railway - still very much in use - belonged to the Cheshire Lines Committee, an amalgamation of the Great Central, Great Northern and Midland companies.

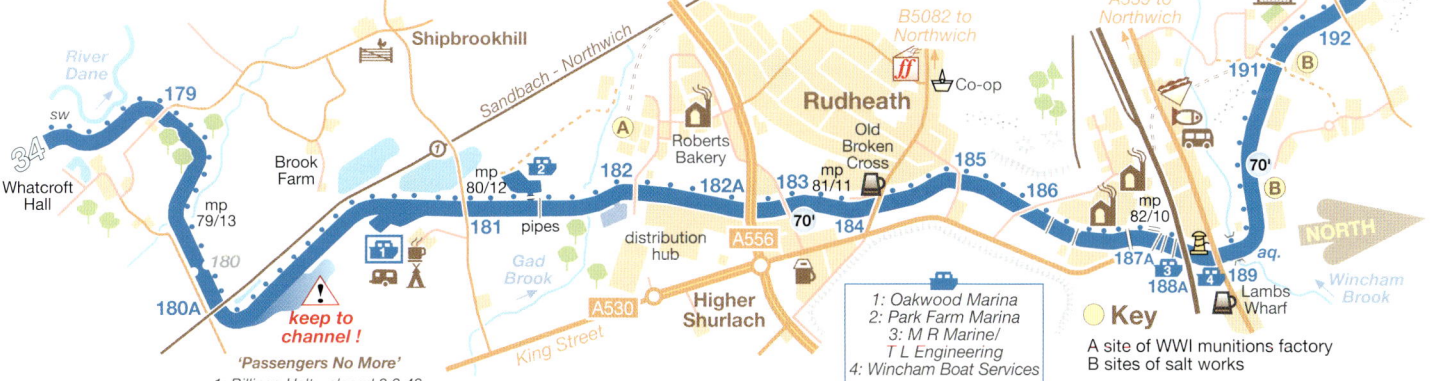

87

36 TRENT & MERSEY CANAL Anderton & Barnton 5mls/0lks/2hrs

EXCITEMENT mounts, whatever your mode and direction of travel, as the canal nears Anderton and its famous Boat Lift. Of all the so-called "Seven Wonders of the Waterways", Anderton Lift is arguably the most ingenious, though its track record doesn't always bear scrutiny. Indeed, it wasn't in operation at all between 1983 and 2002, and though ostensibly functionable since the latter date, it has often been side-lined by one niggle or another. Indeed, as we went to press we learned that it would again be out of action throughout 2025, and a good part of the following year as well, undergoing further refurbishment.

Down on the banks of the Weaver a popular visitor centre supplies the facts and figures behind this Heath Robinsonesque contraption. Suffice it here to say that it dates from 1875 and was designed by Edwin Clark who, *Canal Companion* aficionados will pretty much uniquely know, hailed from Marlow; and who, some three years earlier, had engineered the railway to that pretty Thameside town.

Either side of Anderton, the Trent & Mersey Canal continues in its unhurried, Brindleyesque manner, negotiating a scarred landscape destabilised over the years by salt extraction. In 1958 a new length of canal had to be dug at Marston to bypass a section bedevilled by subsidence.

Barnton and Saltersford tunnels were amongst the earliest essays in the art of canal tunnel digging. They are far from straight. Neither are they wide enough for narrowboats to pass inside. Their lack of width also prevented widebeam barges from traversing the Trent & Mersey between Preston Brook and Middlewich as had originally been planned. They are short enough, however, not to cause undue traffic delays. Both bores are towpathless, but walkers have the bonus of a charming walk, by way of the old horse paths, across the wooded tops. Separating the two tunnels is an idyllic, leafy pool, which provides a pleasant mooring. You could linger here to your heart's content, watching the boats emerge from the tunnels. Or descending for a stroll along the Weaver.

Key
A former Winnington Works *(due for redevelopment)*
B site of Wallerscote Works *(under redevelopment)*

1: Anderton Marina ABC Boat Hire
2: Uplands Marina.

Exercise care entering Barnton Tunnel: check first to see that no boat is approaching from the oposite end. Northbound boats may enter Saltersford Tunnel for 20 minutes on the hour, southbound similarly on the half hour.

Broken Cross
Map 35
Eating & Drinking
OLD BROKEN CROSS - Broken Cross Place (Bridge 184). Tel: 01606 333111. 18th century inn refurbished in the modern manner. Food served from noon daily. CW9 7EB.
Shopping
Garage with Spar shop less than five minutes walk to south-east. Co-op ten minutes west.

Wincham Wharf
Map 35
Eating & Drinking
BIG BAPS - Manchester Road. Freshly made baps, sandwiches, pies etc. Eat-in or takeaway, 7am-2pm daily. Tel: 0751 394 7596. CW9 7NE
THE CODFATHER - Manchester Road. Tel: 01606 42342. Award-winning fish & chips. CW9 7NE
LAMBS WHARF - Manchester Road (Bridge 189). Tel: 01606 514053. Canalside bar and live music venue. CW9 7NT
Connections
BUSES - services 89 & CAT9 to/from Northwich and Knutsford and Warrington respectively.

Marston
Map 35
Former salt mining village still wrought by the lop-sided scars of the past.
Eating & Drinking
SALT BARGE - Ollershaw Lane (Bridge 193). Tel: 01606 246628. Welcoming local open from noon daily. Food status uncertain awwtp. CW9 6ES
Nicho's cafe/sandwich bar 2 mins west of Bridge 192.
Things to Do
LION SALT WORKS - Ollershaw Lane (Bridge 193). Tel: 01606 275066. Award-winning heritage centre devoted to the history of salt-making. Open Tue-Sun 10.30am-5pm. Gift shop, cafe, play area. CW9 6ES

Anderton Lift

Anderton
Maps 36/56
Even if you're not planning to use the magnificent Boat Lift, it's difficult to resist the urge to pause and take a gander: Boat Lifts don't exactly grow on trees!

Eating & Drinking
THE MOORINGS - restaurant and coffee shop at Anderton Marina. Tel: 01606 79789. CW9 6AJ
STANLEY ARMS - canalside opposite Anderton Lift. Tel: 01606 77661. Food from noon daily. Greene King ales. Offside customer moorings. CW9 6AG
LIFT CAFETERIA - canalside. Boaters breakfasts available from 9.45am daily at this cafe offering fine views of the Lift. Tel: 01606 786777. CW9 6FW
Things to Do
ANDERTON BOAT LIFT - Tel: 01606 786777. Visitor Centre celebrating the Lift and local canals in all their historic glory. A widebeam trip boat named *Edwin Clark* after the Lift's designer offers trips up or down the Lift (but *not* in 2025!). River trips to Northwich and back are also usually available. CW9 6FW
ANDERTON NATURE PARK - waymarked trails through reclaimed wasteland where many plants usually confined to coastal environments thrive.
Connections
BUSES - Network Warrington service 9A runs to Northwich bi-hourly Mon-Sat.
TAXIS - Northwich Taxis. Tel: 01606 46666.

Barnton
Maps 36/56
Barnton provides a modest range of facilities - convenience store, butcher, pharmacy - as depicted on the map. Buses 9A and N4 connect with Northwich.

Dutton
Map 37
BLUEBELL COTTAGE GARDENS can be found just downhill from Bridge 213. Tel: 01928 713718. The garden showcases a range of herbaceous hardy perennials available to purchase from the adjoining organic nursery. Additionally there are bluebell woods and a wildflower meadow to explore. Light refreshments. WA4 4HP

37 TRENT & MERSEY CANAL Bartington & Dutton 5mls/11k/2hrs

FORTY years ago, we'd urge travellers on the Trent & Mersey to keep their eyes peeled for the passage of coastal vessels along the Weaver Navigation. Nowadays you're more likely to see a UFO, for waterborne trade on the river petered out at the end of the 20th century. Hopeless romantics, Pearsons believe it could have formed an ideal short-sea link with Ireland, but realists will tell you that it makes economic sense for everything to go by road, more's the pity.

Wasted opportunities apart, this is an extremely beautiful length of the Trent & Mersey. Rolling farmland, interspersed with belts of deciduous woodland, characterise the canal's progress along a ledge above the Weaver's widening valley. Picturesque, but prone to instability, and after the especially wet summer of 2012 a significant breach in the vicinity of Dutton Hall, resulted in the newly formed Canal & River Trust's first public appeal being launched to raise the £1.5m required for the canal's reinstatement. Canals - as recounted elsewhere in this guide - have an irritating habit of breaking both sorts of banks.

Dutton Locks come into view on the Weaver Navigation, together with Joseph Locke's imposing viaduct of twenty sandstone arches erected by the Grand Junction Railway in 1837. Footpaths lead from bridges 211 and 213 for a closer view. Snaking delightfully at the foot of brackeny banks, the canal encounters Longacre Wood, cared for by the Woodland Trust. In the background trains swoosh their urgent way over the pointwork at Weaver Junction where the route to Liverpool bifurcates from the West Coast Main Line.

Milepost 91/1 informs you that the Trent & Mersey Canal has all but completed its journey from Shardlow near Derby. Dutton Stop Lock was belatedly put in by the Trent & Mersey Co. to protect their water supply. 19th century maps imply that it was roofed-over at one time. Nearby stands a drydock covered by a valanced canopy with a distinct sense of railway styling. Little wonder, the dock was built by the North Staffordshire Railway for the maintenance of the tugs which pulled strings of boats (apparently up to twenty at a time) through the tunnels, a practise which continued up until the 1940s. Presided over by two whitewashed cottages, the canal disappears into the mouth of Preston Brook Tunnel. It must be fun to lean out of one of those upstairs windows and watch a boat vanish into the bowels of the earth beneath you.

A strict timetable of entry times is in operation at Preston Brook Tunnel: northbound on the hour for 10 minutes; southbound on the half hour for 10 minutes.

38 BRIDGEWATER CANAL Preston Brook 4½ mls / 0 lks / 1½ hrs

PRESTON BROOK is one of those nodal points on the inland waterway follower's emotional compass that none of their more rationally grounded friends and acquaintances will have ever heard of. Here - just inside the northern portal of Preston Brook Tunnel - that doyen of the canals, the Bridgewater, meets the Trent & Mersey. In the heyday of water transport Preston Brook was one of the busiest canal centres in the north-west. An inland port where cargoes were transhipped between wide-beam Mersey 'flats' and narrowboats. A substantial number of warehouses were erected to cater for this activity, which continued up until the end of the Second World War. Indeed, narrowboats continued to trade here until the late 1960s, following which the majority of warehouses were regrettably demolished. And, consequentially, Preston Brook, whatever its historic status, lacks the obvious appeal of peers such as Shardlow or Stourport. A notable survivor, however, is a former flour warehouse converted into flats, whilst there are plenty of boats usually to be seen on the move; a marina sees to that.

North of the M56 motorway - which connects Manchester with North Wales - the Bridgewater Canal rapidly establishes a rural atmosphere. Norton's prominent water tower was built in 1892 as part of the system which supplies Liverpool with water from Lake Vyrnwy in mid-Wales. Closer to hand, the village of Daresbury has connections with Lewis Carroll, but is these days perhaps better known as home to a world renowned Science & Innovation Campus.

1: Preston Brook Wharf
2: Preston Brook Marina

'Passengers No More'
1: Preston Brook - closed 1.3.48
2: Moore - closed 1.2.43
3: Daresbury - closed 7.7.52

for details of facilities turn to page 93

38A BRIDGEWATER CANAL Runcorn 3mls/0lks/1hr

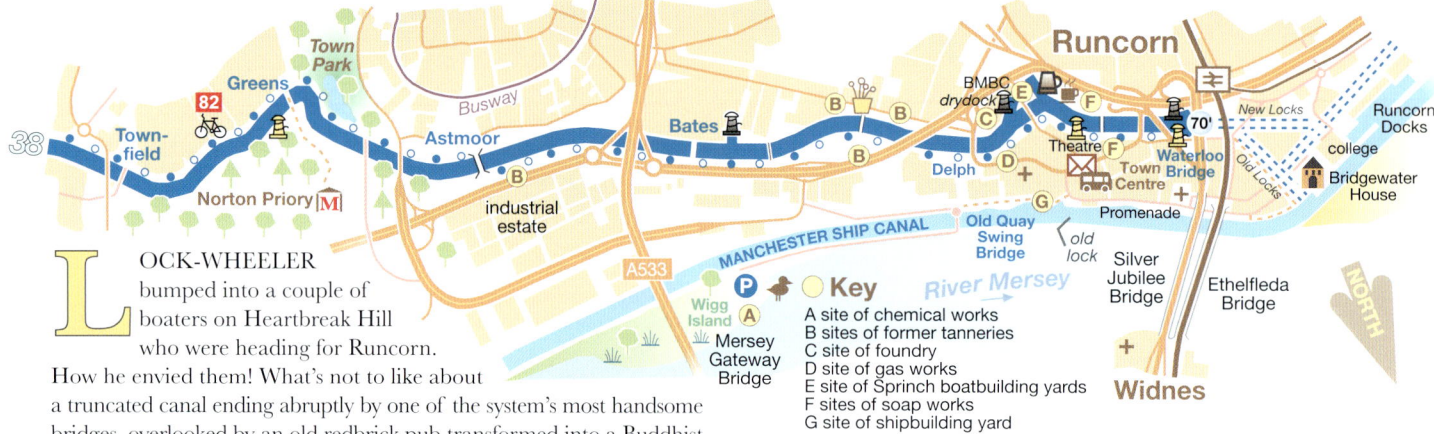

Key
A site of chemical works
B sites of former tanneries
C site of foundry
D site of gas works
E site of Sprinch boatbuilding yards
F sites of soap works
G site of shipbuilding yard

LOCK-WHEELER bumped into a couple of boaters on Heartbreak Hill who were heading for Runcorn. How he envied them! What's not to like about a truncated canal ending abruptly by one of the system's most handsome bridges, overlooked by an old redbrick pub transformed into a Buddhist Temple? How quirky can you get! Indeed, anyone with an affinity with the flotsam and jetsam of small coastal ports is likely to find a detour off the main route of the Cheshire Ring into Runcorn a rewarding experience. Less perceptive observers have been flippantly dismissive of the arm's five lockless and predominantly urbanised miles, and visiting boats are a relatively rare phenomenon. Most vessels on the move seemingly belong to members of the Bridgewater Motor Boat Club (est. 1952) which has premises in the old Sprinch boatbuilding yards at the western end of the canal; what's more they welcome visitors.

But if boats are comparatively rare, towpath walking and cycling are activities enthusiastically embraced by the native population, as is angling. And there are rural interludes of a sort: notably in the vicinity of Greens Bridge, where rhododendron shrubs fill the woods bordering the lily-fringed canal, and a bosky mooring is provided for boaters wishing to visit Norton Priory. Here too lies the northern edge of Runcorn's Town Park, which boasts an extensive miniature railway.

West of Norton views open out over the Manchester Ship Canal and the widening river with its Mersey Gateway toll bridge, opened in 2017. This length used to be bordered by tanneries - producing leather for shoes and suitcases, harnesses and handbags - and soap works. During the Great War mustard gas was produced at an alkali works on Wigg Island, now it's a nature reserve offering panoramic views across the Mersey. Public rights of way shadow the ship canal, now overlooked by apartments where once there was an extensive shipbuilding yard. The graving dock's slipway intriguingly survives. Hereabouts too, the Guinness boats use to dock, bringing vital supplies of Dublin's finest stout.

But back on the Bridgewater, a pair of arms, employed by the BMBC as a drydock and moorings, indicates the site of the old Sprinch boatbuilding yard. The original line of the canal looped south at this point, encountering a natural lake called the Big Pool in the process.

Visitor moorings are provided alongside Runcorn's Brindley Theatre, and again at the end of the canal, where the former Waterloo Hotel has become Wat Phra Singh, a Buddhist Temple with adjoining Peace Garden. The arm terminates prematurely at an elegant cast iron bridge which spanned the top chambers of the much-mourned Runcorn Locks. From here two flights of ten locks each - the Old and New locks - led down to link with the Manchester Ship and Runcorn & Weston canals.

The course of the Old Locks (abandoned in 1948) has become a public footpath, encountering evidence of former chambers. An even more exciting survivor at the bottom of the flight is Bridgewater House, the 'Canal Duke's' residence of 1777, erected so that he might personally oversee completion of his canal. It is now a Wellbeing Enterprise Centre.

Preston Brook   Map 38
Spar convenience store with post office counter just a couple of minutes walk west of canal. Arriva X30 buses run hourly to Runcorn Mon-Sat.

Daresbury   Map 38
A bracing ten minute walk uphill from Keckwick Bridge leads across the A56 into the peaceful core of Daresbury (pronounced 'Dars - as in stars - bury') village. Uplifted by a visit to All Saints parish church (Lewis Carroll souvenirs obtainable) and having viewed the handsome Sessions House, you can justifiably seek out refreshment at the Ring o' Bells (Tel: 01925 740256 - WA4 4AJ) a Chef & Brewer pub which serves food from 11.30am weekdays and from 9.30am weekends. Arriva X30 bus links Daresbury with Chester, Runcorn and Warrington.

Moore   Map 38
Peaceful village despite its proximity to Runcorn. Home of the charmingly named Gentlemen of Moore Rugby Club. Good pub called the Red Lion (Tel: 01925 740101 - WA4 6UD). Convenience store and post office adjoining canal, and buses to/from Warrington and Runcorn. Moore Nature Reserve can be reached by walking down Moore Lane and crossing the Manchester Ship Canal. The reserve, consisting of two hundred acres of woodland, meadows, lakes and ponds, intriguingly incorporates an abandoned length of the old Runcorn & Latchford Canal.

Runcorn   Map 38A
There is a ruggedness to Runcorn old town likely to appeal to certain psyches. Two contrasting bridges span the Mersey. The castellated railway bridge dates from 1869; the neighbouring suspension bridge from 1961: the bridges are known as Ethelfleda and Silver Jubilee respectively. The latter replaced a transporter bridge which could carry only four road vehicles at a time. Marriott Edgar immortalised the ferry which preceded it in his comic monologue (popularised by Stanley Holloway) *Tuppence Per Person Per Trip*. A bracing walk across its haughty replacement can be heartily recommended, perhaps coupled with a visit to Catalyst the science discovery centre. Or one might perhaps go and pay homage at Widnes railway station to the plaque which records that Paul Simon ('on a tour of one-night stands') wrote *Homeward Bound* on its westbound platform in 1965.

Eating & Drinking
THE BRINDLEY - Tel: 0151 907 8360. Canalside arts centre with bar and terrace cafe. WA7 1BG
SOCIETY TAP ROOMS - Ashridge Street. Tel: 01928 775628. Characterful backstreet bar housed in former Runcorn & Widnes Co-operative Society building of 1928. Open Thur-Sun afternoons and evenings. WA7 1HU
TEN LOCK FLIGHT - Crosville Way. Tel: 01928 352094. Newbuild Marston's pub overlooking canal. Food served from 11.30am daily. WA7 5TW

Shopping
Enough shops remain in the town centre to meet canallers' needs. Tucked away in Granville Street (opposite the library) is Monk's delicatessen, excellent for both cooking ingredients and take-away food. Family run, it can trace its origins back to 1884. Staunchly independent, Curiosity Books (Tel: 01928 575956) are on High Street. The Market Hall is open daily and there's a street market on Tuesday.

Things to Do
NORTON PRIORY - Warrington Road. Tel: 01928 569895. Canal access from Green's Bridge. Open daily (ex Wed) from 10am-5pm. Three distinct layers of history which peel back to reveal: life in the original monastery dissolved by Henry VIII in 1536; the Tudor mansion which grew up in its place; and the Georgian country house of 1740 that succeeded it. WA7 1SX

Connections
BUSES - an unusual feature of the town is its segregated 'busways' which provide a fast 'interurban' network worth sampling for its own sake. Try Arriva's 3A/C for a circular run via Weston village commanding exhilarating views over the Mersey, Weaver, and Manchester Ship Canal.
TRAINS - station adjacent to canal terminus well served by trains to Liverpool, Chester, and London Euston. Runcorn *East* station is on the Manchester, Warrington, Chester and North Wales route and is handily placed for Preston Brook.

39 BRIDGEWATER CANAL Stockton Heath 4mls/0lks/1½ hrs

IDEALLY, one needs access to an old large scale map to grasp the former complexity of Warrington's waterways: that and a time machine, preferably. The big game changer, of course, was the advent of the Manchester Ship Canal, ceremoniously opened by Queen Victoria on 21st May 1894. Pop down from London Bridge on the Duke of Bridgewater's Canal, opened on 21st March 1776, and compare the two waterways, separated by half a mile and a hundred and eighteen years of civil engineering progress. How perverse that the older canal is now the busier!

Whilst in the neighbourhood, it would be a missed opportunity not to go and pay homage to Warrington's Transporter Bridge which spans the River Mersey in the vicinity of Crosfields once famous soap works. One of only three extant in the UK, it dates from 1916, and is unique in that it was built to convey railway wagons across the river, as opposed to road vehicles. Intact but derelict, a society was formed in 2015 to campaign for its long term future - *www.warringtontransporterbridge.co.uk*

Long derelict, Walton Lock provided access to a link between the Ship Canal and the Mersey. Lock-wheeler has fond memories of passing through it in 1980 aboard the motor barge *Panary*, on which he had voyaged up from Birkenhead with a consignment of Canadian wheat for Fairclough's Mill. The lock was bi-directional, and which gates were used depended on whether the water in the river was higher or lower than that in the canal. But even with this useful facility, *Panary* got stuck on the mud, and required the assistance of a tug to free it.

Trade on the Ship Canal continues to fluctuate, but is inevitably a pale shadow of its heyday. *Naomi B*, pictured on page 106, was conveying

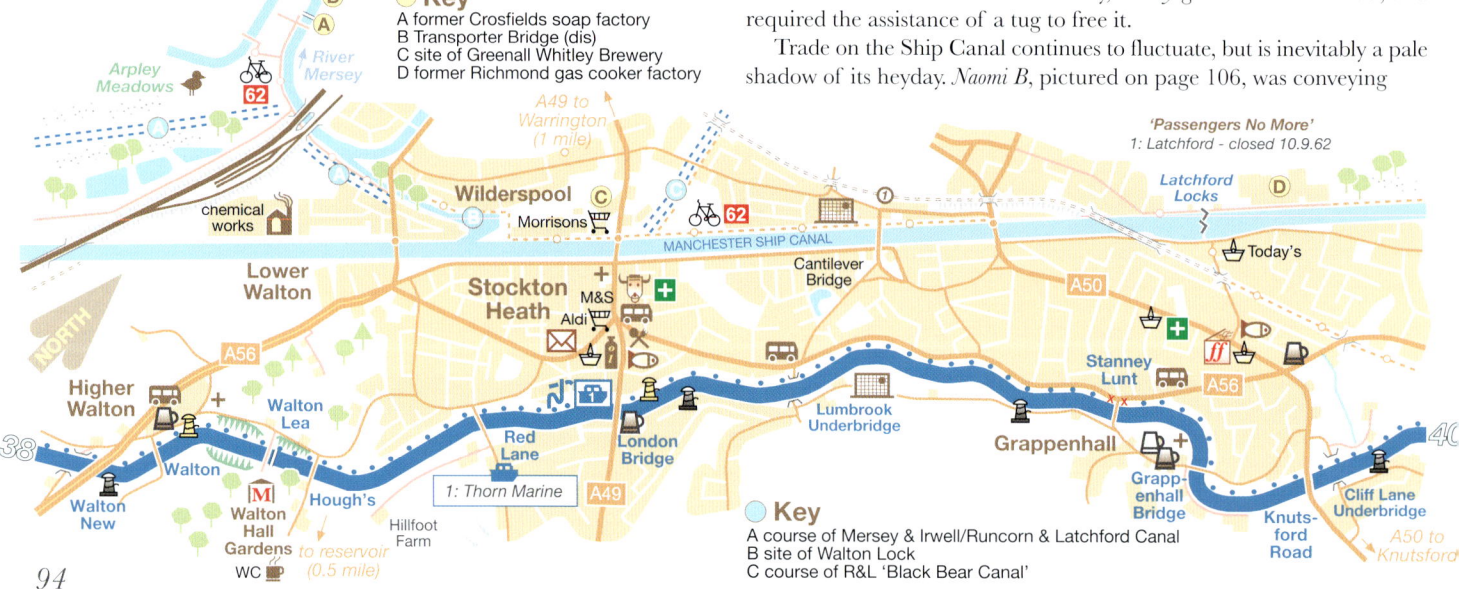

Key
A former Crosfields soap factory
B Transporter Bridge (dis)
C site of Greenall Whitley Brewery
D former Richmond gas cooker factory

1: Latchford - closed 10.9.62
'Passengers No More'

1: Thorn Marine

Key
A course of Mersey & Irwell/Runcorn & Latchford Canal
B site of Walton Lock
C course of R&L 'Black Bear Canal'

construction materials for a Manchester Brewery, and is typical of the ad hoc nature of sailings now. The only regular traffic at the Manchester end of the Ship Canal is bulk cement imported from Ireland. Silica sand is brought in from the West Highlands to Runcorn Docks, as is cement once or twice a week. Weston Point Dock is mostly used for dredging operations.

Meanwhile, back on the Bridgewater Canal, at London Bridge the premises of Thorn Marine (a most friendly and useful establishment catering for all boaters' needs) were originally a Bank Rider's house with stabling for boat horses. The bridge itself dates from the 1930s when London Road was upgraded. The A49 is three-quarters of the way on its journey from Ross-on-Wye to Bamber Bridge on the outskirts of Preston; its sublime Marches scenery but a memory. On the south-eastern side of the bridge, look out for the semi-circular flight of steps down to the water's edge. This was Stockton Quay where 18th century canal passengers would embark aboard packet boats linking Runcorn with Manchester.

With suburbia to the north and open country to the south, the canal passes Grappenhall Football Club, who are nicknamed 'The Canalsiders'. Back in the 1890s plans were laid for a railway linking the Manchester Ship Canal with a new port to be built on the Lincolnshire coast. It was to be known as the Lancashire, Derbyshire & East Coast Railway and would have crossed the Bridgewater Canal in the neighbourhood of Lumbrook Underbridge. In the event only a central section between Chesterfield and Lincoln materialised: an outcome not without its parallels in the present day!

Higher Walton   Map 39

Picturesque estate village built on the brewing fortunes of the Greenall family. The church of St John the Evangelist is by the Lancaster architectural partnership Paley & Austin, designers of many railway stations.

Eating & Drinking
WALTON ARMS - Old Chester Road. Tel: 01925 262659. Vintage Inns pub/restaurant open from 11.30am daily, food served throughout. WA4 6TG

Things to Do
WALTON HALL - Higher Walton. Tel: 01925 262908. Mansion of the brewing magnate, Sir Gilbert Greenall. The house itself is used as a wedding venue, but the grounds and gardens, which include a Children's Zoo and Heritage Cafe, are open to the public. WA4 6SN

Connections
BUSES - Arriva X30 runs hourly (ex Sun) to/from Runcorn and Warrington. Ditto Ashcroft Travel 62 (Mon-Fri only) which runs via Moore.

Stockton Heath   Map 39

An unexpectedly prosperous suburb of Warrington. The imposing sandstone church dates from 1868 and is the work of E. G. Paley, architect of many fine Victorian churches in the north-west, and partner of Hubert Austin mentioned at Higher Walton.

Eating & Drinking
ANCHOR & HOPS - Walton Road. Tel: 0780 972 1143. Bottle shop and tap room. WA4 6NL
CORKS OUT - London Road. Tel: 01925 267700. Wine shop/bar open from 11am daily. WA4 6LE
COSTELLO'S BAR - Walton Road (at crossroads). Tel: 01925 600910. *Good Beer Guide* listed modern bar operated by the Dunham Massey Brewing Co. (see Map 41). Open from noon daily. WA4 6NJ
EGO - Walton Road. Tel: 01925 602606. This stylish Mediterranean restaurant and bar is part of a growing M&B chain, sister branches of which feature on Maps 28 & 40. Open from 11am daily. WA4 6NJ
LONDON BRIDGE INN - London Road. (adjacent canal at London Road Bridge). Tel 01925 267904. Imposing J.W. Lees (of Manchester) pub. Food served from noon throughout daily.   WA4 5BG
TOMAHAWK - London Road. Tel: 01925 982920. Popular all day restaurant (from 9am) and steak bar. Open from noon on Sundays. WA4 6LG

Shopping
Sainsbury's Local just downhill from London Bridge; Aldi on Walton Road; M&S Foodhall in Forge Shopping Precinct; and large Morrisons across the Ship Canal.

Connections
BUSES - frequent Cheshire Cat services 7/8/9 to/from Warrington town centre. 'Not at all bad' was how the architectural historian and critic, Nikolaus Pevsner, restrainedly described the town in the *South Lancashire* volume of his Buildings of England series. And on that somewhat tentative recommendation alone, who could resist a short bus ride to see it for oneself!

Grappenhall   Map 39

A pretty cobbled lane leads to the church and village stocks. Suggestions that the grinning cat carved on the tower of St Wilfrid's church inspired Lewis Carroll's Cheshire Cat are perhaps best treated as apocryphal.

Eating & Drinking
PARR ARMS - Church Lane. Tel: 01925 212120. Whitewashed and well-appointed village pub. Food served throughout from noon daily. WA4 3EP

95

40 BRIDGEWATER CANAL Lymm & Thelwall 4mls/0lks/1½ hrs

CANAL Companion loyalists will know of the hold ferries have on our imagination, and the Thelwall Ferry (operating hours 7-9am ex Sun, 12-2pm and 4-6pm) has always been one of our Cheshire Ring treats. The ferryman will take you over to the far bank of the Manchester Ship Canal aboard *Bollin*, a small motorised craft which in recent years replaced the aluminium boat formerly sculled between the banks. Having gained the far side, a short walk westwards (along what used to be the course of the MSC's own elaborate internal railway system) will bring you to the giant Latchford Locks (Map 39). The larger of the two chambers measures 600 x 65ft - just think how many narrowboats you could fit in that. You can complete the circle by turning right at Today's convenience store and going up on to the Trans Pennine Trail, following the old railway back to Thelwall, mildly cussing that the nanny state denies access to the lofty girder bridge which once carried the trains across the Ship Canal. There is no fare as such for the ferry, though donations for the RNLI are gratefully accepted.

The M6 Motorway crosses the Manchester Ship Canal in one giant leap and a bound called Thelwall Viaduct. In fact there are two of them, the original dating from 1963, a second added, as traffic levels soared exponentially, in 1995.

The classical pianist, Stephen Hough, was raised in Thelwall and Grappenhall. In 2018 he collaborated with the Thelwall Morris Men to compose a dance called Primrose & Blue in a nod to the colours of the local rugby league team, Warrington Wolves. Rather a far cry from the concert halls of the world Hough inhabits now.

Unostentatiously true to its 83ft contour, the Bridgewater Canal slips through the dainty little town of Lymm. In canal terms, this twenty-five mile pound constitutes what the French would call the *longueurs* of the

'Passengers No More'
1 Thelwall - closed 17.9.56
2 Lymm - closed 10.9.62
3 Heatley & Warburton - closed 10.9.62

Cheshire Ring. So one welcomes the charm of Lymm and is grateful for an excuse to leave the canal behind and renew one's relationship with dry land. Whitbarrow Aqueduct carries the canal over a brook which cleaves a dramatic gorge through a sandstone outcrop on its way down to the Mersey. The gorge has been turned into an attractive park, but once there was a mill here, the sluice and water wheel of which remain to tickle your historic fancy. Lymm was an early victim of transport engineering. Brindley surveyed a route which sliced the old town square in half, so that even today houses overhang Lymm Bridge like interrupted conversations.

South of Lloyds Bridge, Oughtrington's parish church is seemingly displaced from the rest of the village. In common with Higher Walton's (Map 39) it was built from Victorian profits, in this instance by one of the 'cotton kings', George Charnley Dewhurst, who resided in Lymm. To the north of Lloyds Bridge stands a three-storeyed terrace of former fustian-cutting cottages, the raw cloth being brought in from Manchester by canal boat, treated and returned as velvet. A fine example of a canalside warehouse stands to the east of Burford Lane Underbridge. The adjoining house has been beautifully restored but the warehouse has patently seen better days. In the 1980s it was used as a workshop producing spare parts for the iconic Vincent motorbike.

Thelwall Map 40
Eating & Drinking
LITTLE MANOR - Bell Lane. Tel: 01925 212070. Brunning & Price establishment, and you know how gushing we can get about them. Open from 11am daily, food served throughout from noon. WA4 2SX
PICKERING ARMS - Bell Lane. Tel: 01925 555956. Pretty half-timbered pub close to the ferry. Food served from noon weekdays, from 9am Sat, and from 10.30am Sun. WA4 2SU

Lymm Map 40
One of the most appealing ports of call on the 'Cheshire Ring', and its facilities could not be handier. An enigmatic sandstone cross occupies the centre, and there are several picturesque nooks and crannies. Lymm Dam dates from the construction of the Stockport to Warrington turnpike in 1824.

Eating & Drinking
BREWERY TAP - Bridgewater St. Tel: 01925 755451. *Good Beer Guide* listed pub serving Lymm or Dunham Massey (see Map 41) beers. WA13 0AB
CHIA - The Cross. Tel: 01925 753079. Tapas bar, open 4pm Wed/Thur; 2pm Fri; noon weekends. WA13 0HU
ELMAS - Pepper Street. Tel: 01925 756049.

Colin Warne, Thelwall Ferryman

Mediterranean restaurant and take-away. Open from 4pm Mon-Thur, from noon Fri-Sun. WA13 0JB
EIGHTEEN - The Cross. Tel: 01925 751702. Kitchen bar. Opens 5pm Thur/Fri; noon Sat/Sun. WA13 0HU
GREEN DRAGON - Mill Lane. Tel: 01925 757070. Ego restaurant open from 11am daily. WA13 9SB
LA BOHEME - Mill Lane. Tel: 01925 753657. French restaurant. Closed Mon & Tue. WA13 9SD
SEXTONS - Eagle Brow. Tel: 01925 753669. Cafe serving fresh baking. 8.30am-5pm daily. WA13 0AD
There are opportunities for connoisseurs to sample Manchester brewed beers by Hydes (Bulls Head) and Lees (Spread Eagle).

Shopping
Conscious of its charm, boutique and antique outlets have infiltrated Lymm's more traditional retailers, amongst which are Hopkinsons butchers, Sextons bakery (which does take-away/ready cooked meals), and a pharmacy. Sainsbury's boast both 'Local' and 'Superstore' outlets. Post office. Canalside Makers and Artisan markets on selected Sundays.

Connections
BUSES - service X5 provides an hourly (bi-hourly Sun) link with Warrington and Altrincham.

41 BRIDGEWATER CANAL Dunham 4½ mls/0lks/1½ hrs

OUTSKIRTS exude their own remoteness; a quality exaggerated by the sense of contrast between what is urban and what is rural. Greater Manchester's sprawl hasn't quite extended to its boundary with Cheshire. Oldfield Brow marks the beginning (or end in the case of westbound travellers) of the conurbation. Dunham Town sits prettily in the fragility of no-man's-land. From hereabouts to Romiley - the first semblance of countryside on the far side of Manchester - it is ten hours cruising. Long gone, though, are the days when we would have exhorted you to avoid mooring overnight in the city.

The Bridgewater Canal is not as shallow as most: clearly a case, as Cat Stevens so perceptively put it, that "the first cut is the deepest." But long lines of moored craft force you to throttle down to a sedate pace, so the opportunity to accelerate without a wash must be postponed. Why hurry? The flat, rural landscape has its own refreshing charm; peaceful and timeless being epithets which spring easily to mind.

Coal used to be unloaded at Bollington Wharf. On the adjacent road, the Olde No.3 pub gained its name from the fact that it was the third stop on the coaching route from Liverpool to London. Of a shy and solitary nature (a default-setting disposition where many canal enthusiasts are concerned), Maurice Egerton, the 4th and last Baron Egerton of Tatton Park, continued his forebears enthusiasm for canals by keeping an ex-army launch here in the 1950s. Maurice was descended from Francis Egerton, the third Duke of Bridgewater, who had so famously promoted the Bridgewater Canal, whilst his uncle, Wilbraham Egerton, was Chairman of the Manchester Ship Canal, cutting the first sod in 1887. A great traveller, pioneer motorist and aviator, Maurice left the family's seat at Tatton Park (4 miles to the south-east) to the National Trust, dying on his Kenyan estate in 1958.

There are pleasant views across parkland roamed by fallow deer to Dunham Massey's 18th century mansion, open to the public under the aegis of the National Trust. Towards the end of the Second World War the estate was used as a prisoner of war camp whose inmates built a large model of a Bavarian castle made from scrap materials. Post-dating the estate, the canal slices across an avenue leading from the house to an

obelisk in an oak wood which was erected to commemorate a racehorse called Bay Malton, though there is no inscription as such. The horse, which anecdotally won enough prize-money to save the owner of Dunham Massey's fiscal bacon, used to be remembered by the name of a canalside pub at Oldfield Brow.

Between Warrington (Map 39) and Broadheath (Map 42) the canal often keeps company with the Trans Pennine Trail, a 215 mile multi-user route from Southport to Hornsea, hereabouts occupying the course of the former Warrington & Stockport railway, closed to passenger trains as long ago as 1962, but used by freight (mostly Yorkshire coal bound for Fiddler's Ferry power station) until 1985. Suddenly, one finds oneself traversing mosses reminiscent of those on the Llangollen Canal between Whitchurch and Ellesmere. A sense of loneliness and isolation descends, all the more palpable in its juxtaposition to so vast a conurbation.

Approaching the outskirts of Altrincham, Lock-wheeler was gratified to see that the bulk of the former Linotype factory had been incorporated - rather tastefully in his opinion - into a housing development, and that even more appropriately its streets bore the names of typefaces. Typesetting was a subject close to his heart. Literally. As a student on a printing course in the 1970s (see page 3, if you haven't already), he had recoiled in panic as his best blazer was liberally spattered with molten metal from an errant Lintotype machine. Back in the present day, solely the iconic canalside engine house of 1897, earmarked for conversion into apartments, proved beyond redemption. A replica is reputedly promised. Yeah, right!

Agden Wharf Map 41
BARN OWL - Warrington Lane. Tel: 01925 752020. *Good Beer Guide* listed canalside pub. Food served Tue-Fri lunch and evening (from 5.30pm) and weekends 12-8.30pm. WA13 0SW

The Dunhams Map 41
Picturesque estate villages, Woodhouses and Town, lie on either bank of the canal and repay exploration. St Mark's, at Dunham Town, is a quaint little Victorian church dating from 1865 with Stamford tombs.
Eating & Drinking
AXE & CLEAVER - School Lane. Tel: 0161 928 3391. Chef & Brewer pub/restaurant. Food served from 11.30am daily throughout. WA14 4SE
DUNHAM BARN - School Lane. Tel: 0161 941 6889. Charming tea room and gift shop, open 10am-4pm, closed Mondays and Tuesdays. WA14 4TR
SWAN WITH TWO NICKS - Park Lane. Tel: 0161 928 2914. A classic country pub featuring locally-brewed Dunham Massey ales amongst others, with food served from noon daily. WA14 4SU
VINE INN - Barns Lane, Dunham Woodhouses. Tel: 0161 928 3275. Quaint country pub offering an all too rare opportunity to sample Sam Smith's ales from Tadcaster. Open from 11am (noon Sun). WA14 5RU
YE OLDE NO.3 - Lymm Road (A56). Tel: 0790 869 0199. Roadside pub adjoining off-side visitor moorings. Food served from noon daily. WA14 4TA
Shopping
Little Heath Farm Shop (Tel: 0161 928 0520 - WA14 4SE) is a cornucopia of home-reared beef, lamb and pork, sausages, vegetables and New Cheshire potatoes. Dunham Massey Brewing (Tel: 0161 929 0663 - WA14 4PE) sell their own bottled beers (together with some wines and chutneys) from their premises on Oldfield Lane. On Station Road, Dunham Woodhouses, Dunham Massey Farm sells home-made ice cream, and they are open daily 12-5pm. Tel: 0161 928 1230.
Things to Do
DUNHAM MASSEY - Tel: 0161 941 1025. House (including 17th century watermill) open late Feb-early Nov, Sat-Wed, 9am-4pm. Gardens, parkland, restaurant and NT shop open daily throughout the year.
Admission charge. Dunham Massey Hall was bequeathed to the National Trust by the 10th Earl of Stamford in 1976. It features one of Britain's most sumptuous Edwardian interiors. Over thirty rooms are open to the public housing an admirable collection of furniture, paintings and Huguenot silver. Heaps of family history: the 7th Earl infamously married a bareback circus rider. Fallow deer roam in the 250 acres of delightful parkland. WA14 4SJ
Connections
BUSES - Arriva/Belle Vue service 280 links Altrincham hourly (bi-hourly Sun) with Partington, and there is a handy bus stop outside main gate of the Hall.

Oldfield Brow Map 41
Facilities for canallers include a convenience store, post office/pharmacy (with cash machine), sandwich bar (Tel: 0161 929 8100) and fish & chips/Chinese (Tel: 0161 941 1127).
Connections
BUSES - Arriva service 282 runs hourly to/from Altrincham.

42 BRIDGEWATER CANAL Sale 4½ mls/0 lks/1½ hrs

THE Bridgewater Canal traverses the apparently boundless suburbs of Altrincham and Sale, an urban sprawl broken only by the green corridor of the Mersey's flood plain.

It is odd to reflect that none of these buildings were here when Brindley charted the Bridgewater across this flat landscape in the middle of the 18th century. Market gardens and gentlemen's residences defined the neighbourhood. Indeed, it remained predominantly agricultural (its fecundity enhanced by daily cargoes of 'night soil' from inner Manchester) until construction of the Manchester, South Junction & Altrincham Railway brought an explosion of house building in its wake from the 1840s onwards. Before they actually built the railway there were proposals to convert the canal into one. Thankfully, nothing came of that, but the trains did bring an end to the passenger packet boat services hitherto operated with aplomb.

Broadheath (aka Altrincham) Bridge in its present guise dates from 1935, and exudes Art Deco overtones to prove it. In contrast, a few hundred yards short of it to the west, stands an old cotton warehouse of 1833. Dwarfed by Urban Splash's projecting apartment blocks (inspired by the bows of ocean liners) at the rear of their redevelopment of the Budenberg Gauge Company's premises, it is immensely sad that such an intrinsically handsome building should be abandoned and in such a bad state of repair, and it is difficult to understand why it could not have been incorporated into such an otherwise excellent regeneration scheme. Another of the many works drawn to this part of Altrincham by the presence of canal and railway transport facilities, was Thornton-Pickard, manufacturers of photographic apparatus.

Remnants of two old railways (LNWR & CLC respectively) cross the canal before it swings round to run alongside the Manchester, South Junction & Altrincham Railway and its numerous Metrolink stops. Walton Park boasts a railway of quite a different kind, the miniature line of the Sale Area Model Engineering Society whose circular elevated track is designed to accept locomotives of both three and a half and five inch gauge. They get up steam most Sunday afternoons. Literally!

Prior to the coming of the railway, Sale was just a barren waste with a rifle range. When Napoleon was threatening to invade in 1804, the Duke of Gloucester held a grand review of regulars and volunteers on the open expanse of Sale Moor, as vividly described by Mrs Linnaeus Banks in her 1876 novel *The Manchester Man* whose entertaining narrative also takes in Whaley Bridge - see Map 47B.

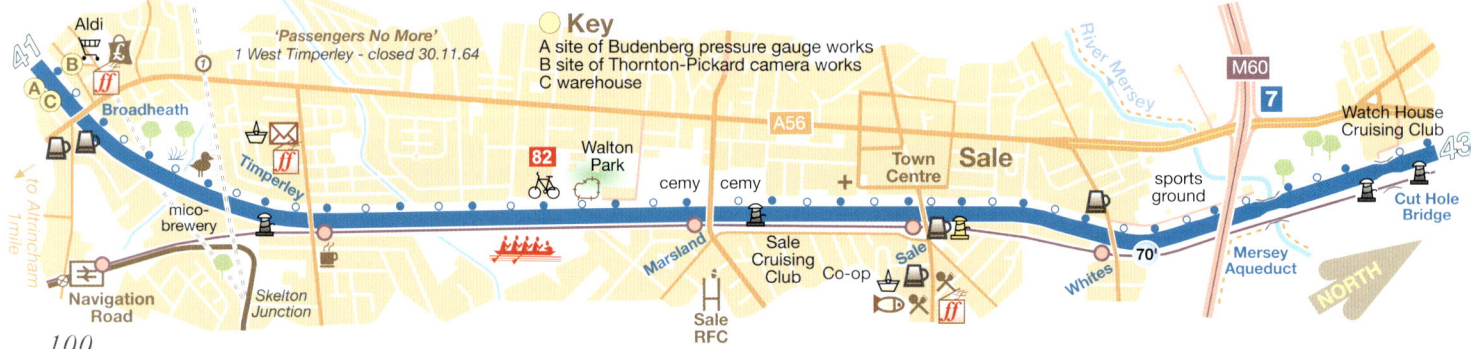

100

Trafford Rowing Club, established in 1957 operate out of premises which were once used as a canalside grain store. Two years after the club's formation, they faced competition for the Bridgewater Canal's turgid waters in the shape of Sale Cruising Club.

Sale Brooklands Cemetery was opened in 1862. Amongst its illustrious occupants are the scientist James Prescott Joule, and the husband of suffragette Emmeline (and three equally committed daughters), Richard Pankhurst. Curving round to pass beneath the M60, the canal passes Manchester University's athletics track and rowing club. Beyond the M60 stands Mosley Acre Farm, premises of the Society for Abandoned Animals who take in and try to rehome unwanted dogs, cats and rabbits. Sale Water Park has been created out of gravel extraction cavities associated with the construction of the motorway and is popular with windsurfers, water skiers and small boat sailors.

Watch House Cruising Club occupy a former length-man's cottage overlooking a series of arches which carry the canal over the Mersey Valley. Boat clubs are a feature of the Bridgewater Canal these days, but it wasn't until 1952 that pleasure cruising was permitted at all. In the Fifties the Watch House was base for a horse-drawn hotel boat operation which plied canals all over the country.

Altrincham (Map 42)

All too easily (and unfairly) dismissed as a residential appurtenance to Manchester, Altrincham hasn't entirely forgotten that it was once an independent Cheshire borough. If you're dashing round the Cheshire Ring it wouldn't be high on your wish list, but with more time at your disposal it can rewardingly be reached by bus from Dunham or Oldfield Brow, or by tram from Sale.

Eating & Drinking
BELGIAN BAR - Greenwood St. Tel: 0161 941 6800. Bruges comes to the Bridgewater! WA14 1RZ
COCO'S - Regent Road. Tel: 0161 928 2303. Well-appointed Italian restaurant. WA14 1RP
COSTELLO'S BAR - Goose Green. Tel: 0161 929 0903. *Good Beer Guide* listed brewery tap for Dunham Massey Brewery (see also Map 41). WA14 1DW
ESSENCE - Manchester Road. Tel: 0161 928 1504. Indian just south of Broadheath Bridge. WA14 4RJ
OLD PACKET HOUSE - Navigation Rd. Tel: 0161 900 6044. Historic pub by Broadheath Bridge which once served the canal. WA14 1LW
PHANTHONG - Regent Road. Tel: 0161 928 5808. Town centre Thai. WA14 1RY

Shopping
Altrincham can trace its status as a market town back to the 13th Century and remains a good shopping centre as befits its prosperous suburbs. The handsome market hall dates from 1849 and operates on Tuesdays, Fridays and Saturdays for general merchandise, and on Thursdays for antiques. Abacus (Tel: 0161 928 5108) is a good secondhand bookshop on Regent Road.

Connections
BUSES - X5 operates hourly (bi-hourly Sun) to/from Warrington via Lymm.
METROLINK - frequent trams to/from Manchester via Sale. Tel: 0161 205 2000.
TRAINS - hourly Northern service to Chester (via Northwich) and Manchester.
TAXIS - Trafford Cars. Tel: 0161 928 1111.

Sale (Map 42)

A town arguably best known for its rugby union club who ground share now with their rugby league counterparts, Salford City Reds, at the Salford City Stadium. Overlooking the canal, the cupola-topped, neo-William & Mary style Town Hall dates from the First World War and, unfortunately, sets an architectural tone that the town centre fails to sustain.

Eating & Drinking
BORELLO - School Road. Tel: 0161 962 4455. Italian just west of Sale Bridge. M33 7XY
J. P. JOULE - Northenden Road. (just east of Sale Bridge). Tel: 0161 928 9889. Wetherspoon. M33 3LF
KING'S RANSOM - Britannia Road (by Sale Bridge). Tel: 0161 969 6006. Canalside Greene King. M33 2AA
SOKRATES - Northenden Road. Tel: 0161 282 0050. Greek restaurant east of Sale Bridge. M33 2DH
VERANDA - Northenden Road. Tel: 0161 282 7200. Charming Mediterranean restaurant east of Sale Bridge. Open from 4pm daily. M33 3BR

Shopping
There's a handy Nisa convenience store east of Sale Bridge, but the town centre lies to the west of the canal and incorporates a pedestrianised shopping centre called 'The Square'. Tesco, Sainsbury's and Aldi have supermarkets either side of School Road, but we were drawn to a nice little fishmongers on Claremont Road boasting that the occupants of its slabs came 'fresh from Fleetwood'.

Connections
METROLINK - frequent trams to/from Manchester and Altrincham. Tel: 0161 205 2000.

43 BRIDGEWATER CANAL Waters Meeting 3½mls/0lks/1hr

Key
A site of Metropolitan Vickers
B site of Ford Motor Company
C site of Trafford Park MPD
D site of Edible Oil Refinery
E site of Power Station
F former Cotton Warehouses
G site of Pomona Docks

HONKING geese; hooting trams: here comes Manchester! Love it or loathe it, it's all nigh impossible to ignore the impact it will have on your itinerary, let alone your sensibilities. But let's not get ahead of ourselves, there's Stretford to consider first, notable for the canalside Roman Catholic Church of St Ann's, erected to the designs of E. W. Pugin (A. W. N.'s eldest son) in the 1860s. Neighbouring Trafford Grove is unusual that its terrace houses face each other across small front gardens separated solely by a footpath. Longford Road Bridge marks the temporary terminus of the Bridgewater Canal from Worsley between 1761 and 1765, before Castlefield was reached. On the outside bend, south of the bridge, stood Rathbone's, a notable dry-dock and boatbuilding yard. Stretford Marine provide welcome boating facilities in an area not exactly over-endowed with them. A large gas works once stood opposite.

Waters Meeting sounds misleadingly idyllic, yet the truth is it's not somewhere you'd necessarily want to linger. Under a graffitied side-bridge, the original section of the Bridgewater Canal, threading its way through the industrial heart of Trafford Park, heads sullenly towards its end-on junction with the Leeds & Liverpool Canal at Leigh.

Prior to the Ship Canal's opening in 1894, Trafford Park was the sylvan country seat of the de Trafford family who had held sway hereabouts since the 11th century. Fierce opponents of the Manchester Ship Canal - on the grounds that its construction would render Trafford Hall uninhabitable - the family put the estate on the market in 1896. Amidst considerable controversy, it was purchased by the developer Ernest Hoole, who joined forces with Marshall Stevens, General Manager of the Manchester Ship Canal, to create Trafford Park, the world's first industrial estate. At its zenith, during the Second World War, Trafford Park employed over seventy thousand people. Trafford Park Village was developed to house the workforce. It was modelled on the American grid-iron pattern, with streets and avenues given numbers rather than names. A gas-powered tramway provided transport facilities for both passengers and freight. Kelloggs built a works beside the canal as part of an initially ill-timed drive to enter the European health food market. Merchant ships carrying up to 10,000 tons of American grain would come up the Ship Canal to Manchester Docks and tranship their cargoes into a fleet of Bridgewater barges for onward transport to the works. A custom which continued until 1974.

East of Waters Meeting, the canal skirts a busy rail/road transhipment depot. Logistics have come a long way since the days of those barges: via Felixstowe, Tilbury and Southampton, containerised freight from all over the world is unloaded here in the same time that it used to take to arrive from East Lancs. For all the activity on its doorstep, the canal exudes an air of loneliness: the sole preserve of runners, cyclists and guidebook compilers; the latter vying with each other to come up with lugubrious epithets.

Manchester United's Old Trafford stadium overlooks the canal, the nearest stand commemorating Sir Alex Ferguson, the club's revered manager between 1986 and 2013. Ironically, it's rivals Manchester City - the club who Sir Alex once famously referred to as 'noisy neighbours' - that have enjoyed the bragging rights in recent times, and we shall encounter their equally impressive stadium on Map 45. Barges, travelling down from collieries in the vicinity of Worsley, Leigh and Wigan, delivered coal to Trafford Park power station until 1972.

Another Old Trafford lies a boundary catch to the south, home, of course, of Lancashire County Cricket, and an historic venue for Test Matches. Perhaps less well known, however, was a third sporting venue called White City, where greyhound racing took place for over half a century before its closure in 1982. Athletics, speedway and stock car racing also thrived. Trafford Park motive power depot provided locomotives for services emanating from Manchester Central. It closed in 1968.

The Liverpool Warehousing Company's variously dated cotton warehouses overlook the canal and remind us of lost trade as it threads its way under numerous concrete road crossings. At Throstle Nest Bridge the towpath changes sides. Extending the Metrolink tram network to Salford Quays and Eccles has had a remarkable effect on this once heavily industrialised area of Manchester. The trams snake across the canal on a bridge, but we're all far too late to see this environment at its most interesting. Half close your eyes and imagine Pomona's once busy dockland: swinging cranes, shouting stevedores, tank engines shunting wagons along tracks set in cobbles: ropes being thrown, oaths sworn, hooters blown. In the Fifties Manchester was the third busiest British port after London and Liverpool, twenty million tons of cargo being handled annually, and the docks at Salford and Manchester were awash with shipping from all over the world.

Pomona Lock was installed in 1995 as a replacement for Hulme Locks (Map 44). Given sufficient boating confidence and insurance policies, arrangements can be made with the Bridgewater Canal Company (see page 157) to negotiate the lock and gain access to the Irwell. Convoys of lesiure craft occasionally use the lock for passages along the Manchester Ship Canal.

Manchester's burgeoning skyscrapers loom ahead. In London such premises are the preserve of offices, here they consist of apartments. Vying vertiginously, some aspire to seventy floors: 'playground bullies' in some eyes, 'elegant footprints' to others. Given their city's notoriously damp climate, will the occupants of these interlopers spend half their lives with their heads in the clouds?

Descending 'Heartbreak Hill' (Maps 16/31)

Preston Book Tunnel (Map 37)

Inbound on the MSC at Latchford (Map 39)

A Rare Damp Day in Manchester (Map 44)

Disley Swing-bridge (Map 47A)

Clarence Mill, Bollington (Map 49)

Bosley Locks (Map 51)

Saltersford Locks (Map 56)

Misty morning on the Weaver (Map 57)

44 ROCHDALE CANAL Manchester 2mls/9lks/3hrs

Eating & Drinking
1 Akbar's
2 Albert's Shed
3 Briton's Protection
4 Cask*
5 Dakota*
6 Dimitri's
7 Dom's
8 Dukes 92
9 Erst*
10 Kitten
11 Little Yang Sing
12 Maray
13 Pollen*
14 Port Street Beer House*
15 Peveril of the Peak
16 Rump 'N Ribs
17 Sapporo Teppanyaki
18 TNQ
19 The Wharf
* see enlargment page 118

Convenience Stores
1 Sainsbury's Local
2 Tesco Express
3 Morrisons Daily
4 Costcutter

this map to approximate scale: 3½ inches to a mile
for details of facilities in Manchester turn to pages 118 and 119

114

IF Manchester hasn't been quite so conspicuously successful repurposing its canal heritage as that cheeky upstart down the road, Birmingham, you can't say it hasn't tried. It is handicapped, of course, by the Rochdale Canal's clandestine, partly subterranean and - not to put a finer point on it - truculent passage through the city centre: a boorish lump of a canal featuring nine recalcitrant wide-beam locks which have never been particularly well-maintained; well not in living memory, anyway. True, Manchester's canals have been given 'a biodiversity and wellbeing boost' thanks to the Canal & River Trust and Whitehall's Green Recovery Fund, and volunteers have altruistically given their free time to brighten the canal corridor with vegetable gardens, linear orchards and wild-flower meadows. But it doesn't help that the Rochdale's towpath is inherently narrow and not ideal for languid promenades; nor that it has a reputation for the alcoholically worse for wear falling into it, and occasionally not emerging.

The Canals of Castlefield

Doyen of the Canal Age, the Bridgewater arrived at Castlefield in 1765: George III was on the throne and America was still a British colony. Forty years were to pass before the Rochdale Canal came to join the Bridgewater. Everyone knows that the latter was dug to carry the Duke of Bridgewater's coals from his mines at Worsley to the market place of Manchester, but the canal soon developed as a general carrier and numerous warehouses sprang into being at Castlefield for the storage of multifarious cargoes. Several remain intact. Dominating the junction, the Merchants Warehouse has been refurbished, as has the vast Middle Warehouse overlooking the arm leading to the River Medlock - known as Castlefield Quay now and offering the city's best visitor moorings to our way of thinking. At the end of this arm, at a point where the original canal tunnelled beneath the sandstone outcrop, stands the Grocers Warehouse. Dating from the 18th century, the building originally consisted of five floors with a central arch over the canal. Later a second arch was added. An ingenious system of sluices fed a water wheel which drove the warehouse's lifting machinery. Two floors topped by a viewing promenade have been reconstructed, whilst the former bays are fronted by a pair of not entirely appropriate metal lift bridges.

But it would be churlish to be pedantically critical of Castlefield. Some observers have cited the Merchants Footbridge of 1995 (which spans the junction) as being out of keeping with the largely 19th century environment surrounding it, but we feel it compliments the adjoining railway structures without ingratiatingly replicating them. It is wider at its centre to provide space for pedestrians to pause to take in the view, and was inspired by Santiago Calatrava's La Devesa Footbridge at Ripoll in Spain. The adjoining railway viaducts are of enormous aesthetic appeal as well. See how the original masonry arches have been parodied in cast iron. One set of tracks carries conventional trains, another, at a higher level, forms the Metrolink tramway approach to the former Central Station, reborn as a convention complex. A third viaduct dates from 1892. It was the work of the engineering firm of Heenan & Froude, structural engineers for the Blackpool Tower. Disused since the 1960s, it has recently been repurposed as an urban park in the vein of New York's High Line. A series of arms extend beneath these railway arches towards Liverpool Road. This area was known as Potato Wharf, a name reflecting the use of these arms as an unloading point for market garden produce brought in by boat from the farmlands of Cheshire.

The Rochdale Nine

Hard work, by any standards, the Rochdale Nine (locks 92-84) vouchsafe canal explorers an off-beat, quirky and stimulating perspective of the city, an adventurous insight denied mere tourists. The bottom chamber is known as Duke's Lock because it was actually built by the Bridgewater company. Later it was renumbered in the Rochdale sequence. The 92nd lock on the canal's epic Trans-Pennine journey from Sowerby Bridge. Looming imperiously over all this is Beetham Tower: its former status as Manchester's tallest building (554ft) has, however, been usurped during the currency of this edition by Deansgate Square South Tower (659ft).

The Bridgewater Canal at Cornbrook

Passing beneath yet another highly decorative railway bridge, the Rochdale Canal negotiates a short tunnel under Deansgate before encountering, between locks 91 and 90, a split level boardwalk development of clubs and bars which occupies former railway arches. By Bridge 99 the Hacienda Apartments derive their name from the famous night club which stood on the site between 1984 and 1997. Heart of the 'Madchester' scene of that heady 'acid house' and 'rave' era, the club was closely associated with the band New Order, though it's worth noting that The Smiths played the club on several occasions and that Madonna's first UK appearance took place here.

Lock 89 marks the former junction with the Manchester & Salford Junction Canal, a section of which was rewatered to connect with the Bridgewater Hall, home of the celebrated Halle Orchestra. It seems to us that an opportunity was lost to provide city centre visitor moorings at the end of this arm where it opens out into a small basin beside the Bridgewater Hall. But the basin has been cosmetically enhanced by a half-hearted fountain. As it passed beneath Deansgate, the M&SJC connected with the basement of the Great Northern Railway goods warehouse, now a retail and entertainment complex.

Manchester's very own Oxford Street spans the canal at Bridge 98, the view here being dominated by the terracotta tower of Sir Alfred Waterhouse's Refuge Assurance building, now the Kimpton Hotel. Bloom Street Power Station overlooks the pound between locks 88 and 87. It was built in 1902 to provide power for the city's tramways, but surplus steam was harnessed to provide heating for shops and offices in the vicinity, and even to raise the curtain at the Palace Theatre.

Abandon the towpath for a moment and sneak down the cobbled confines of Atwood Street, to be confronted by the astonishing Edwardian baroque of India House. Built in 1906 as a packing and shipping warehouse, it featured in Adolphe Valette's painting of the same name. Moreover, having been converted into flats, it was here, in the early 1990s, that Noel Gallagher of Oasis wrote much of the band's debut album *Definitely Maybe*.

Purring over Princess Street (Bridge 97), double-decker buses create a kaleidoscope of colour, enlivening the muted tones of massive textile warehouses refurbished as flats, hotels and restaurants. Canal Street (along which towpath users must divert between bridges 97 and 94) lies at the heart of Manchester's Gay Village, venue of the annual Manchester Pride festival. Pavement cafes provoke an incongruous juxtaposition with a canal environment which was once the sole preserve of burly bargees who would scarcely believe their eyes at the scenes enacted here now. By Bridge 96, a Beacon of Hope sculpture is dedicated to all affected by HIV and AIDS. In neighbouring Sackville Gardens the sculptured figure of a man on a park bench holding an apple in his palm commemorates Alan Turing, codebreaker at Bletchley Park during World War Two, and father of computer science at Manchester University in the early Fifties. Turing ate an apple laced with cyanide in 1954 because his sexuality had been exposed and he had become a victim of prejudice. It seems entirely apt, then, that prejudice has given way to pride.

Manchester's Crown Court overlooks the canal between Minshull and Aytoun streets. It dates from the 1870s and was designed in Venetian Gothic by Thomas Worthington who also did the Albert Memorial by the Town Hall. Over Bridge 93A many a doomed prisoner must have trudged to their fate. The city's German-built trams purr their way over Bridge 93, lending a continental aspect to the passing scene, before the canal briefly becomes subterranean. Lock 85 used to do a passable impression of what the Styx would have looked like if Brindley had ever been called in to make it navigable. It has, however, been illuminated in recent times. More, admittedly, as a deterrent to the 'rough trade' which this subfusc zone attracts, than to make life easier for boaters whose needs are invariably of secondary consideration. Oh, and don't worry if you do encounter shadowy loiterers, their minds will be on other matters.

Emerging Orpheus-like from the underworld into the dank chamber of Dale Street Lock (No.84), boat crews may feel entitled to a round of fist-bumps and high-fives. Celebrations, however, will have to be curtailed if continuing eastwards, where more locks lie, devilishly in wait!

Lock 90 on the Rochdale Canal

The Canals of Piccadilly

Once upon a time Piccadilly Basin (formerly Dale Street) boasted numerous wharves and warehouses. Now, in place of tethered barges, there are parked cars, and the past enjoys a joke at our expense. The basin adjoins the junction of the Ashton and Rochdale canals, a stone's throw from Piccadilly railway station on the south-eastern edge of the city centre. In amongst the apartment blocks and hotels there are a few tangible remains of the Rochdale Canal's proud heritage: a crenellated entry arch off Dale Street itself; the canal company's offices; and a substantial millstone grit-built warehouse converted into offices. Its date-stone (1806) bears the initials 'WC', which at a guess relate to William Crosley, John Rennie's assistant. Round the side it plaintively reveals its water arches. On neighbouring Ducie Street the Native Manchester apartment hotel occupies a corresponding warehouse of the railway era. Piccadilly Basin offers visitor moorings at the east end of the city centre, though not perhaps as generally salubrious as those to be found at the Castlefield end of the Rochdale Canal. Here, however, one is at least handy for the 'Northern Quarter', a regenerated cornucopia of independent outlets and eating places.

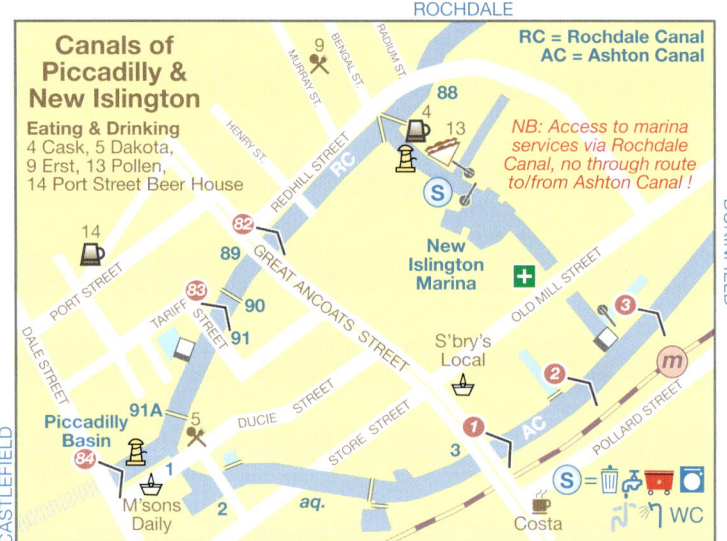

Manchester — Map 44

Still smarting from having its leg of the High Speed Railway amputated; still puzzled as to what part of the Levelling-Up Process that act of Whitehall parsimony comprised; Manchester appeared to be going about in a 'business as usual' mien on the occasion of our most recent research. Though 'business' is perhaps a misnomer nowadays. The city seems busier after dusk, as if pleasure and hospitality are its real money-spinners now. The sadness, from a canaller's perspective, is that Manchester's act of embrace with its waterways appears unrequited. Unlike Birmingham, canalside redevelopments here appear less well integrated; more a matter of passive reflection than passionate response. Forty years have passed since a wand was waved over Castlefield's hitherto dissolute canals, but boat movements remain at such a relatively low level that it can feel like a gig few fans have bothered to attend.

Architecturally, however, Manchester remains one of the most handsome cities in the post-industrial world, and we would urge you to moor and explore; nothing's very far away, the city centre being astonishingly compact and approachable. 'Musts' include the three squares: Albert, with Waterhouse's imposing Town Hall; St Ann's, an oasis of relative peace in the city centre; and St Peter's, dominated by the circular Central Library and flamboyant terracotta of the Midland Hotel, meeting place (4th May, 1904) of a certain Mr Rolls with a certain Mr Royce. More esoterically, try venturing into the rag trade zone east of Piccadilly and thence to High Street where the skeleton of the old Wholesale Fish Market features entertaining friezes illustrating fishing, landing and selling scenes. Manchester boasts thousands of buildings like this, evoking its plutocratic zenith. Thence wander down to the banks of the Irwell where, in the shadow of the modest cathedral lies Chetham's Music School, Victoria Station and the stolidly confident Co-operative buildings. These are the parts of the city reassuringly Northern in character. The smoke palls may have been blown away by the winds of change, but there are moments when it is still possible to feel that you've walked on to a canvas by Adolphe Valette or his better known pupil, a certain L. S. Lowry.

Eating & Drinking

AKBAR'S - Liverpool Road. Tel: 0161 834 7222. Indian restaurant opposite S&I Museum. M3 4NQ
ALBERT'S SHED - Castlefield. Tel: 0161 839 9818. Classy restaurant housed in old Bridgewater Canal Co. warehouse. Open from noon weekdays, 10.30am weekends. Access Lock 92/Bridge 101. M3 4LZ
BRITON'S PROTECTION - Great Bridgewater Street. Tel: 0161 236 5895. Listed in the CAMRA National Inventory of Historic Pub Interiors. M1 5LE
CASK - Liverpool Road. Tel: 0161 832 2633. Bar for beer lovers. No food, but you can bring your own. *Also at New Islington Marina.* M3 4NQ/M4 6SQ
DAKOTA - Ducie Street. Tel: 0161 674 9180. Stylish grill and bar in canalside hotel. M1 2JL
DIMITRI'S - Campfield Arcade, Castlefield. Tel: 0161 839 3319. Greek tapas bar and taverna. M3 4FN
DOM'S - Deansgate. Tel: 0161 834 2649. Italian restaurant open from noon daily. M3 4LY
DUKES 92 - Castlefield Junction. Tel: 0161 839 8642. Canalside bar and restaurant. Open daily from 11.30am, food served from noon throughout. Meat, fish & cheese sharing boards, sandwiches, small plates, grills, pizza etc. Access Lock 92/Bridge 101. M3 4LZ
ERST - Murray St. Tel: 0161 547 3683. Michelin listed small plates restaurant: from 1pm Tue-Sat. M4 6HS
KITTEN - Owen Street. Tel: 0161 392 7913. Japanese izakaya and bar. Open daily from 5pm. M15 4TW
LITTLE YANG SING - George Street. Tel: 0161 228 7722. Renowned restaurant in 'Chinatown'. Open from 12.30pm daily. M1 4HE
MARAY - Brazennose Street. Tel: 0151 347 0214. Middle Eastern cuisine. HQ in Liverpool; hence the telephone number. Open from noon daily. M2 6LW
PEVERIL OF THE PEAK - Great Bridgewater Street. Tel: 0161 236 6364. *Good Beer Guide* listed green-tiled pub named after a stagecoach. M1 5JQ
POLLEN - cafe/bakery specialising in sourdough and viennoiserie. Branches at Cotton Field Wharf, New Islington M4 6FQ and Aytoun Street M1 3GL.
PORT STREET BEER HOUSE - Port Street. Tel: 0161 237 9949. *GBG* listed pub in the Northern Quarter for beer enthusiasts. Open from noon daily. M1 2EQ
RUMP 'N RIBS - Liverpool Road. Tel: 0161 228 2284. Steak house opposite S&I Museum. M3 4AQ
SAPPORO TEPPANYAKI - Liverpool Rd. Tel: 0161 831 9888. Japanese restaurant opp. S&IM. M3 4JN
TNQ - High Street. Tel: 0161 832 7115. Acronym for 'The Northern Quarter', this vibrant restaurant definitely has Lock-wheeler's seal of approval. Open noon-10pm daily (7pm Sun). M4 1HQ
THE WHARF - Slate Wharf, Castlefield. Tel: 0161 507 4240. Brunning & Price new-build pub in warehouse vernacular handily placed for Castlefield visitor moorings. Open daily from noon, food throughout. B&P never fail to impress on our canal travels, and this couldn't be closer to the best moorings. M15 4ST

Shopping

The principal shopping area lies to the north of the Rochdale Canal. If you're just passing through, there are convenience stores at various strategic points, as shown on the map.

Things to Do

VISITOR INFORMATION CENTRE - Central Library, St Peter's Square. M2 5PD
CASTLEFIELD VIADUCT - Castlefield. Taking its cue from New York's celebrated High Line, this former Cheshire Lines Committee viaduct is progressively being re-purposed as an elevated urban park under the auspices of the National Trust. M3 4LG
CITY ART GALLERY - Mosley Street. Tel: 0161 235 8888. Access is free (though donations welcome) to this inspiring gallery, particularly strong on British painting. Shop and cafe. 10am-5pm Tue-Sun. M21 3JL
HOME - Tony Wilson Place (off Whitworth Street West). Tel: 0161 200 1500. Film, theatre and visual arts centre. Cafe bar and bookshop. M15 4FN
PEOPLE'S HISTORY MUSEUM - Spinningfields. Tel: 0161 838 9190. A look at the lives of ordinary people in Britain over the last two hundred years. Much Trade Union material. M3 3ER
SCIENCE & INDUSTRY MUSEUM - Liverpool Road. Open daily 10am to 5pm. Tel: 0330 058 0058. A first rate celebration of Manchester's industrial prowess and scientific endeavour. Includes the first purpose-built passenger railway station in the world, opened in 1830 for the Liverpool & Manchester Railway. It's disappointing, however, that they have never spilled out across Liverpool Road to display some appropriately Mancunian canal craft. Free admission (donations welcome). Nice Warehouse cafe 8am (9.30am weekends)-5pm Shop. M3 4FP
SIGHTSEEING MANCHESTER - 90 mins open top bus tours taking in city centre and Salford Quays. Start from Princess Street adjacent the Art Gallery.
NATIONAL FOOTBALL MUSEUM - Urbis Building, Cathedral Gardens. Tel: 0161 605 8200. M4 3BG

Salford Quays   Map 43

Boosted by MediaCity, Salford Quays are a 21st century manifestation of Salford Docks: commerce, leisure and retail where there used to be ships and dockers.

IMPERIAL WAR MUSEUM NORTH - Trafford Wharf Road. Tel: 0161 836 4000. 'Powerful stories of over a century of war'. Daily 10am-5pm. M17 1TZ
THE LOWRY - Salford Quays. Tel: 0343 208 6000. Multi-art venue. What would the curmudgeonly old bachelor of Mottram have made of it? M50 3AZ
ORDSALL HALL - Ordsall Lane. Tel: 0161 872 0251. Remarkable Grade I listed Tudor hall. Admission free. Closed Fri & Sat. Small shop and cafe. M5 3AN

45 ASHTON CANAL Ancoats, Clayton & Fairfield 4mls/18lks/4hrs

Largely de-industrialised and drained of its former atmosphere, the once macho Ashton Canal cuts an emasculated figure these days, and it's the beligerent Canada Geese you have to be wary of as opposed to hooligans now. Which is not to say the Ashton does not repay exploration. Canal travellers - especially those armed with Pearsons - are adept at prising the maximum pleasure from the minimum circumstance and can approach this much maligned canal with their eyes wide open: not expecting to be attacked by feral gangs, but neither under the misapprehension that the perverse rewards of an assault course no longer await them.

Connection with the Rochdale Canal at Ducie Street was made in 1800, and it is from these same (if much altered in ambience) environs that those exploring the Ashton depart (or, of course, arrive) today, dog-legging (Map 44) through bridges 1 and 2; the latter carrying vertiginously cobbled Jutland Street which L. S. Lowry sketched in 1929 when it was known as Junction Street. Paradise Wharf precedes Store Street Aqueduct (another subject matter of Lowry's) dating from 1798 and quite possibly the first such structure to be built at a 'skew' angle. Originally it spanned a watercourse known as Shooters Brook, but as the area developed industrially the brook was culverted and a road built over it. Piccadilly Village is a rather tepid and inscrutable approach to canalside redevelopment, token cranes and 'cast-iron' footbridges hardly constituting vernacular veracity. Architecturally more imaginative is Will Alsop's 'Chips' apartment block erected by Urban Splash alongside the short pound between locks 2 and 3 in 2009, though when we last passed it was heavily scaffolded, after it had emerged that the cladding was non fire retardant.

The Ashton Canal's notoriously arduous eighteen locks - for the most part fitted with hydraulic paddle gear and time-consuming anti-vandal locks - comprise the following flights: Ancoats (3); Ashton (formerly Beswick) (4); Clayton (9) and Fairfield (2). On aggregate they raise the canal by a hundred and sixty-six and a half feet, and, oddly enough, boaters find their spirits correspondingly rising the nearer they get to the top.

Fragments of the Ancoats so vividly described by Howard Spring in *Fame is the Spur* continue to manifest themselves; here a mill, there a backstreet replete with corner 'chippy'. You can try and take the chip shop out of Manchester but you

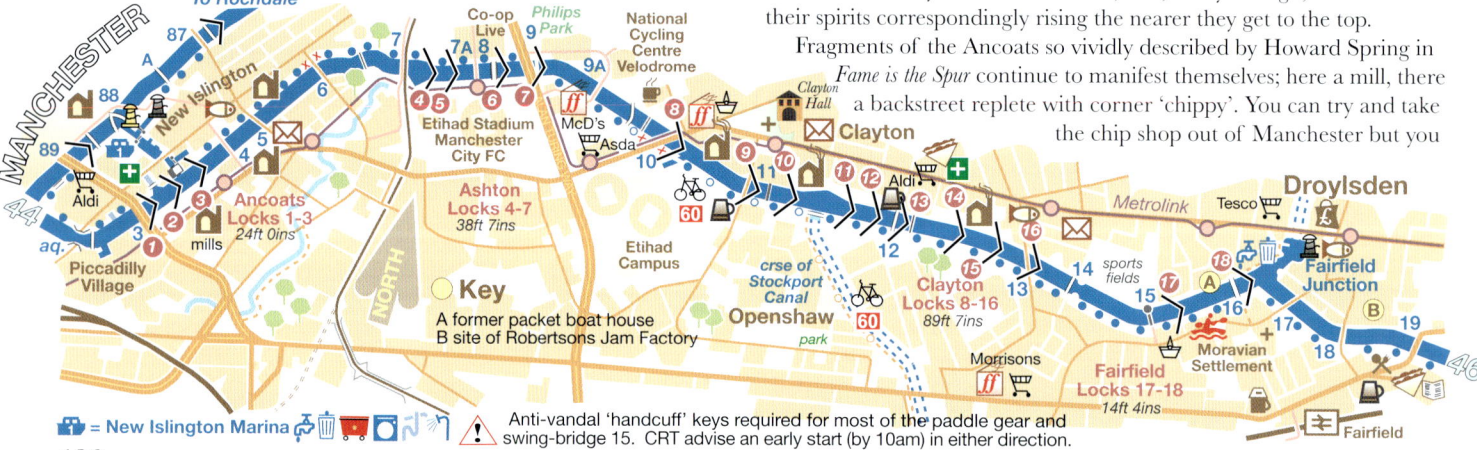

can't take Mancunians out of their chip shops. Thus they still emerge from their smart apartment eyries, hair in curlers, to queue for a fish supper.

Overlooked by a gas-holder, the canal crosses the River Medlock, passes beneath the former Lancashire & Yorkshire Railway's connecting line between Ardwick and Miles Platting, and threads its way through 'Sportcity'. 19th century boatmen would be astonished by such scene changes. Where now cluster Co-op Live, Manchester City FC's Etihad Stadium, and the National Cycling Centre's Velodrome, previously stood textile mills, coal mines, gas works and an electricity generating station. Philips Park dates from 1846 and can lay claim to being one of the first municipal parks in the world. It was named after the local member of parliament who campaigned for green open spaces for working people. The River Medlock runs through it, and there is an extensive cemetery to the north. Alan Turing Way (Bridge 9) is named after the codebreaker and computer genius, previously encountered in Sackville Gardens on Map 44.

A sprinkling of canalside chemical works reaffirms that at least some industrial activity remains in Greater Manchester. Between locks 10 and 11, 'Stockport Junction' marked the egress point of a five mile branch which never actually reached the centre of Stockport, petering out instead by the flour-caked, redbrick mills of South Reddish. Trade had petered out too by the 1930s though it wasn't officially abandoned until 1961. Infilled long ago, its course now forms part of National Cycle Route 60 and can be followed down through Openshaw (name-checked in Flanders & Swann's *Slow Train*) and beyond across an aqueduct (sans water, of course) still straddling the old Great Central Railway's main line at Gorton.

Unreconstructed Ancoats

Fairfield Locks (17 & 18) were duplicated in the heyday of the canal. The short pound between them is spanned by a stone footbridge (known locally as the camel's hump) with a strong family resemblance to the roving bridge at Portland Basin (Map 46). Also of interest is a boat-house which housed a packet boat prior to the coming of the railways. Near at hand is Fairfield Moravian Settlement, a secluded and strangely unworldly estate of Georgian town housing built about cobbled avenues lit by cast-iron lamps. The Moravians are a Protestant sect founded in Europe during the 15th century.

From Fairfield Junction a branch canal was built to Hollinwood on the outskirts of Oldham where its terminus lay less than a mile from the Rochdale Canal to which a link was mooted but never dug. Whilst collieries provided the branch with the bulk of its trade, a recreational element flourished at 'Crime Lake', a Tixall-like widening which attracted boathouses, tea rooms and fairground booths to its banks. The winter of 1854 was so bad that the lake froze over for three months and stalls were erected on the ice to cater for skaters. A property development has seen the first few hundred yards of the Hollinwood Branch rewatered and provided with a mooring basin.

Robertson's marmalade and jam factory was located by Bridge 18. Sadly it closed in 2006 and the twenty acre site has been redeveloped as housing. We miss the fruity aromas which once emanated from the works, and though the company's golliwog logo proved an embarrassment in later years, we will always have a soft spot for Roberton's; after all the company's founder was a 'Paisley Buddy', just like Lock-wheeler.

46 ASHTON & PEAK FOREST CANALS Portland Basin 5½ mls/0lks/2hrs

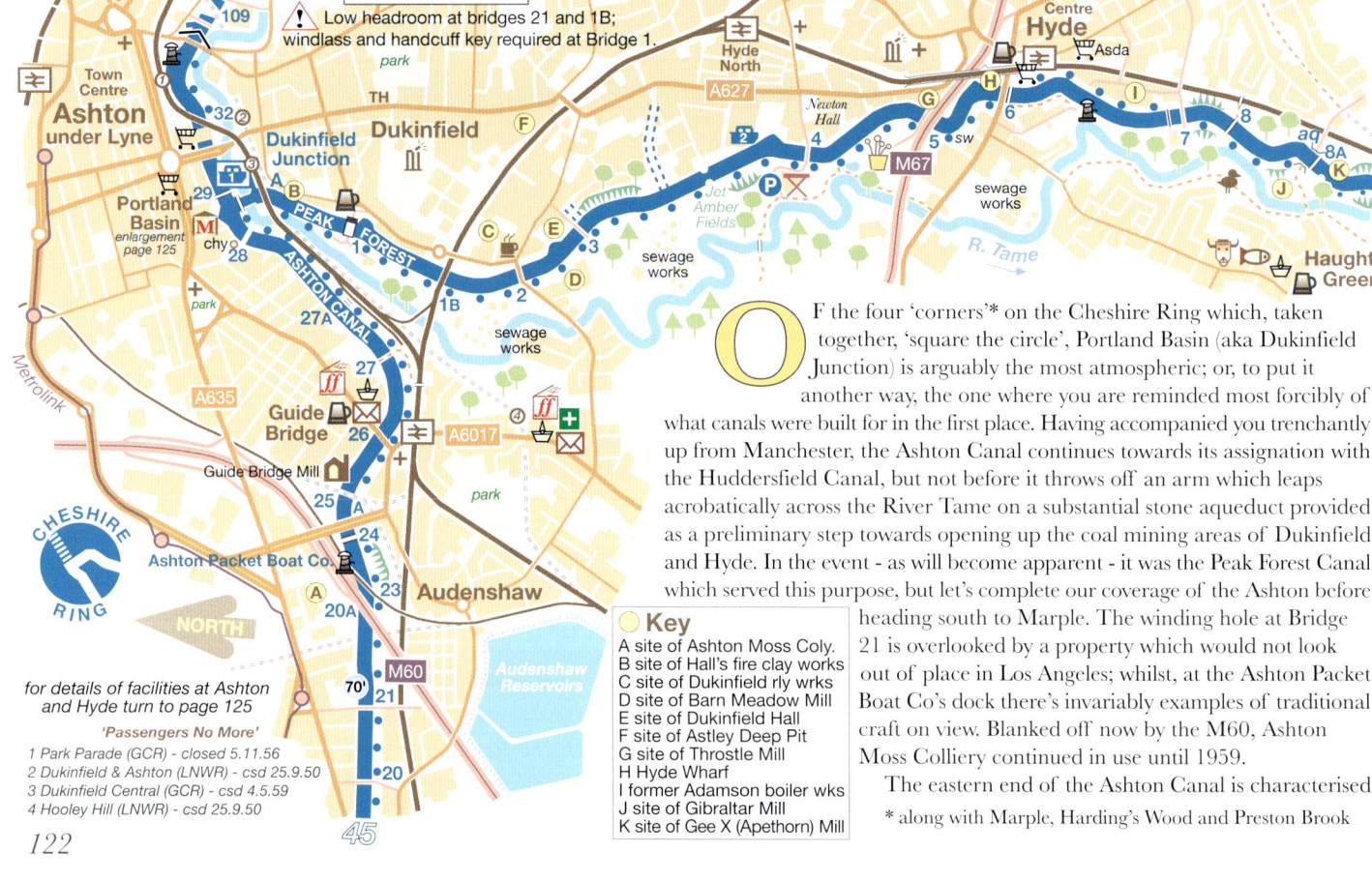

Of the four 'corners'* on the Cheshire Ring which, taken together, 'square the circle', Portland Basin (aka Dukinfield Junction) is arguably the most atmospheric; or, to put it another way, the one where you are reminded most forcibly of what canals were built for in the first place. Having accompanied you trenchantly up from Manchester, the Ashton Canal continues towards its assignation with the Huddersfield Canal, but not before it throws off an arm which leaps acrobatically across the River Tame on a substantial stone aqueduct provided as a preliminary step towards opening up the coal mining areas of Dukinfield and Hyde. In the event - as will become apparent - it was the Peak Forest Canal which served this purpose, but let's complete our coverage of the Ashton before heading south to Marple. The winding hole at Bridge 21 is overlooked by a property which would not look out of place in Los Angeles; whilst, at the Ashton Packet Boat Co's dock there's invariably examples of traditional craft on view. Blanked off now by the M60, Ashton Moss Colliery continued in use until 1959.

The eastern end of the Ashton Canal is characterised

* along with Marple, Harding's Wood and Preston Brook

by knotted railways and textile mills both past and present. Railways were attracted to Guide Bridge like iron filings, notably the illustrious Great Central, whose renowned route between Manchester and Sheffield through Woodhead Tunnel passed this way. Had Sir Edward Watkin, its ambitious chairman, had *his* way, this would have formed a through route to Paris, a century before the Channel Tunnel was built. In the early 1950s it became the first main line in the country to be electrified. But to many people's lasting regret, this pioneering route was closed to passengers in 1970, and to freight just over a decade later. When we were researching the first edition of this guide back in 1981, disconsolate rows of electric locomotives were lined up in the sidings at Guide Bridge awaiting the breaker's torch. Much rationalised now, Guide Bridge's current claim to railway fame is that it is a stopping point for the Saturdays only Stockport to Stalybridge service, retained to save the railway operators from going through the tedious and contentious procedure of applying legally to close the line.

Bridge 27A carries the Ashton Canal's towpath over what was once a short arm called Princess Dock, from which a packet-boat operated. Bridge 28 is overlooked by the 210ft high Junction Mills chimney of 1867. Octagonal, and unusual for its 'tulip' shaped crown, the chimney was purchased for a pound by Tameside Council to prevent its demolition along with the mill it served, and now provides an appropriately plangent landmark for Portland Basin.

The canalscape at Portland Basin is immensely appealing. Everywhere

Bridge 28 and Junction Mills Chimney

you look something catches the eye. Pride of place goes to an extensive, three-storey warehouse originally built by the Ashton Canal Co. in 1834, destroyed by fire in 1972, but rebuilt to house a museum devoted to Tameside's rich industrial and social history. Directly opposite lies the aforementioned arm, handsomely spanned by a slender, stone-built roving bridge dated 1835. And then, once across the stone aqueduct which spans the Tame, you are officially on the Peak Forest Canal, and anticipating a whole new and exciting chapter of canal exploration.

Peak Forest Canal

Astonishing, to recall, that fifty years ago all three canals converging on Ashton-under-Lyne were officially abandoned. It took a crusade by enthusiasts to both lobby authority to revive these waterways, and to provide the muscle at the mucky end of their proposals. The Ashton and Peak Forest canals were reopened in 1974 (the Huddersfield had to wait another twenty-seven years) but only after tens of thousands of voluntary man and woman hours had been spent removing vast tonnages of often quite revolting rubbish from the beds of both canals.

Fourteen and a bit miles long, and with sixteen locks concentrated into one flight, the Peak Forest Canal was constructed between 1794 and 1803, the final five, drawn out years concerning the locks at Marple being delayed by financial constraints. Its most important and profitable traffic flow was in limestone from Derbyshire quarries, but coal and cotton were also significant cargoes.

For its first four miles the Peak Forest finds itself journeying along a shoulder above the River Tame which once formed the boundary between Lancashire and Cheshire. This Tame - not to be confused with the one which travellers on the Coventry Canal encounter - rises on the moors above Saddleworth and merges with the Goyt to form the Mersey at Stockport. Initially it feels as if the canal will have its work cut out to extricate itself from the canker of urbanisation, but canals - as you well know - have a facility for shedding their skin, and this one soon gets merrily into its stride, offering hints, here and there, of past glories.

Bridge 1 is a lift bridge (requiring an anti-vandal key and a windlass to operate) which carries a track down over the canal to Plantation Farm. A nearby plaque recalls that Mary Moffat was born on the farm in 1795, that she became an African missionary, and that she was an inspiration to her son-in-law, David Livingstone. Yes, the 'Doctor Livingstone' famously encountered on the shores of Lake Tanganyika in 1871 by the explorer, Henry M. Stanley.

With sewage farms on one side, and anonymous industrial units on the other, the canal proceeds southwards towards Hyde. James Lees-Milne recounts, in *Prophesying Peace*, how he inspected Dukinfield (Old) Hall in 1944 on behalf of the National Trust, finding it located 'in dreary surroundings, on one side an ungainly factory, and on the other a canal, filled with detritus.' In the event it wasn't taken under the trust's wing, being demolished circa 1950, though the ruins of the hall's chapel miraculously remain. The Duckenfield (sic) family's most famous son was Lieutenant Colonel Robert Duckenfield who was appointed Commander of Cromwell's army in the north-west in 1648. There is a memorial to him in St Lawrence's church, Denton, a couple of miles to the west.

By Bridge 3 stood a basin serving coal mines at Dewsnap and Astley, linked to the canal by tramway. Astley Deep Mine lived up to its name and was notorious for its safety record. In 1874 fifty four men and boys lost their lives in a huge explosion. The mine finally closed in 1901, though a slag heap remained until being flattened in the 1970s.

Five minutes on foot from Bridge 4 stands Newton Hall, a reconstructed half-timbered house which dates back to the 14th century. It was rebuilt at the behest of Sir George Kenyon, a pillar of local life and chairman of a firm manufacturing, amongst many other items, rope. Sir Edmund Hillary visited the company's erstwhile works near Bridge 4 in 1953, presumably to vouch for himself the integrity of the ropes which were going to help him and Sherpa Tenzing conquer Everest. In the opposite direction lies a public open space called Jet Amber Fields, apparently on account of a local coal seam.

The canal had to be realigned to accommodate the M67 motorway in the mid 1970s. Thankfully Hyde Wharf with its loading shed and handsome warehouse was spared. The towpath changes sides between bridges 6 and 7 to preserve the privacy of one of the promoters of the canal who dwelt at Hyde Hall, demolished, alas, in the 19th century. This length is overlooked by the remains of Adamson's engineering works, manufacturers of many a textile mill boiler. Daniel Adamson was a keen promoter of the Manchester Ship Canal and a preserved steam-powered tug named after him offers trips on the Weaver Navigation - see photograph on page 147.

Like a pair of worn out bloomers, the bottom fell out of the cotton industry as man-made fibres became more fashionable and less expensive to produce. So the mills were made redundant. Laid up like obsolete oil tankers on a Cornish tidal creek. The maritime analogy is apt. Like ships the mills bore proud names. They lay, chimneys belching smoke, in the folds of the landscape like ocean going vessels in a swell. Two vanished examples of the breed lay adjacent to Apethorn Aqueduct by Bridge 8A. Gibraltar Mill on the towpath side and Gee X (or Apethorn) Mill on the offside. There is access here to Lower Haughton Meadows Local Nature Reserve, a bosky area of ancient woodland west of the canal.

The neighbouring suburb of Hyde was known as Gee Cross. Workers at the mills arrived and departed aboard the dainty green & cream trams of the Stalybridge, Hyde, Mossley & Dukinfield Co. until 1945. Between 1950 and 1963 Gee Cross was the terminus of Manchester trolleybus service 210, the best part of nine, 'swift and silent' miles from Piccadilly.

Ashton-under-Lyne   Map 46

It's perhaps not widely remembered that Ashton-under-Lyne was name-checked in Flanders & Swann's *The Gnu Song* of 1960. But since when did anything appear in the Canal Companions that was widely remembered anyway? Once of Lancashire, now the foremost town of Greater Manchester's Metropolitan Borough of Tameside, Ashton's economy was built on textiles and coal-mining. Nowadays it revolves around retail and local government. The Town Hall exudes Corinthian-columned dignity. The parish church of St Michael was taken in hand by the Victorians but retains some notable 15th century stained glass devoted to St Helena. And last, but not least, this was the birthplace, in 1892, of the prolific travel writer, Henry Canova Vollam Morton.

Eating & Drinking
BRIDGE VIEW CAFE - Portland Basin Museum. Tel: 0161 343 6785. Open 11am-3pm weekdays, 10.30am-3pm weekends. OL7 0QA

Shopping
The Market Hall is vast, and it is quite possible to lose your womenfolk in it for hours on end while you attend to more manly matters ... like a meat pie from S. Williams & Sons. The Ladysmith shopping centre houses a cornucopia of well-known retailers, and is so-named, we imagine, because it's a 'relief' to leave it. An Asda supermarket spans the canal to the east of Portland Basin, whilst a branch of Lidl looms nearby, but you'd be mad to miss the market.

Things to Do
PORTLAND BASIN INDUSTRIAL MUSEUM - Portland Place. Tel: 0161 343 2878. Open Tue-Sun 10am-4pm, admission free. Provides a hugely enjoyable insight into the area's industrial and social past. It is housed in a canalside warehouse built by the Ashton

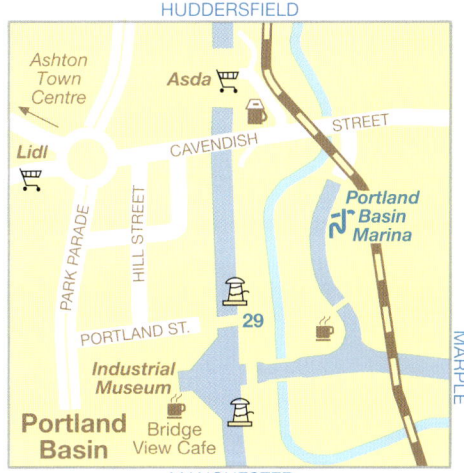

Canal Company in 1834. Highlights include a 1920s recreated street scene evoking the sights and sounds of bygone Ashton-under-Lyne. OL7 0QA

Connections
TRAINS - Northern services to/from Manchester Victoria, Stalybridge and Huddersfield.
TRAMS - Metrolink. Tel: 0161 205 2000.
TAXIS - Radio Cars. Tel: 0161 330 2090.

Dukinfield   Map 46

Another victim of the crass boundary changes of 1974. The red brick, clock-towered Town Hall mulls over the town's lost status like someone reflecting on the unfair set-backs of their past. Lees-Milne considered it 'hideous', and whilst normally only too happy to concur with his penetrative opinion, on this occasion we beg to differ. Go and see for yourself: these 'forgotten' towns invariably repay exploration.

Hyde   Map 46

'One of the Cheshire cotton towns close to the Lancashire border' was Pevsner's opening gambit. Naturally, neither claim remains true; poor, subsumed Hyde being undeservedly remembered for its associations with the mass murderers Shipman, Brady and Hindley. Nevertheless, Hyde is the sort of town one has a duty of care to visit, if only to see how these once proud boroughs, disembowelled by distant government edicts, have been left to cope on their own, underfunded resources. Redemption comes with minor, joyful details such as the Let's Talk Tripe shop in the Market Hall. Hyde market was the subject of local artist Harry Rutherford's evocative painting *Northern Saturday*. A mural by the artist, which visitors are welcome to view, adorns the foyer of the substantial Town Hall. The dance-hall scene in *Yanks*, a 1979 film starring Richard Gere, Lisa Eichorn and Vanessa Redgrave, was filmed here. The screenplay was by Colin Welland, famous for announcing 'The British are coming!' on accepting an Oscar for the screenplay of *Chariots of Fire* in 1982, a cheeky allusion to Paul Revere's Midnight Ride.

Eating & Drinking
PAGLIACCI - Market Street. Tel: 0161 351 1457. Homely Italian. Open from 5pm Tue-Fri and from 2pm weekends.
Fish & chips from Bosuns on Clarendon Street.

Shopping
Aldi and Asda within easy reach of Bridge 6. Open market and market hall daily (ex Sun)

Connections
TRAINS - Northern run an hourly service (Mon-Sat - no Sunday trains) to/from Manchester and Rose Hill Marple, providing useful towpather links with Woodley, Romiley and Guide Bridge.

125

47 PEAK FOREST CANAL Marple 5mls/16lks/4hrs

FROM its post-industrial origins in the vicinity of Ashton-under-Lyne, the Peak Forest Canal gradually transmogrifies into one of the loveliest in the country, and by the time it skirts Romiley the reinvention is well under way. Two tunnels heighten the sense of expectation and adventure. Woodley Tunnel is prefaced (from the north) by an imposing stone-built, skew-arched, ivy-clad and pigeon-haunted railway bridge erected by the grandiloquently titled Cheshire Lines Committee, whose tracks Cheshire Ring travellers encounter on a number of occasions. Watch out for the containerised rubbish trains which rumble lugubriously across this bridge, conveying Manchester's refuse to a big hole on the outskirts of Scunthorpe.

Bridge 13A carries another railway line; though in fact it once carried two, the useful link with Stockport Tiviot Dale having succumbed to Marples & Beeching in 1967. More like a short tunnel, the structure's echoing properties are well worth indulging in. Bridge 14 provides access to Romiley. The Boat House Inn once abutted the north-west corner of the bridge, an important stop on a fly-boat passenger service which linked Dukinfield with Marple in the pre-railway era. South of Bridge 14 the canal widens at the site of Hatherlow Wharf where there were limekilns, whilst, on the towpath side, stood a hat works, one of many in the Stockport area.

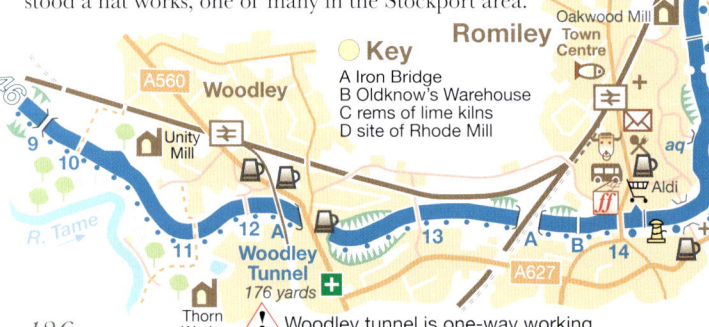

A pair of charmingly named aqueducts - Hatherlow and Burymewick respectively - carry the canal at rooftop level around the heavily suburbanised fringe of Romiley. The latter offers access to Chadkirk Chapel - see page 129. Oakwood Mill dates from the middle of the 19th century. Originally employed in cotton spinning, during the First World War it made margarine. Nowadays, known as Romiley Board Mill, it produces cardboard products from recycled materials. Hyde Bank Tunnel is just about wide enough for boats to squeeze past each other inside, though boaters of a nervous disposition may prefer to wait. The towpath, meanwhile, goes entertainingly over the top, itself bridged by the carriageway to Oakwood Hall. Ormerod Heyworth, builder of Oakwood Mill in

for details of facilities at Romiley and Marple turn to page 129 the 1830s, erected this baronial pile on the opposite bank of the canal and lived there in considerable style. The House was designed by Edward Walters, architect of Manchester's Free Trade Hall. A later occupant was Ephraim Hallam. What melodramatic names these Victorian gentlemen were christened with. But like many an overblown property, time was unkind to the hall, and after a period as a Jesuit seminary, it became a remand home for wayward girls. Now it has been broken up into apartments.

Achingly beautiful, the canal glides through woodland, buttressed above the Goyt between Hyde Bank Tunnel's eastern portal and Marple Aqueduct. The supports date from a major earth slip in 1833. Bridge 15 heralds a narrow, retaining-walled section which was originally another tunnel.

Referring obliquely and somewhat misleadingly to it in his classic Victorian travel book *Wild Wales*, George Borrow rather memorably termed Marple Aqueduct a 'stupendous erection'. Completed in 1800, it bears the canal a hundred feet above a steeply wooded ravine carved by the impatient River Goyt*. Alongside, in juxtapositions reminiscent of Chirk on the Llangollen Canal, and Slateford on Scotland's Union Canal, stands an even loftier railway viaduct. From the aqueduct's western end, a stepped path - on which you may have to come to terms with vertigo - leads precipitously down to offer a worm's eye view of the structure, this time allowing appreciation of its unusual cylindrical hollowed sections, so built to lessen the weight of masonry resting on support piers. Boatmen, it's said, were in the habit of burying their horses at the foot of the aqueduct. Over two hundred years old, Marple Aqueduct remains a monument to its Alfreton-born engineer, Benjamin Outram, who died from a stroke just five years after its completion, at the ridiculously early age of forty-one. We forget what a toll their tireless work took on these pioneering engineers of the industrial revolution.

By Bridge 16, Aqueduct House is thought to have been the inspiration behind a canalside dwelling featured in Agatha Christie's Thomas and Tuppence Beresford crime novel *By the Pricking of My Thumbs*. Christie's

*Up until the end of the 19th century the river was known as the Mersey downstream of the Goyt's confluence with the Etherow opposite Brabyns Park.

sister, Margaret lived at Abney Hall near Stockport, and the world famous crime writer was a frequent visitor to these parts. The inspiration behind Miss Marple, one of her best loved sleuths, is said to have come from a visit to a sale at Marple Hall which coincided with her working on the first mystery featuring Jane Marple, a collection of short stories entitled *The Thirteen Problems* first published by Collins Crime Club in 1932.

Satisfying for the spectator and participant alike, the sixteen Marple Locks raise the canal by over two hundred feet. They'll take the latter a leisurely two and a half hours to negotiate, but they took ten years to build, largely because the canal company was experiencing financial problems. This was far from unusual, for huge capital outlay was involved in advance of any profits which could come from completion. Indeed, for a number of years goods were laboriously transhipped from boats at either end of the flight onto a temporary tramway. In recent years the flight has shown its age and been closed to navigation for one reason or another. Most recently the chamber of Lock 7 had to be stabilised with inner walls of concrete piling, a task which took contractors the best part of a year.

Highlight of the locks is undoubtedly Oldknow's Warehouse above Lock 9, a handsome, three storey stone structure now housing a suite of enviable offices. Samuel Oldknow - one of the main promoter's of the Peak Forest Canal - had a mill at Mellor, and bales of finished cotton were brought here by road for storage before onward transit along the canal.

Bridge 18 is known as Posset Bridge, apparently because Oldknow promised the navvies a posset of ale apiece if they finished the bridge on schedule. History records it proved sufficient inducement! The bridge incorporates separate horse and foot tunnels and, on the offside, an arch indicates a former arm to the foot of a bank of limekilns. Another short arm left the canal at this point and led to Hollins Mill. Green's coal boats traded here as late as 1959, one of the last commercial traffics on the canal. Take a moment before continuing along the canal to see 'Lock 17' (a few yards to the east along Strines Road) a memorial to local historian Gordon Mills. The top four chambers of the flight must be unique in their setting alongside the neat front gardens of a street of suburban villas.

The faded splendour of Goyt Mill

Macclesfield Canal

Marple is the meeting place of the Peak Forest Canal and its junior - by some thirty years - the Macclesfield Canal. Surveyed by Thomas Telford and engineered by William Crosley, the latter was promoted to provide a more direct route between Manchester and The Potteries than previously offered by the Bridgewater and Trent & Mersey canals, though its completion in 1831 coincided with the onset of the Railway Age and its full potential was never realised. Indeed, along with the Ashton and Peak Forest canals the Macclesfield was absorbed into its APM group of canals by what became known as the Great Central Railway, which, at the railway grouping of 1923, went on to become a constituent of the LNER.

Transport politics apart, Marple is a superbly photogenic junction, abounding in great sweeps of stonework and cobbles. Amongst the most obvious attractions are the Macclesfield Company's perishable goods warehouse, a durable stone building with an arched loading bay adjoining a former stop lock, and a functionally stylish roving bridge which enabled horses to haul boats through the junction without the need to unhitch the towing rope. With support from the Department for Levelling Up and the National Lottery Heritage Fund, Marple Wharf is in the process of being refurbished and the warehouse is due to become a heritage centre and cafe. Boater facilities are earmarked for 2024.

Evidence of the important transport role the canal played can be found by Bridge 3. Still splendid with its turrets and terracotta, Goyt Mill was erected in 1905 and spent its working life spinning cotton imported through Manchester Docks and brought here by canal. Indeed, the loading apparatus still hangs hopefully over the water awaiting the next consignment of bales. A landmark for miles around, the mill's lofty chimney was felled in the 1980s. Nowadays, the mill's six floors are occupied by an an array of small enterprises, not least a Scalextric Racing Course. It was to Goyt Mill that the last commercial traffic on the Macclesfield Canal - coal from Stoke-on-Trent - survived until 1957. Curiously, another mill stood alongside the canal by Bridge 4. This was Rhode (aka Shepley's) Mill, demolished in the mid-1930s, though if you nip up onto the road which crosses the bridge you'll encounter stone walling which obviously pre-dates the industrial estate that now occupies its former site.

Romiley
Map 47

Suburban settlement with bustling main street best reached from Bridge 14 or Hyde Bank Tunnel.

Eating & Drinking
DUKE OF YORK - Stockport Road. Tel: 0161 406 9988. Comfortably appointed inn dating from 1786. Wide choice of food (ex Mon) and real ales. Two minutes walk from Bridge 14. SK6 3AN
QURASHI - Stockport Road. Tel: 0161 406 9000. Indian restaurant and take-away. SK6 3AN
SPREAD EAGLE - Hatherlow. Tel: 0161 494 5723. Nice refurbished 18th century pub easily accessed from Hatherlow Aqueduct. Open from noon daily; food served lunch and evening weekdays and from noon throughout at weekends. SK6 3DR

Shopping
Good little shopping centre. Sainsbury's Local (on Compstall Road to east of station) and branch of Aldi adjacent Bridge 14.

Things to Do
CHADKIRK CHAPEL - Vale Road. Ancient chapel, walled garden, and nature reserve. Usually open on the last Sunday in the month 12-4pm at which time refreshments are available. Access from the towpath at Burymewick Aqueduct. SK6 3LD

Connections
BUSES - services 383/4 provide circular connections with Marple and Stockport. .
TRAINS - local Northern trains provide connections with Marple, Hyde, Rose Hill, New Mills etc

Marple
Maps 47/47A

Subtract the canal, and its setting on the cusp of the moors, and Marple would amount to little more than an innocuous suburban annex of Stockport. That said, the little town's position on the 'Cheshire Ring' makes it a popular overnight mooring point and it has some of the handiest and best facilities on this side of the circuit. Christopher Isherwood, author of *Goodbye to Berlin* - from which the musical *Cabaret* was derived - was born here.

Eating & Drinking
FISHERMAN'S TABLE - Church Lane. Tel: 0161 536 4389. Fleetwood sourced fish restaurant open from 5.30pm Mon-Wed and from noon Thur-Sat. SK6 7AR
HATTERS ARMS - Church Lane. Tel: 0161 427 1529. Stone-built, wood-panelled local. SK6 7AW
MARPLE SPICE - Stockport Road. Tel: 0161 427 9166. Indian restaurant near Bridge 18 PF Canal. SK6 6BJ
RING O' BELLS - Church Lane. Tel: 0161 427 2300. Robinson's pub by Bridge 2 on the Macclesfield Canal. Open from noon (ex Mon) food served lunch and evenings, though only until 5pm Sun. B&B. SK6 7AY
SAMUEL OLDKNOW - Market Street. Tel: 0161 425 9530. Award-winning two-storey town centre establishment named after the celebrated local industrialist. Open throughout from 1pm Mon-Thur and from noon Fri-Sun. Pork pies on sale, but you're welcome to bring your own take-aways. SK6 7AD

Shopping
Handy shopping centre (including a large Asda supermarket) within easy reach of bridges 2 or 18. Nice bakery called Archers on Hollins Lane: oh those corned beef and vegetable pies! Littlewoods butchers on Church Lane. Launderette on Market Street.

Things to Do
REGENT CINEMA - old-fashioned, one-screen cinema adjacent Bridge 18. Tel: 0161 427 5951. SK6 6BJ

Connections
BUSES - frequent services to/from Stockport which is an interesting town (with a Hat Museum) to visit in its own right.
TRAINS - station just down hill from Bridge 17. Services to/from Manchester, Romiley, Guide Bridge, New Mills etc. Rose Hill station, just over half a mile west of the town centre, is the terminus of an hourly service to/from Manchester, but it also marks the northern end of the Middlewood Way (converted from its abandoned trackbed after closure in 1970) and has thus potential for walkers.
TAXIS - VIP. Tel: 0161 494 1234.

Marple Bridge
Maps 47/47A

Thriving little community grouped about the bridge which carries the road to Glossop across the Goyt.

Eating & Drinking
FOLD - Town Street. Tel: 0161 302 6114. Bistro and bottle shop open Wed-Sun. SK6 5AA
LIBBY'S - Town Street. Tel: 0161 427 2310. Family-run artisan bakery/cafe which morphs into a pizza/wine bar Thur-Sat evenings. SK6 5AA
MAPLE TREE - Town Street. Tel: 0161 484 5555. Chinese open from 5pm daily ex Mon. SK6 5DS
NORFOLK ARMS - Town Street. Tel: 0161 427 8090. Comfortable pub, open from noon daily, food served throughout. SK6 5DS
PURPLE PAKORA - Brabyns Brow (just downhill from Bridge 17, Peak Forest). Tel: 0161 427 7748. Indian restaurant with sister establishment in Congleton. Open daily from 5pm (4pm Sun). SK6 7DA
TOWN STREET FRYER - Town Street Tel: 0161 449 7290. Fish & chip shop open lunchtimes and evenings (until 7.30pm) daily ex Sun & Mon. SK6 5AA

Shopping
Make a bee-line for Dutsons deli/take-away on Town Street, a couple of shops along from a friendly convenience store and post office. Pharmacy. Antiques.

Things to Do
BRABYNS PARK - woodland and riverside walks.

47A PEAK FOREST CANAL   Marple & Newtown   3mls/0lks/1½ hrs

KNOWN in some elevated circles as the *Upper* Peak Forest Canal, the route southwards from Marple, to the twin termini of Bugsworth and Whaley Bridge, is one of the most exhilarating on the system. Lockless, and punctuated but occasionally by moveable bridges, it is the setting as opposed to the canal itself which lifts this section out of the commonplace, like an otherwise ordinary tune rendered memorable by sumptuous orchestration. A vigorous landscape of fells, wind-bent woods, lonely stone cottages, railway viaducts and colossal mills places this particularly beautiful canal in an austere, northern mould, and canal explorers, whatever their means of propulsion, are blessed with a sense of privilege to be viewing the world from such a sublime perspective.

   Your departure from Marple Junction may be subject to some delay as there is much to see. The sturdy stone house opposite the roving bridge was once part of James Jinks' boatbuilding yard. A former drydock has been transformed into a sunken garden. It became disused in the Thirties, the story being that it leaked so badly that Mrs Jinks' cellar was flooded every time a boat entered or left the dock. Adjoining the old boatyard, below an arm now used for moorings, is a bank of lime kilns which once had about them the look of medieval ruins. It is thought that Samuel Oldknow - who had his finger in every money-spinning pie between Manchester and Stockport - had the kilns so built to romanticise the view from Mellor Lodge, his home across the valley.

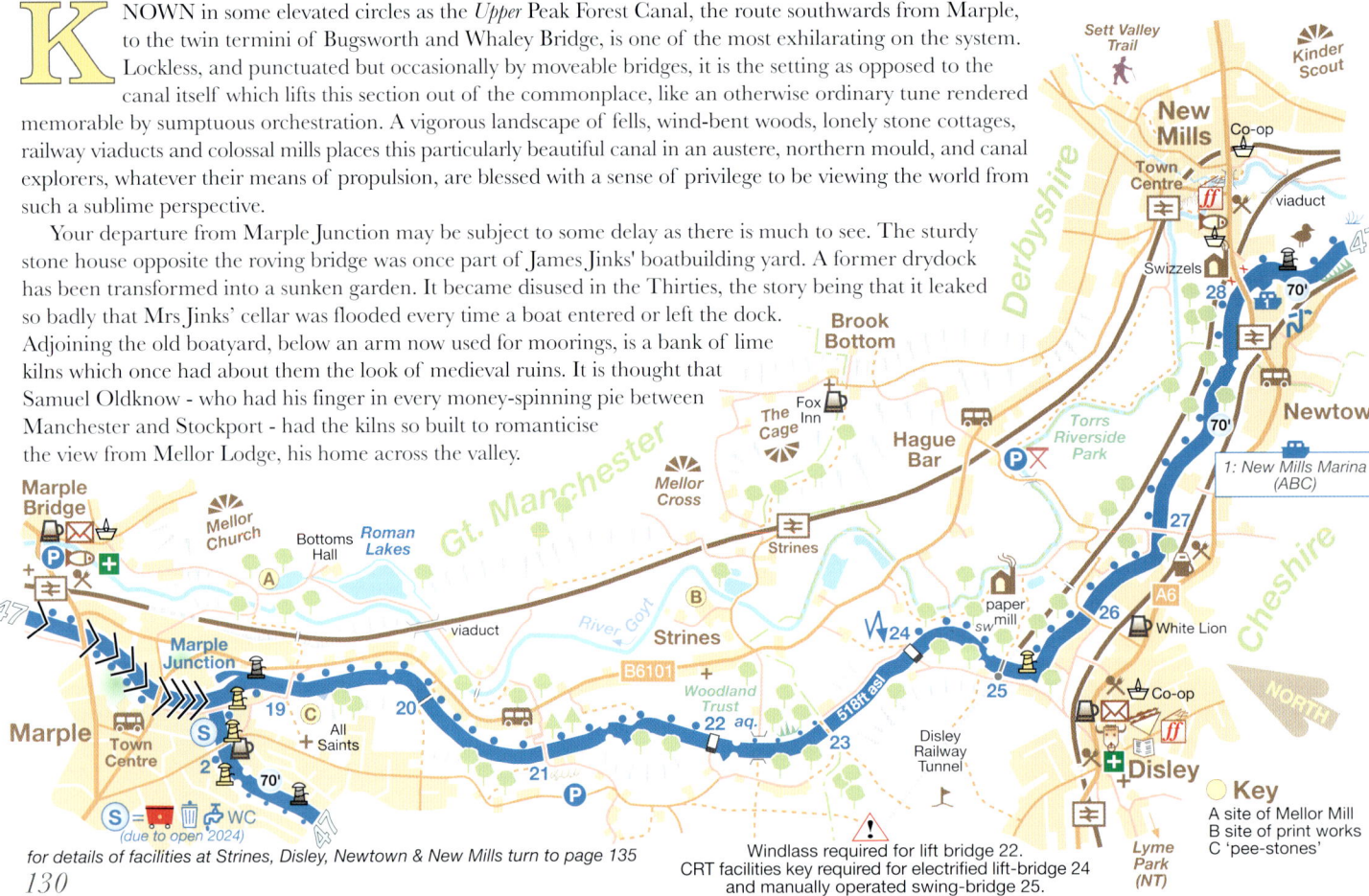

for details of facilities at Strines, Disley, Newtown & New Mills turn to page 135

Windlass required for lift bridge 22.
CRT facilities key required for electrified lift-bridge 24 and manually operated swing-bridge 25.

Alongside Mellor Lodge stood Mellor Mill, a massive enterprise destroyed by fire in 1892. A group of industrial archaeologists are painstakingly restoring the wheel pit and associated water tunnels at the site of Mellor Mill which can easily (and entertainingly) be reached by footpath from Bridge 19, by which an interesting fleet of ex working boats are more or less permanently moored.

The towpath changes sides at Bridge 19 which, unusually for the Peak Forest Canal, is constructed of brick. Oldknow's apprentices crossed the bridge on Sundays on their way from Bottoms Hall beside the river - where they were accommodated in conditions advanced for the day - to All Saints Church on the hillside to the west. On the way they'd make full use of two 'pee stones', thoughtfully provided - for what we'd now call a personal facility break - before the rigours of the service. If you walk up to All Saints now (encountering a capped-off mine shaft and those 'pee stones' en route) you'll see that only the tower of the earlier church (which Oldknow, with typical altruism had funded) remains, isolated in its extensive graveyard adjoining an imposing Gothic Revival replacement of 1880.

Milestones, with a family resemblance to those on the Macclesfield Canal, intermittently measure the canal's progress, though they are not all in situ and their faces are too weatherbeaten to retain any inscriptions. Keep your eyes peeled for a large wooden cross on the horizon to the east. It was erected in 1970 to commemorate a spot where John Wesley preached, and a service is held beside it every Easter. A landmark no longer visible was the lofty chimney of Strines Print Works, demolished in 2007 and replaced now by housing. The printing was on textiles rather than paper. The works had a wharf by Strines Aqueduct between bridges 22 and 23 for the unloading of raw materials and the loading of finished goods before the railway was built through the Goyt Valley. Incidentally, Strines station - which astonishingly, given its remote location, survived the Beeching massacre - has been suggested as the inspiration for the station in Edith Nesbit's *The Railway Children*. Certainly she came to stay with her step-sister at Mellor next door to a house known as 'Three Chimneys', intriguingly there is a scene in the book (though not the film) where a canal child throws stones at the railway children, whilst additionally Edward Ross, secretary of the Manchester, Sheffield & Lincolnshire Railway lived at Marple and may well have inspired the character of the 'old gentleman'.

Seasoned canal travellers may well find themselves reminded of the Mon & Brec, another canal which clings tenaciously to precipitous hillsides. Waterside Mill, visible as the canal curves round between bridges 24 and 25, can trace its history back over two centuries. Originally it belonged to Oldknow (who else!) but since the turn of the 19th century it has concentrated on the manufacture of paper, tissue being a speciality now. The Midland Railway's direct main line from Manchester to London emerges from Disley Tunnel (over two miles long) just below the canal. The portal is crowned by the MR's trademark wyvern and dated 1901. Bridges 21-23 & 26 sport good old fashioned British Waterways 'blue & yellow' number plaques, a nice custom to have been revived.

New Mills Newtown is the largest settlement encountered by the Upper Peak Forest Canal, indeed, in most respects its development was brought about by the canal's construction. Here, in premises adapted from the old Brunswick cotton mill, is Swizzels confectionery works, purveyor of sherberty smells and origin of all the sticky substances you invariably discover abandoned in your children's pockets - even when they're in their forties. Swizzels-Matlow can trace their origins back to 1928. They relocated here during the Second World War to escape London's bombs. The works appears in several of Clare Allan's works; a New Mills based artist and printmaker of increasing renown.

There are two more mills and a foundry overlooking the canal from various angles which, between them, continue to evoke a very 'northern industrial' atmosphere. One of the mills is home now to Trafalgar Marine Services, fender makers and providers of rope.

As the canal twists around the hillside to reveal superb views of Kinder Scout - at 2,088 ft, the highest point in Derbyshire - there is access to Goytside Meadows, a local nature reserve whose trio of unimproved fields retain their delightfully euphonious nomenclature: Nice Eyes, Little Eyes, and Higher Flowery Croft.

47B PEAK FOREST CANAL Whaley Bridge & Bugsworth 2mls/0lks/1hr

THERE is going to be no escape from these glacially moulded hills and the canal knows it, but seems determined to enjoy itself nonetheless. Similarly obliged is the explorer, on foot, cycling or afloat, for it would be churlish to be otherwise. Within the increasing confines of its valley, it is as if the Goyt has thrown a party and been overwhelmed by the number of attendees: the canal, two railways and the A6 trunk road, well on its way north from Luton to Carlisle. The railways, Midland to the east and London & North Western to the west, were absorbed at the 1923 grouping into the LMS, whereas the Peak Forest Canal, railway owned since as early as 1846, became part of the LNER. Co-ordinated transport is an elusive concept where the British psyche is concerned.

Furness Vale Marina creates regular tidal surges of pleasure craft. The long row of terraced cottages opposite would have provided homes for workers at the neighbouring calico printing works now used as an industrial estate. Raised above the level of the canal, trains to Buxton rattle by at hourly intervals; the signal box beside the level-crossing retains its London Midland Region 1950s maroon coloured enamel nameplate. On the opposite side of the valley the former Midland line hosts long trains of limestone quarried in the vicinity of Buxton, the modern equivalent of the narrowboats which once carried the same commodity so successfully on the canal.

Is this canal more conducive to happiness than any in the country? Pearson's, notorious for shifting (or perhaps more kindly, cyclic) allegiances, could certainly present an affirmative, if fleeting case. Bridge 34 is merely a footbridge now, but until relatively recently there was a lift-bridge here as well. Surplus to requirements, it has found a new lease of life on the Lichfield & Hatherton Canals. A pair of concrete road bridges introduces the junction of the original main line to Bugsworth Basin and the branch to Whaley Bridge; boat horses

1: Furness Vale Marina
2: Phoenix Day Boats

⚠ CRT facilities key required for swing-bridge 30.

'Passengers No More'
1: Buxworth - closed 15.9.58

132

Departing from Bugsworth

gained access to the latter via a tunnel, and it is recorded that well broken-in animals would nonchalantly find their own way through the tunnel while their owners rope-hauled the boat across the junction by way of the footbridge.

An aqueduct carries the main line over the Goyt then it passes beneath the A6 before curving round to the reconstituted splendours of Bugsworth Basin. The Bugsworth Basin Heritage Trust (formerly known as the Inland Waterways Protection Society) are a small, dedicated group of enthusiasts who have painstakingly restored Bugsworth Basins to something approaching the glory of their commercial heyday. Their tireless efforts came to fruition with reopening of the basins in 1999. Unfortunately this proved a false dawn, and leakage brought about an abrupt closure of the basins to boating traffic, a hiatus lasting half a dozen years. Happily, however, the complex reopened for the second time at Easter, 2005. The event was marked by the symbolic departure of a horse-drawn narrowboat loaded with 16 tons of crushed limestone bound for Guide Bridge.

Bugsworth today enjoys Ancient Monument status and what the BBHT have achieved amounts to the successful excavation of an archaeological site of considerable importance. The complex comprises a series of transhipment arms and basins which radiate from a gauging stop overlooked by a wharfinger's house and canal office. A six mile tramway descended from the limestone quarries of Dove Holes. Loaded wagons ran down to Bugsworth by gravity, whilst empty ones were horse-drawn back. These trains were known as 'gangs', and often totalled twenty wagons at a time under the control - if that's not too precise a term - of a brakeman and his 'nipper', or youthful assistant; both of whom somewhat perilously rode the leading wagon. It comes as no surprise to learn that derailments were not exactly an unknown phenomenon on the rudimentary L shaped track. At Chapel-en-le-Frith there was an inclined plane which operated on the principle that empty wagons were hauled upwards by the weight of loaded ones travelling downhill. In the heyday of the basins perhaps twenty narrowboats a day would leave Bugsworth laden with limestone for Lancashire's burgeoning industries. The tramway ceased operating in the 1920s, though one of its wagons has found its way into the National Railway Museum at York, whilst the Peak Forest Tramway Trail can enjoyably be followed eastwards along the valley floor.

It would be difficult to exaggerate the reward to be gained from visiting Bugsworth, especially by boat in which you would have every opportunity to soak up the basin's latent atmosphere as dusk falls. The BBHT have an information centre alongside the entrance to the basins, and their enthusiasm is contagious. Oh, and by the way, the locals took exception to the vulgarity of 'Bugsworth', considering Buxworth more polite.

Whaley Bridge Transhipment Shed Exterior

construction of a canal, but the Railway Age caught up with these heroic, not to say romantic proposals; more's the pity, when you contemplate what could have been one of Britain's most beautiful inland waterways.

Whaley Bridge hit the national headlines in August 2019 when one and a half thousand residents were evacuated amidst fears of a dam burst. The dam - or, more accurately, spillway - is part of Toddbrook Reservoir, which, along with Combs Reservoir, is owned by the Canal & River Trust and feeds the Peak Forest Canal. CRT and their contractors, Kier, have been working to re-open the reservoir ever since, and completion is earmarked for 2025, at a cost in the region of £15 million. Canal maintenance, as we have seen elsewhere in this guide, doesn't come cheap, and one can't help wondering if a charity - however well-meaning its outlook - is the best way of administering a two thousand mile public utility. Isn't it rather like asking those wonderful chaps at the Severn Valley Railway if they'd kindly look after the West Coast Main Line!

Whaley Bridge Transhipment Shed Interior

Meanwhile, back on the 'branch' to Whaley Bridge, yet more private moorings signal the approach to this compact and appealing little Derbyshire town. Shaded by woodlands, the canal runs parallel to the old, now by-passed A6 before terminating in a small, triangular basin dominated by a sizeable, stone-built, transhipment shed which originally boasted three stories. An arm enters an archway in the centre of this handsome structure whilst, in the past, railway tracks were accommodated on either side to facilitate loading and unloading in sheltered conditions. Under the enthusiastic auspices of the Whaley Bridge Canal Group, this Grade II listed structure has been refurbished internally as a community hub - see opposite.

Whereas the link at Bugsworth was by way of a fairly primitive tramway, the railway connection at Whaley Bridge, dating from 1831, was of a more sophisticated design. The Cromford & High Peak climbed right across the Peak District to link with the Cromford Canal, 33 miles to the south. Tantalisingly, the route was originally surveyed for the

Disley
Map 47A

Amiable Cheshire village, even if it's hard to cross the A6 without leaving a limb behind. Nice walk to reach it along the lane from Bridge 25. Shadowing the Macclesfield Canal, the Gritstone Trail sets off for Kidsgrove from the railway station forecourt.

Eating & Drinking
DANDY COCK INN - Market Street. Tel: 01663 765563. Cosy little Robinson's pub. SK12 2AA
MALT DISLEY - Market Street. Tel: 01663 308020. *Good Beer Guide* listed micro pub. SK12 2AA
MR CHONG - Market Street. Tel: 01663 308077. Popular Chinese restaurant/take-away open from 5pm Wed-Sat and 4pm Sun. SK12 2DT
RAM'S HEAD - Buxton Road West. Tel: 01663 767909. Large smartly refurbished former coaching house open from noon (9am weekends). SK12 2AE
SAFFRON - Market Street. Tel: 01663 766016. Indian restaurant open from 5pm daily. SK12 2AA
SASSO - Market Street. Tel: 01663 765400. Italian restaurant open from 5pm; noon Sat/Sun. SK12 2AA
WHITE LION - Buxton Road. Tel: 01663 762800. Pub on the A6 easily reached from Bridge 26. SK12 2HA

Shopping
Facilities include a Co-op open 7am-10pm (8pm on Suns), butcher, baker, pharmacy and post office.

Things to Do
LYME (PARK) - Tel: 01663 762023. Lavish National Trust property set in extensive grounds. Masqueraded as 'Pemberley' in BBC's 1995 version of *Pride and Prejudice*, Colin Firth's wet shirt and all. If on foot, eschew the A6 and follow the lane from Disley station; though beware, it is a three mile hike.

Connections
TRAINS - hourly Northern services to/from Stockport, Manchester and Whaley Bridge.

Strines
Map 47A

Promising 'base camp' for climbs up to Brook Bottom from which there are panoramic views over to Lyme Park's 'Cage'.

Eating & Drinking
FOX INN - Brookbottom. Tel: 0161 427 1634. Cosy whitewashed Robinsons pub tucked away up in the hills. Open from noon daily. Sandwiches. SK22 3AY

Connections
TRAINS - approx hourly Northern services to/from New Mills and Manchester via Marple and Romiley.

Newtown
Map 47A

A 19th century textile-based expansion of the North Derbyshire town of New Mills. Handy shops, pubs and a good fish & chip cafe. Trains as per Disley. Torrside Brewing (est. 2015), housed in canalside warehouse, morphs into a Tap on selected dates and they have an on-site bottle shop open Mon-Wed 12-5pm. Holiday lets at ABC's Newtown Marina.

Eating & Drinking
A TAVOLA - Albion Road. Tel: 0747 874 3293. Quirkily charming Sicilian restaurant open from 4pm Tue-Thur and 1pm Fri/Sat. Good vegetarian choices. SK22 3EY

Connections
TRAINS - as Disley.

New Mills
Map 47A

New Mills itself is a more than worthwhile ten minutes away on foot. Furthermore there's a dramatic trail to be followed (over weirs, under viaducts and through a chasm) along the rivers Goyt and Sett. Plenty of shops (including a nice little s/h bookshop tucked up High Street), banks and eating/drinking establishments.

Connections
TRAINS - Northern services to/from Manchester or via the picturesque Edale Valley to Sheffield.

Whaley Bridge
Map 47B

A charming little Derbyshire town sheltering under the moors of Axe Edge. Make the canal terminus a convenient excuse to explore the surrounding countryside. Go up and see the reservoirs in the Goyt Valley, flooded after the First World War.

Eating & Drinking
CASA DI PIZZA - Market Street. Tel: 01663 734333. Snug Italian open Tue-Sat from 6pm. SK23 7AA
GOYT INN - Bridge Street. Tel: 01663 732710. *Good Beer Guide* listed pub close to the basin. SK23 7LR
MEDITERRANEAN - Market Street. Tel: 01663 732218. Cafe/steak bar open from 9.30am daily. SK23 7LP
C&HP Railway. Unspoilt interior. SK23 7HR
THE FRYERY - Canal Street. Tel: 01663 732902. Fish & chips lunch & evening daily ex Sun. SK23 7LS

Shopping
Plenty of small characterful shops where they are eager to pass the time of day with visiting canallers. Large 24 hour Tesco supermarket situated close to the junction with the Bugsworth Arm.

Things to Do
TRANSHIPMENT WAREHOUSE - Canal Street. Tel: 01663 738016. Volunteer run hub. Secondhand bookshop with extensive (and inexpensive!) stock. Coffee shop. Food & Arts Market on the 2nd Saturday of the month. Open daily ex Tue. SK23 7LS

Connections
TRAINS - Northern Trains hourly service to/from Buxton, Stockport and Manchester with stops at Furness Vale, Newtown, Disley and Middlewood.

Bugsworth
Map 47B

NAVIGATION INN - adjacent Bugsworth Basin. Tel: 01663 732072. Cosy atmosphere and canalia. Food and accommodation. SK23 7NE Bus service 190 runs to/from Whaley Bridge and Chinley Mon-Sat.

48 MACCLESFIELD CANAL High Lane & Higher Poynton 5mls/0lks/2hrs

QUICKLY establishing its character, the Macclesfield Canal gathers momentum, proceeding generally on a north-south axis, employing cuttings, embankments and aqueducts to avoid the need for locks. There is grace in its overbridges - one might even go as far as saying sagacity - and eloquence in its stone mileposts, counting the miles from Marple down to Hall Green (on the outskirts of Kidsgrove) and back. To simplify the maps, we quote only the distance from Marple; attempting to fit in both distances - not to mention the added quarter mile - would have been a challenge!

For the most part, the canal is rural, and it's easy to forget that it relied on industry for its lifeblood. You wouldn't know it now, but on the off-side just north of Bridge 9 there was a sizeable cotton-spinning mill. It led a chequered existence. Rebuilt after a serious fire in the 1890s, it was destroyed beyond viable repair by, of all unlikely things, a hurricane on the 22nd February 1908; fortunately without loss of life; though not, alas, livelihood.

High Lane, an elongated community strung out along the A6, introduces elements of suburbia. Bridge 12 carries the towpath over the originally 'T' shaped High Lane Arm, it's 'L' shaped remains home to the North Cheshire Cruising Club. *Ailsa Craig*, the converted lifeboat chartered by a band of IWA luminaries in 1948 to explore the northern waterways, was based on the arm for a number of years before being sold to the Wyatts at Stone. The NCCC (whose journal is endearingly - and increasingly accurately - known as "The Ditchcrawler") leased the remaining part of the arm from the LNER in 1943. A peculiarity, then as now, was the use of boathouses - the aquatic equivalent of a lock-up garage. This part of the arm was used as a wharf for Stockport, its long vanished counterpart served Middlewood Pit, abandoned, along with the neighbouring Norbury collieries by the end of the 19th century. Out in the wilds - nowhere near a public road - Middlewood's railway station is an odd, if welcome, survival. A useful resource for towpath walkers, it once boasted platforms on two levels belonging to different railway companies, and a 'chord' connected the two lines.

From time to time the trees which line much of the canal recede, and one's gaze is directed eastwards where moorland rears up in dramatic waves. The tower visible in the middle distance

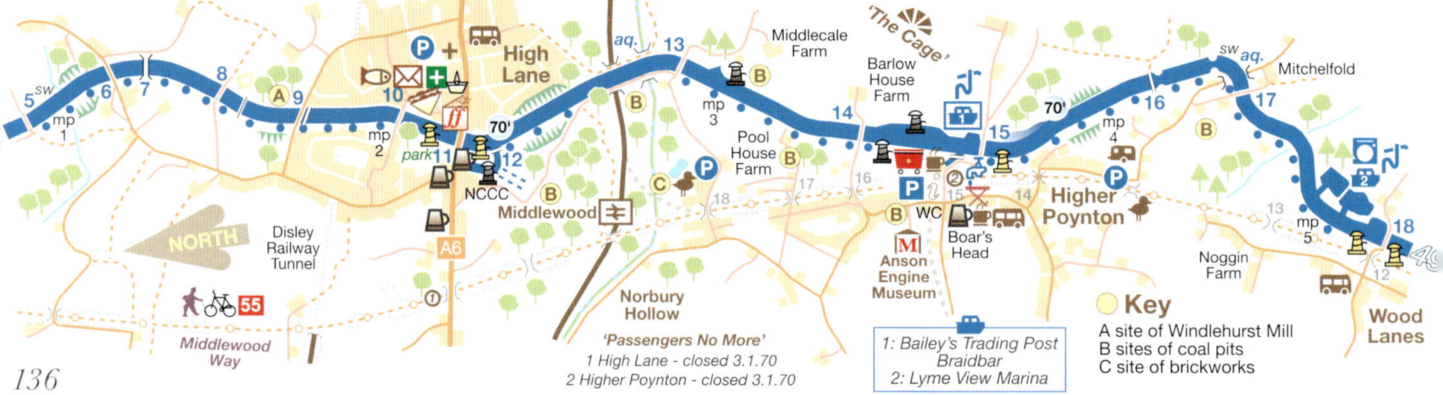

'Passengers No More'
1 High Lane - closed 3.1.70
2 Higher Poynton - closed 3.1.70

1: Bailey's Trading Post
Braidbar
2: Lyme View Marina

Key
A site of Windlehurst Mill
B sites of coal pits
C site of brickworks

136

is in Lyme Park (see page 135) and known as 'The Cage', an 18th century belvedere. Disley Home Guard used it as a lookout during WWII.

In its brief commercial heyday, the Macc's heaviest traffic was in coal mined in the vicinity of Higher Poynton. Much activity centred on Lord Vernon's Wharf (Bridge 15) where a fleet of coal carrying narrowboats was maintained. A network of tramways and inclines connected the canal with Anson, Nelson and Park collieries, and business was brisk, at least until the arrival of the railways. Amongst the carriers was the famous name of Pickfords who could trace their origins back to an 18th century waggoner from Poynton. In the 1950s a pioneering outfit known as Constellation Cruisers began operating a hire fleet from here. Nowadays it is revered in canal circles as the headquarters of Braidbar, award-winning boatbuilders of some repute.

South of Bridge 15 the canal widens into a shallow pool, probably brought about by a burst. Presumably it was cheaper to pay out compensation to the landowner than go to the trouble of repairing the canal bank.

The bridges in this former colliery area differ in design from the ellipsoidal stone arches previously mentioned. Instead they are flat decked and designed to be easily raised in the event of subsidence.

Bridge 16 is a lattice girder footbridge, but the canal narrows at the point of a former swing-bridge as well. The latter swivelled from the off-side, and as it was habitually left in the open position for boats to pass, there had to be some means to access it for operation from the towpath side. Bridge 17 is guarded by a metal, lozenge-shaped weight limit sign of Great Central Railway provenance. The GCR were at one time joint operators, along with the North Staffordshire Railway, of the line between Marple and Macclesfield, now known as the Middlewood Way.

Opposite Milepost 5 lies Lyme View Marina. Two extensive basins provide off-line mooring for private owners. This was previously the site of a basin provided for loading the output of Adlington Colliery onto boats. A neighbouring pub called the Miners Arms (now closed) echoed the area's old occupation long after the last coal was brought to the surface.

High Lane   Map 48

Strung out along the A6, with its interminable traffic, this suburban satellite of outer Stockport is of little attraction in its own right but canallers might find its facilities of use: pubs, fish & chips, fast food outlets, a Chinese restaurant, a well-stocked Spar with cash machine, post office/pharmacy. Talisman Books (late of Marple Bridge) have an excellent secondhand book outlet to the rear of 32 Buxton Road, hard by Bridge 11. Half-hourly buses (Centrebus 199) to/from Stockport and Buxton: ditto hourly trains from Middlewood, accessible by footpath from the canal.

Higher Poynton   Map 48

The elaborate, orange-brick Boar's Head, and one or two other Victorian properties (39 Shrigley Road housed the station-master) hint at Higher Poynton's industrial pedigree, and the station platforms remain intact, otherwise all is innocuously residential now.

Eating & Drinking
BAILEY'S TRADING POST - Lyme Road (adj. Br. 15). Tel: 01625 872277. Canalside dealer in boating accessories (fenders, gas, oil etc) plus canalia, refreshments and day boat hire. - SK12 1TH
BOAR'S HEAD - Shrigley Road. Tel: 01625 409853. Refurbished pub popular with boaters and walkers. Open noon daily, food served throughout. SK12 1TE
COFFEE TAVERN - Tel: 01625 873826. Cosy cafe dating back as far as 1876 when it was opened by Lord Vernon, owner of the Poynton coal mines, as a public reading room. 10am-5pm ex Mon. SK12 1TE

Things to Do
NELSON PIT VISITOR CENTRE - two minutes walk from Bridge 15. Interpretive material relating to Higher Poynton's coal mining past and the railway origins of the Middlewood Way. Toilet facilities. SK12 1TH
ANSON ENGINE MUSEUM - Anson Road (five minutes walk from Bridge 15). Tel: 01625 874426. Delightful museum celebrating the internal combustion engine, located on the site of Anson Pit, closed in 1926. Xanadu of fabled names - Gardner, Ruston, Hornsby, Tangye, National, Mirrlees etc etc. Open Fri & Sun, Easter to October, 10am-4pm. SK12 1TD

Connections
BUSES - Belle Vue services 391/2 operate Mon-Sat to Stockport and Macclesfield (via Bollington).

Wood Lanes   Map 48

Once the location of Adlington Colliery, though you wouldn't know it now. A footpath leads idyllically eastwards up onto the slopes of Park Moor.

49 MACCLESFIELD CANAL Bollington 5mls/0lks/2hrs

SEEMINGLY in cahoots with the trackbed of the Macclesfield, Bollington & Marple Railway, the canal ducks in and out of woodland, alternating between cuttings and embankments.

Typically handsome stone-built bridges appear at frequent intervals, appearing to 'staple' the canal together. The railway closed in 1970 but was repurposed as the 'Middlewood Way' in 1985. Arguably, the 'roaring twenties' bypassed this sequestered corner of Cheshire, nevertheless a petrol-electric railcar, nicknamed 'The Bug', provided a frequent shuttle service between Bollington and Macclesfield.

Eastwards the Pennine escarpment keeps inspirational company with the canal. Westwards, Alderley Edge ends abruptly on the Cheshire Plain. On a clear day Stockport and Manchester, are well defined on the horizon, whilst nearer at hand lies Woodford Aerodrome. Two famous aircraft designs made their inaugural flights from here: the Lancaster bomber in 1941 and the Shackleton reconnaissance plane eight years later.

The parapet of Bridge 25 bears the inscription 'Lovers Leap June 1894' which apparently relates to the sobering story of a married man who'd turned out his wife and three children in preference for another woman. Public opinion was so against the erring individual that his home was set alight and a 'safe house' had to be found for the 'other woman'. Finally, feelings were running so high against the lovers that they made a suicide pact and drowned themselves in the canal.

Pride came before profit margins when the Swindells (unfortunate name) came to erect their two massive cotton mills at Bollington - Clarence and Adelphi - in the middle of the 19th century. With their flamboyant architectural embellishments they have the air of baronial country seats rather than places where hundreds toiled to earn a meagre living. In retirement, however, they lend Bollington a plausibility it might otherwise lack and act as stately guardians to this rarely less than exciting length of canal. Soaring above this atmospheric former textile town on a high, stone-laid embankment pierced by a lofty aqueduct the canal traveller is treated to a series of eye-catching views.

South of Bollington, Kerridge Drydock, formerly known as Endon Wharf, was a busy site where locally quarried stone was loaded onto boats.

In the small hours of 29th February 1912 a large breach occurred in the canal opposite the dock, draining the

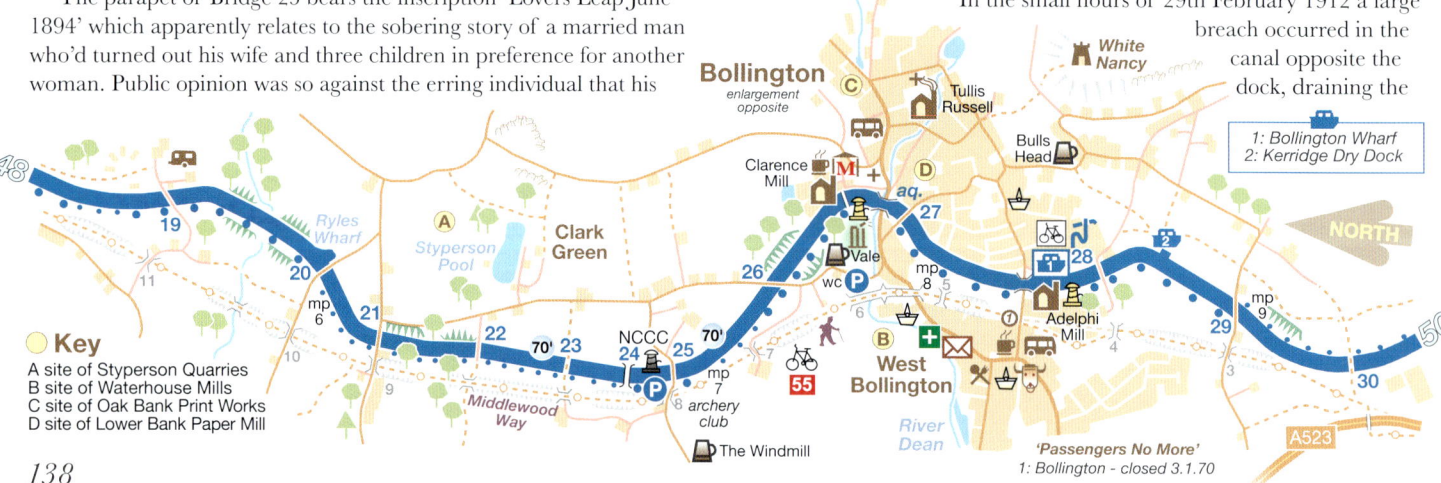

Key
A site of Styperson Quarries
B site of Waterhouse Mills
C site of Oak Bank Print Works
D site of Lower Bank Paper Mill

'Passengers No More'
1: Bollington - closed 3.1.70

1: Bollington Wharf
2: Kerridge Dry Dock

whole twenty-mile pound between Bugsworth and Bosley Locks. Considerable damage was done to Bollington, and the town's gas works was rendered inoperable. 160 boat-loads of clay puddle were brought in to mend the breach. In stark contrast to the Dutton breach (Map 37) of a century later, it took three weeks as opposed to nine months to repair.

The towpath changes sides at Bridge 29, a typically attractive Macclesfield roving bridge - reminiscent of a neatly folded cardigan, wouldn't you agree? To the north-east the wooded slopes of Kerridge Hill dominate the skyline, topped by a whitewashed, sugarloaf-shaped stone monument. Built as a summerhouse to commemorate the Battle of Waterloo, it is known to all and sundry as 'White Nancy'. In 2012 'Nancy' was adorned with regal insignia to commemorate Queen Elizabeth II's Diamond Jubilee.

Bollington
Map 49

'A Derbyshire Town in Cheshire peopled by Lancashire Folk' it used to be said of Bollington, reflecting its former status as a cotton town. But nowadays the locality is nicknamed 'the Happy Valley' and boasts its own community radio station 'Canalside 102.8fm'. In the absence of smoky mill chimneys, Bollington is as spick and span and as pretty as any hill town in Umbria. Is it a village, is it a town? It's anyone's guess! But with a population bordering on eight thousand souls, it's certainly far from insubstantial, and so if you are going to 'drop anchor' anywhere on 'The Macc' this is the place to do so.

Eating & Drinking
BAY LEAF LOUNGE - Wellington Road. Tel: 01625 576465. Indian restaurant and take-away down from Adelphi Mill. Open from 5pm daily. SK10 5HT
BULLS HEAD - Oak Lane. Tel: 01625 575522. Open Thur/Fri from 4pm; Sat/Sun from noon. SK10 5BD
CAFE WATERSIDE - Clarence Mill. Tel: 01625 575563. Nicely appointed cafe for coffees, lunches and afternoon tea within Clarence Mill. SK10 5JZ
THE GREEN - High Street. Tel: 01625 576691. Stylish little cafe serving 'rustic food'. SK10 5PH.
HOLLY BUSH - Palmerston Street. Tel: 01625 576059. Cosy wood-panelled Robinson's local. SK10 5PW
KIRA - Palmerston Street. Tel: 01625 575752. Indian bistro and lounge bar open from 5.30pm Tue-Sat. SK10 5PW

LIME TREE - High Street. Tel: 01625 578182. Restaurant/wine bar serving 'meat from the family's farm'. Open 11am Wed-Sat, 10am Sun. SK10 5PH
MULBERRY LEAF - Wellington Road, West Bollington. Tel: 01625 571100. Coffee shop open 9am-4pm Tue-Sat. SK10 5HT
TAPA - High Street. Tel: 01625 575058. 'Small plates & wine bar' open 5pm daily ex Sun. SK10 5PH
VALE INN - Adlington Road. Tel: 01625 575147. *Good Beer Guide* recommended pub owned by neighbouring Bollington Brewing Co. established in 2008. Food is served 12-2.30pm & 5-9pm weekdays and from noon throughout at weekends. SK10 5JT

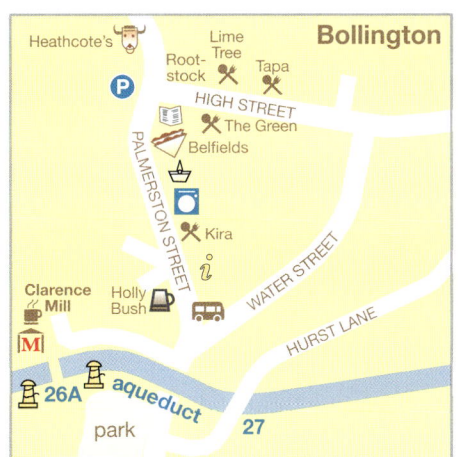

Shopping
Lots of nice individual shops whose owners seem genuinely interested in visitors 'off the cut'. In Bollington itself (amongst other useful outlets) you'll come upon the fabulous Rootstock organic grocery and refill shop (closed Tue & Sun), Belfield's bakery, a small convenience store, newsagent and launderette, plus a branch of the alliteratively initialled J. J. J. Heathcote, the butchers up at the top end of Palmerston Street. But don't ignore West Bollington's facilities which include Tesco and Co-op convenience stores, Barrow's Butchers, Knowles Green wine & cheese shop and a pharmacy. The post office can be found here too, on Wellington Road.

Things to Do
DISCOVERY CENTRE - Clarence Mill. Open Wed 1.30-4pm; Sat & Sun 11am-4pm. Admission free. Bollington Civic Society heritage display. SK10 5JZ
BRIDGEND CENTRE - Palmerston Street. Tel: 01625 576311. Local information, internet access. Heritage Trails, cafe and charity shop. SK10 5PW.

Connections
BUSES - D&G service 10 runs half-hourly (ex Sun) to/from Macclesfield. Belle Vue services 391/2 connect hourly (ex Sun) with Stockport (via Higher Poynton).
TAXIS - Bollington Black Cabs. Tel: 0797 145 1424.

50 MACCLESFIELD CANAL Macclesfield 5mls/0lks/2hrs

LOCATION of the second Inland Waterways Association National Rally in 1953, Macclesfield was the headquarters of its eponymous canal. Brook Street Wharf is overlooked by a handsome mill which once belonged to Hovis the breadmakers. That the canal played an important part in transport to and from the mill can be seen from the arched loading bay at water level. Hovis transferred their milling activities to Trafford Park, Manchester, where ships could deliver imported grain and wheat direct to their door, but they still used this mill as a print works for their packaging and publicity material.

A cutting of high-sided stone retaining walls frames the canal's southern exit from Macclesfield. Perhaps Crosley, the canal's engineer, was already aware of construction techniques on the Liverpool & Manchester Railway, for there is a strong 'railway' character to this cutting. At Gurnett another cutting of this kind lies just north of an aqueduct which carries the canal above the road to Sutton Lane Ends

and the nascent River Bollin. East of here Tegg's Nose dominates the view, a former gritstone quarry which has become a country park in its retirement. The view from its tawny summit is spellbinding.

Dry-stone walls criss-cross little fields climbing bravely up the hillsides, with here and there a knotty tentacle of stone terrace housing. This is Tunnicliffe Country. That much esteemed wildlife artist was born at nearby Langley in 1901. Though best known as an illustrator of other author's works - Henry Williamson's *Tarka the Otter* for example - Charles Tunnicliffe also wrote and illustrated his own nature diaries, a number of which feature local scenes, such as the canal reservoir at Bosley.

By swing-bridge No.47 a gnarled wood marks the perimeter of Danes Moss, a peat bog reminiscent of Whixall Moss on the Llangollen Canal. A footpath leads over the railway from Bridge 47 onto the moss, part of which is managed by the

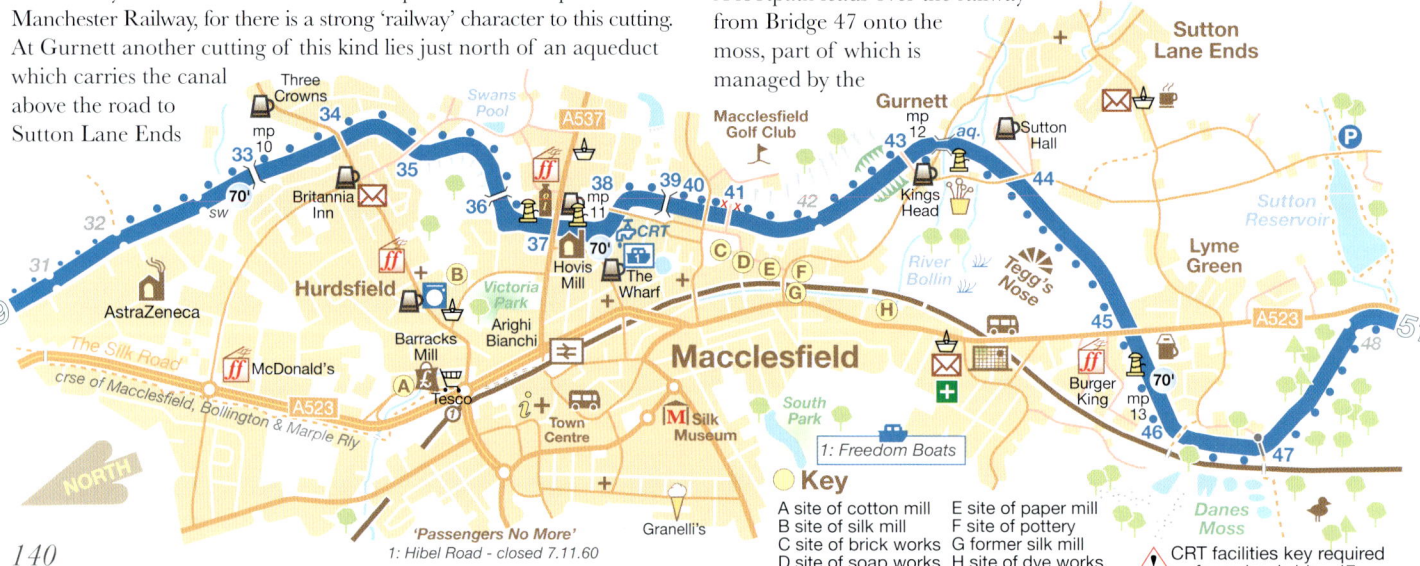

'Passengers No More'
1: Hibel Road - closed 7.11.60

Key
A site of cotton mill   E site of paper mill
B site of silk mill   F site of pottery
C site of brick works   G former silk mill
D site of soap works   H site of dye works

CRT facilities key required for swing-bridge 47.

1: Freedom Boats

Cheshire Wildlife Trust as a nature reserve, an agreeable wilderness of woodpeckers and willow warblers, dragonflies and damselflies, moths, butterflies and lizards. Another worthwhile detour from the canal is CRT's very own Sutton Reservoir, reached via Bridge 48A (Map 51).

Macclesfield   Map 50

The former silk weaving town of Macclesfield has some charming nooks and crannies which make it worth at least a semi-colon in the punctuation of any canal itinerary. Follow Buxton Road down from Bridge 37, past Arighi Bianchi's flamboyant furniture store, pass under the railway and you'll find yourself in Waters Green, where Wesley preached and which Tunnicliffe painted. Cobbled Church Street leads steeply up to the town centre and the fine, Greek Revival style Town Hall designed by Francis Goodwin in 1823. Adjoining this, the well-stocked Tourist Information Office makes an excellent point of departure for further exploration of this old silk making town. St Alban's Church on Chester Road is the work of A.W. N. Pugin. Culturally, Macclesfield has become inextricably linked with the late 1970s post-punk band Joy Division, largely on account of its associations with Ian Curtis, the band's charismatic but ill-fated leader. It was also the birthplace, in 1933, of the blues singer, John Mayall. Film buffs might be interested to learn that Macclesfield was used for the film version of James Hilton's *So Well Remembered* in 1947, starring John Mills and Martha Scott.

Eating & Drinking

CAFE BAR ARIGHI - The Silk Road. Tel: 01625 613333. Cafe/restaurant in stylish Italian furniture shop. Open Mon-Sat 9.30am-5pm, Sun noon-4pm. SK10 1LH
CHERRY BLOSSOM - Church Street. Tel: 01625 615999. Tea room open (ex Sun) 9am-4pm. SK11 6LB
THE CASTLE - Church Street. Tel: 01625 462646. Quaint, half-timbered, *Good Beer Guide* listed pub on a cobbled street. Open from noon daily. SK11 6LB
CHESTERGATE BISTRO - Chestergate. Tel: 01625 611103. Lunches (from 11.30am) Thur-Sat; dinner (from 5.30pm) Tue-Sat. SK11 6DY
CHILLI BANANA - Buxton Road. Tel: 01625 422332. Thai restaurant on road down from canal. Lunch 12-2pm Tue-Sun; dinner from 5pm Tue-Sun. SK10 1JX
FIVE CLOUDS - Market Place. Tel: 01625 429214. Microbrewery & bar, daily ex Sun. SK11 1EX
PICTUREDROME - Chestergate. Atmospheric pop up food hall housed in former cinema. SK11 6DU
PRIME CUT - Castle Street. Tel: 01625 410686. Steak bar open daily from 11.30am. SK11 6AF
PUSS IN BOOTS - Buxton Road (canalside Bridge 37). Tel: 01625 611615. Open noon daily. SK10 1NF
REDWILLOW - Park Green. Tel: 01625 830718. *GBG* listed brewery tap converted from a shop. SK11 7NA
WHARF - Brook Street (to rear of Hovis Mill, access via Bridge 37 and Union Road). Tel: 01625 261879. *GBG* listed drinking pub to rear of marina. Open from 4.30pm (4pm weekends). SK11 7AW

Shopping

Full facilities in the town centre 10 minutes walk from the canal. Cheshire Fish is an excellent fishmongers and stands, appropriately enough, on Roe Street. Two providers of local delicacies are Spearing's (pies and sausages) on Park Green and Granelli's (ice cream) on Newton Street. Cheshire Cat deli on Chestergate. Indoor market daily (ex Sun) outdoor markets on Tue, Fri & Sat. The Treacle Market (last Sunday of each month) is a venue for local food, antiques, books etc.

Things to Do

TOURIST INFORMATION - Town Hall, Market Street Tel: 01625 378123. SK10 1DX
SILK MUSEUM - Park Lane. Tel: 01625 612045. Open Wed-Sat 10am-4pm. The Silk Museum is housed in Macclesfield's Victorian art school where Charles Tunnicliffe once studied. Adjoining this is Paradise Mill, home to Europe's largest collection of Jacquard silk looms. Cafe and gift shop. SK11 6TJ

Connections

TRAINS - 10 minutes downhill from Bridge 37. Avanti and Cross Country provide fast and frequent connections with Manchester and Stoke. Through Avanti trains to/from London. Northern stopping services run to/from Congleton, and as such provide a handy link for one-way towpath walks.
BUSES - bus station on Sunderland Street adjacent to rail station. D&G service 10 runs half-hourly Mon-Sat to/from Bollington. Aimee's service 109 runs to/from Leek via Oakgrove and Bosley.
TAXIS - Silvertown. Tel: 01625 616666.

Gurnett/Sutton   Map 50

KINGS HEAD - Gurnett Aqueduct. Tel: 01625 611444. Good moorings make this a popular stop with boaters. Food and accommodation in quaint pub dating from late 17th Century. SK11 0HD
SUTTON HALL - Bullocks Lane (access via Bridge 44). Tel: 01625 253211. Impressive Brunning & Price conversion of a former manor house. Seven dining areas, terraces and gardens. Substantial menu and up to five real ales. Food served from noon daily, plus breakfasts (9.30am) at weekends. SK11 0HE
SUTTON VILLAGE CAFE - Tunnicliffe Road, Sutton. Tel: 01260 252438. Charming cafe open 8am-4pm daily (9am-3.30pm Sun). Part of the village's post office stores. SK11 0EB

141

51 MACCLESFIELD CANAL Oakgrove & Bosley Locks 5mls/12lks/3hrs

TRAVERSING its summit level of 518ft, the canal skirts the foothills of the Peak District. Bridge 48A is a footbridge affording access to a canalside cottage and Sutton Reservoir (Map 50). It is of comparatively recent construction, prior to which the cottage's inhabitants used a floating bridge to access their isolated property. It must have felt like living on an island. The footbridge is undoubtedly handier, but one can't help feel an element of adventure has been lost, like replacing a friendly coal fire with central heating.

Bridge 49 is an electrically operated swing-bridge, and whilst it only carries a by-road over the canal, traffic can be busy at times, especially during the 'school run', when Cheshire's mothers take to the roads in SUVs better suited (as Keith Goss memorably put it) to delivering aid packages to remote villages in the Third World. A dealer in classic cars occupies the car park of the former Fool's Nook pub.

A deep, ferny bank ensues, foliated with alder trees. In early summer the air here is heavy with the scent of wild garlic. On the towpath side the land falls away precipitously, in a manner reminiscent of a West Country coombe.

Insouciantly gliding along the Macclesfield Canal, marvelling at how they managed to engineer it without locks in so hilly a region, you're suddenly rudely interrupted by a dozen of them in quick succession. Not that there isn't something inherently impressive about the Bosley Flight. It is one of the most superbly engineered and magnificently located flights in the country; notable, for a narrow canal, in that both sets of gates to each stone chamber are mitred pairs. Originally each chamber

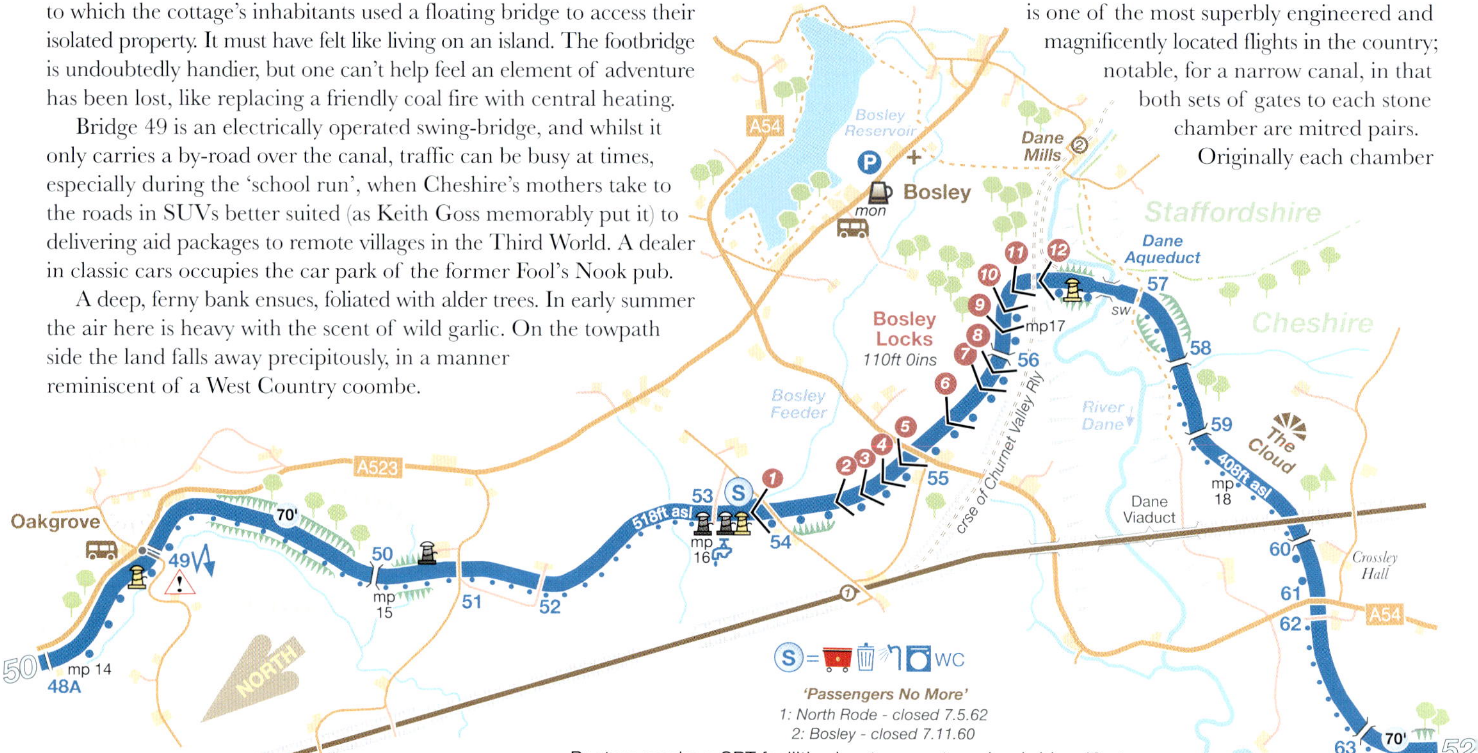

'Passengers No More'
1: North Rode - closed 7.5.62
2: Bosley - closed 7.11.60

⚠ Boaters require a CRT facilities key to operate swing-bridge 49 at Oakgrove. Go about its operation methodically and don't feel pressurised if the road traffic builds up: a bit of patience will do 'em good!

142

had a side pond, a water saving device which acted as a mini reservoir. When the lock emptied, half its contents would run into the side pond to be retained for half filling the chamber when it was next used. Theoretically this system halved the amount of water used by the flight. No one seems to recall exactly when the side ponds went out of use, but at least the one beside Lock 4 has been restored, though regrettably not for general use; even the 'vlockies', generally in attendance, seem not disposed to employ it. Whether you benefit from their help or not, the locks come in easily assimilated clusters, as opposed to intimidatingly like some lock flights we shudder to think of. And, incidentally, whilst there are designated visitor moorings above and below the flight, that at the top end is restricted to just a couple of boats or so; something to bear in mind if you're anticipating a rest before or after negotiating the locks.

Canoeing under The Cloud

The North Staffordshire Railway's Churnet Valley line (familiar to travellers on the Caldon Canal) crossed the canal between locks 11 and 12, the girder bridge (56A) which carried it still being in place, though barbed wire deters access. It wasn't the only railway in the vicinity. A 2ft 6ins gauge tramway ran from Thompstone's flour and corn mills in the neighbouring village of Bosley to a wharf alongside the canal below the bottom lock. A not insubstantial corrugated iron warehouse stood along the off-side of the canal below Lock 12. Apparently Thompstone's grew disenchanted with the service they were receiving from the North Staffordshire Railway, and retaliated by building a link to the Manchester, Sheffield & Lincolnshire Railway owned Macclesfield Canal; as a business might change from DPD to DHL for its logistics now. A diminutive 0-4-0 tank locomotive named *Magnet* was built for the line by Bagnall's of Stafford. Circa 1925 Thompstone's went over from corn milling to wood treatment (an activity which still goes on) and the tramway ceased to be used.

The canal crosses the River Dane on an imposing stone aqueduct, best (though probably illegally) appreciated from the path which descends to the valley floor from the north end of the neighbouring spill-weir. Blissfully peaceful and remote moorings are to be had below Lock 12 under the shadow of The Cloud, a millstone grit eminence rising to 1,126 feet above sea level and straddling the boundary between Cheshire and Staffordshire. In common with most of CRT's designated visitor moorings on 'The Macc', those idyllically sited at the foot of Bosley Locks present the opportunity for some local exploration. Bosley Reservoir, built to feed the canal in general and Bosley's thirsty locks in particular, lies a worthwhile mile to the east. Bosley itself, little more than a scattering of dwellings, a pub and a church on the A523, is famed for its Tug of War team, twice world champions.

By Bridge 57 a lengthy, cobbled spill-weir is spanned by a narrow timber walkway of considerable charm. Walk the plank, or splash through the puddles? What a dilemma! One of the best views of The Cloud can be savoured by Bridge 59. A three arch brick built bridge on a skew carries the North Staffordshire Railway's line across the canal. It opened in 1848, a mere seventeen years after the canal. Transport had been reinvented. Between bridges 60 and 61 the canal runs close to Crossley Hall, a Grade II listed 17th century half-timbered dwelling; a snip at £3m when we last passed!

52 MACCLESFIELD CANAL Congleton 5mls/0lks/2hrs

SOMETHING of a sea-change in the nature of the landscape occurs to the canal as it sashays past Congleton. Southwards the countryside grows softer and exfoliated as you head for the midlands. Northwards, rough-shaven hills with a Pennine hardness about them begin to close intimidatingly in on you.

Congleton's canalside is semi-detached and suburban, the old wharf having been assimilated almost seamlessly within a housing development. H. J. Lea Oakes organic animal feedstuffs mill overlooks an unusual gathering of transport modes by Bridge 75. A high embankment pierced by small aqueducts carries the canal over the steep-sided valley of Shaw Brook. A branch of the North Staffordshire Railway once threaded the valley and its trackbed has become a popular public footpath. A rail/canal transhipment dock known as Vaudrey's Wharf survives in water at Bridge 72. In the not too distant past we manoeuvred into its confines, imagining that we had a cargo to swap with the ghost trains. But word is now that it leaks and that there is no money available to have it relined, so it may well have to be filled in, which would be rather sad. Another memory relating to this length of the Macclesfield Canal concerns the gathering in for milking of a herd of cows by a cart horse. There appeared to be no farmer present whatsoever. As we cruised by, the horse came nonchalantly through a gate at the top of the field which sloped down to the canal. Clip-clopping around the field's perimeter, he got all the cows moving towards the gate, saw the last one safely through, and disappeared with the herd over the horizon: though, yes, it *could* have been two men in a pantomime horse!

By-roads lead from bridges 79 and 80 down to the village of Astbury, just under a mile to the west. The A34 doesn't do the village any favours, but the parish church of St Mary is remarkable and more than compensates. Pevsner considered it 'thrilling' which is about as excited as he ever got. Blink and you'll miss the canal's quiet passage over an aqueduct spanning another country lane.

144

53 MACCLESFIELD CANAL Hall Green & Hardings Wood 4mls/11k/1½ hrs

ITS magical mystery trip of the Pennine foothills drawing to a premature close, the Macclesfield Canal can still strew a few delights in your path. Streams flow down from the neighbouring watershed, with the exuberance of children destined for the coast, in this case the Irish Sea.

From Bridge 86 a footpath leads enticingly to the National Trust's incomparable Little Moreton Hall. Alternatively, you can climb to the top of Mow (rhymes with cow) Cop. That castellated ruin you've watched growing closer for some time now, is Wilbraham's Folly. No, it's not some remnant of a medieval castle, it's an 18th century 'Angel of the North', a pure piece of whimsy plonked there for the entertainment of Squire Wilbraham of Rode Hall, a couple of miles to the west. In any case, the Cop's true claim to fame is that the first open air camp meeting of the Primitive Methodist Revivalists was held on its heights one Sunday morning in May 1807.

As much as anything, you'll miss the Macc's milestones. So 'big ups' to the Macclesfield Canal Society who unearthed as many as they could (they were buried at the beginning of the Second World War to confound would-be invaders) or cut new ones from Kerridge stone to fill the gaps.

Situated (until Beeching got his grubby hands on it) near Bridge 86, Mow Cop & Scholar Green railway station was immortalised (along with a number of other stations with canal connotations) by Flanders & Swann in their elegiac song *Slow Train*. The diarist, James Lees-Milne, alighted here on 27th April 1945, ascending to the folly - 'it blew so hard at the top I could scarcely breath' - and crossing the fields to Little Moreton Hall, both under the aegis of the National Trust for whom he worked.

The smooth lawns of Ramsdell Hall (c1760) sweep down to the canal bank. Untypically ornate cast iron railings (restored in 2008 to lovely effect) separate the towpath from a steep drop into the field below, so that the canal acts as a sort of ha-ha, or sunken wall, at the edge of the gardens.

Older canallers remember with affection the Bird in Hand pub which stood alongside swing-bridge 88, and recall how the landlord would fetch your beer in a jug from the cellar. Swing-bridge 90 is usually open for boats to pass
continued on page 145:

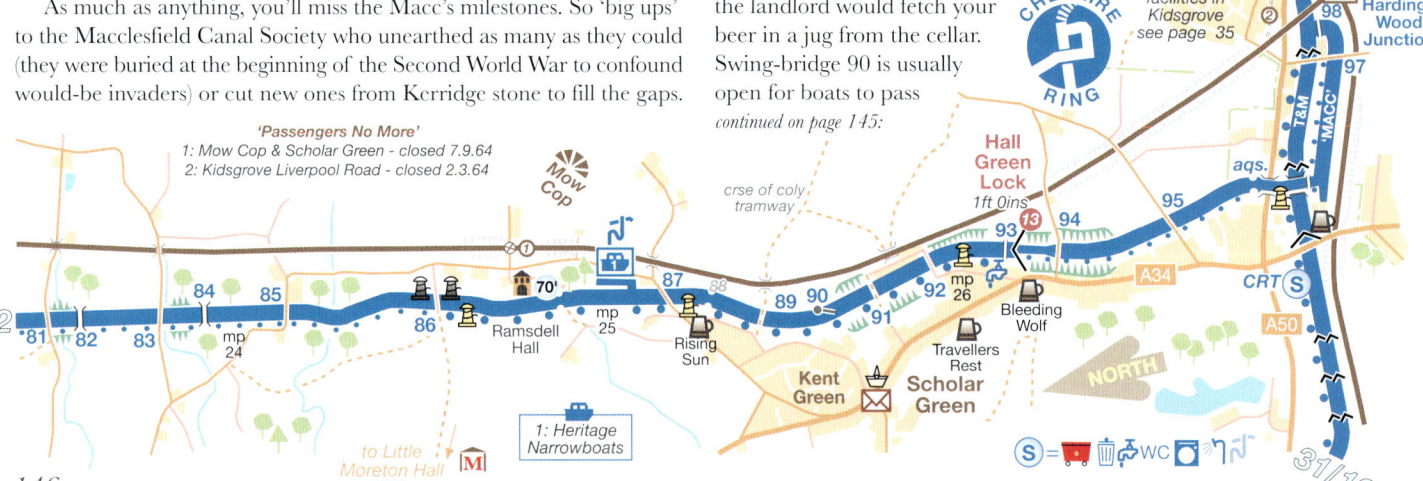

continued from page 146:

through. The pink cottage beside it is eccentrically known as Teapot Hall. Bridge 91 is particularly high, ornate and skewed, as if the Macc is intent on signing-off with a final flourish.

Historically, the Macclesfield and Trent & Mersey canals met at Hall Green as opposed to Hardings Wood. Here, both companies regarded each other in mutual mistrust across a 'Checkpoint Charlie' of paired stop locks, lock-keeper's cottages, and stable blocks. Neither in the railway age was their guard dropped, for the Macclesfield belonged to the Great Central, whereas the T&M was taken over by the North Staffordshire. Accidents of history to be embraced as you proceed dramatically across a pair of lofty aqueducts spanning the A50 and the Trent & Mersey Canal respectively. A dog-leg turn, and an optically bemusing straight, take you back to Hardings Wood Junction, your hugely satisfying circumnavigation of Cheshire completed. Cue for a celebratory pint at the Blue Bell?

Congleton   Map 52

Congleton has an unexpected zest about it, a level of activity which seems almost metropolitan to boaters, down from the cut with mud on their boots and a gauche unfamiliarity with road traffic. The best building in the town is the Town Hall, an imposing Flemish looking building which houses the excellent Tourist Information Centre. Lurking round the back is the town's museum which celebrates its bear-baiting past; the former mayor who ordered the execution of King Charles I; its former textile industries; cigar making; and its connections with Dutch soldiery during the Second World War.

Eating & Drinking
BEARTOWN TAP - Willow Street. Tel: 01260 270775. *Good Beer Guide* listed local dispensing the ales of nearby Beartown Brewery. CW12 1RL
CONGLETON OATCAKES - Lawton Street. Tel: 01260 298040. Fresh filled oatcakes and pikelets, a rare Cheshire example of neighbouring North Staffs' staple diet. Open 6.30am-2pm Wed-Sat. CW12 1RS
FOUR FRIENDS - Mill Street. Tel: 01260 277655. Appropriate Tibetan cuisine after all those hills! Open from 5.30pm Tue-Sun but booking recommended. Take your own wine. CW12 1AB
HIGHTOWN FISH & CHIPS - adjacent Bridge 75. Tel: 01260 276452. Open lunch and evenings (from 4.30pm) daily ex Sun. CW12 3RJ
PRINCE OF WALES - Lawton Street. Tel: 01260 280714. Snug Joules local by Town Hall. CW12 1RP
QUEEN'S HEAD - adjacent Bridge 75, steps up from towpath. Tel: 01260 272546. *GBG* recommended. Food from noon daily. Accommodation. CW12 3DE

Shopping
Hightown offers a bakery, post office and pharmacy accessed via Bridge 75. The town centre is 10 to 15 minutes walk west of the canal, but there are bus connections - see below. Tuesdays, Saturdays and Sundays are Market Days and there's a Morrisons supermarket by the bus station.

Things to Do
TOURIST INFORMATION CENTRE - Town Hall, High Street. Tel: 01260 270350. Closed Sun. CW12 1BN
CONGLETON MUSUEM - Market Square. Tel: 01260 276360. Closed Mondays. Charming little repository of local history. Evidence that boating in Congleton goes back to 930AD. See how far you can get on the touch screen canal test. Closed Mondays. CW12 1ET

Connections
BUSES - Hollinshead's service 91 operates half-hourly Mon-Sat to the centre of town from stops adjacent to Dog Lane Aqueduct and/or the railway station and Bridge 75.
TRAINS - hourly Mon-Sat (intermittent Sun) Northern services to/from Stoke, Macclesfield and Manchester.
TAXIS - A Stars. Tel: 01260 280280.

Scholar Green   Map 53

The annual (May-held) 'Mow Cop Killer Mile' is one of the most gruelling events of the running calendar. The course consists of a climb of 550 feet with a gradient of 1 in 4 at places. The summit is, however, well worth reaching at a more pedestrian pace. Views stretch from The Potteries to the Mersey and are as breathtaking as the climb.

Eating & Drinking
BLEEDING WOLF - access from Bridge 94. Tel: 01782 782272. Incongruous thatched thirties roadhouse on CAMRA's national inventory. Robinson's ales and food from noon weekdays and 9am weekends. ST7 3BQ
RISING SUN - adjacent to Bridge 87. Tel: 01782 971838. Cosy Marston's pub within easy reach of the canal. Food from noon Wed-Sun. ST7 3JT

Shopping
Morrisons 'Daily' convenience store/post office counter on the A34.

Things to Do
LITTLE MORETON HALL - idyllic walk from Bridge 86. Tel: 01260 272018. Refreshments and NT shop. One of the most celebrated examples of a half-timbered house in England, Little Moreton Hall dates from the end of the 15th century. Top heavy, with leaning walls and sagging roofs, it seems like some vast, unstable doll's house. Moat and knot garden. Open mid-Feb to end of Oct 11am-5pm. CW12 4SD

WEAVER NAVIGATION

54 WEAVER NAVIGATION Weston Marsh & Frodsham 4mls/0lks/1hr*

QUITE what inbound, foreign mariners made of Weston Marsh Lock in the glory years of shipping on the Weaver is open to conjecture. Twenty miles of navigable river lay ahead of them, delving into Cheshire's salty belly.

The river was made navigable in the 18th century, but an atypical policy of continual improvement, together with a ready market in salt and chemicals, saw it at its zenith in the first half of the 20th century, and ultimately sea-going vessels of up to 600 tons regularly traded along it. How surreal they appeared, gliding through pasturelands, like dolphins swimming incongruously up an English river.

These days, the Weaver Navigation, to give it its official title, is administered by the Canal & River Trust. Couched in an alien landscape of chemical works and wind farms, Weston Marsh Lock provides a link to the Manchester Ship Canal. Boaters wishing to negotiate it have to pre-book with CRT and comply with Peel Ports (owners of the MSC) stipulations: see page 157 for contact details.

CRT licenced boaters content to stay on the Weaver, are at liberty to explore as far as Weston Point, and though there is no access to the docks (notable for the sadly redundant and inaccessible Christ Church, erected by the Trustees of the Weaver Navigation in 1841) there is plenty of room to wind at the derelict entrance lock to the former Runcorn & Weston Canal. The last authenticated journey along this much mourned link was described in John Seymour's *Voyage Into England* in 1963. Though already officially abandoned, he heroically managed to effect a passage, much to the consternation of the authorities.

Three contrasting bridges span the navigation. The M56 bridge bears all the hallmarks of its lacklustre era. The railway viaduct, on the other hand, was built by the Birkenhead Joint Railway, an amalgamation of the Great Western and London & North Western companies and carries trains between Liverpool and Manchester and North Wales. Sutton Weaver Swing Bridge dates from 1926 and though there is room for most canal craft to pass beneath, it regularly swings for cruises involving the *Daniel Adamson* steam ship which is usually berthed in the vicinity. Frodsham Cut was abandoned in the 1950s. Near the site of Sutton Locks a miry lake contains the skeletons of many Mersey and Weaver 'flats' and 'packets'.

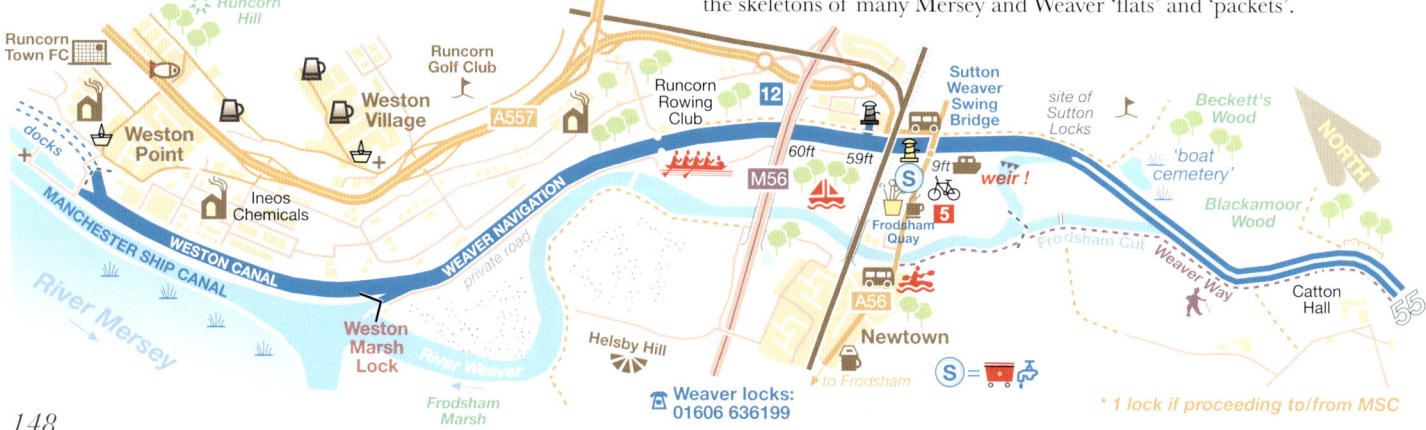

148

* 1 lock if proceeding to/from MSC

55 WEAVER NAVIGATION Acton Bridge & Dutton 4mls/11k/1½ hrs

DEVON's glorious River Dart is evoked as the Weaver negotiates a series of luxuriantly wooded reaches. Tall Lombardy poplar trees are a recurring feature of the riverbank, delineating its progress along the valley's pasturelands. Flying low over the water, cormorants add to the maritime atmosphere. Perhaps they are the souls of seamen, transmogrified.

In earlier times, the river was tidal as far as the long vanished locks at Pickerings. A riverine community flourished here, complete with a Methodist chapel and a public house memorably known as 'Pickering o' the Boat'. The residents of the two former lock cottages on the north bank have to cross the river by boat, as though they dwelt on an island.

Dutton Viaduct flings the West Coast Main Line majestically across the valley on twenty sandstone arches. It was erected in 1837 for the Grand Junction Railway and designed by Joseph Locke; not to be confused with the Irish tenor, Josef Locke, immortalised in the 1991 film, *Hear My Song*.

An elegant timber side-bridge, dated 1919, carries the towing-path over the original navigation channel. Dutton Locks set the tone for its three brethren upstream. Frankly, there is something retrospectively melancholic about them, now that they no longer play host to the sea-going vessels they were built to accommodate. A hand-written signboard poignantly recalls the nationalities of vessels which once plied these waters. Reduced maintenance budgets have resulted in only one chamber being in use. It's wise to check operating times with CRT, either on their website, or by telephoning the number quoted on the map. Amusingly, Dutton Locks, opened in 1880, were built by Glaswegian contractors, apparently necessitating a police presence to keep a semblance of order. The chambers are filled or emptied using the marvellously named Stoney's Patent Cylindrical Equilibrium Sluices.

The river splits into two channels at Acton Bridge. The northernmost is the main, the southern having been adopted for linear moorings by Acton Bridge Cruising Club. Impressively muscular, and dating from 1933, Acton Swing Bridge spans both channels, pivoting on a central pontoon.

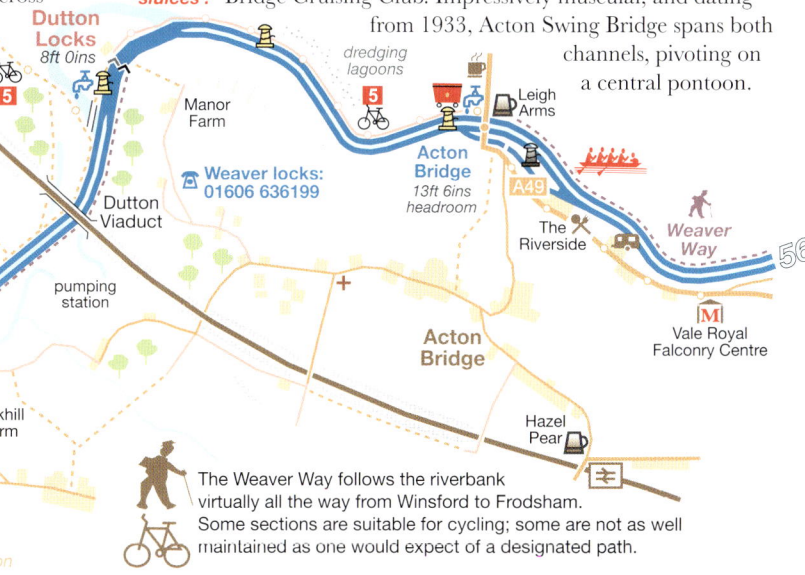

The Weaver Way follows the riverbank virtually all the way from Winsford to Frodsham. Some sections are suitable for cycling; some are not as well maintained as one would expect of a designated path.

for details of facilities at Acton Bridge turn to page 154

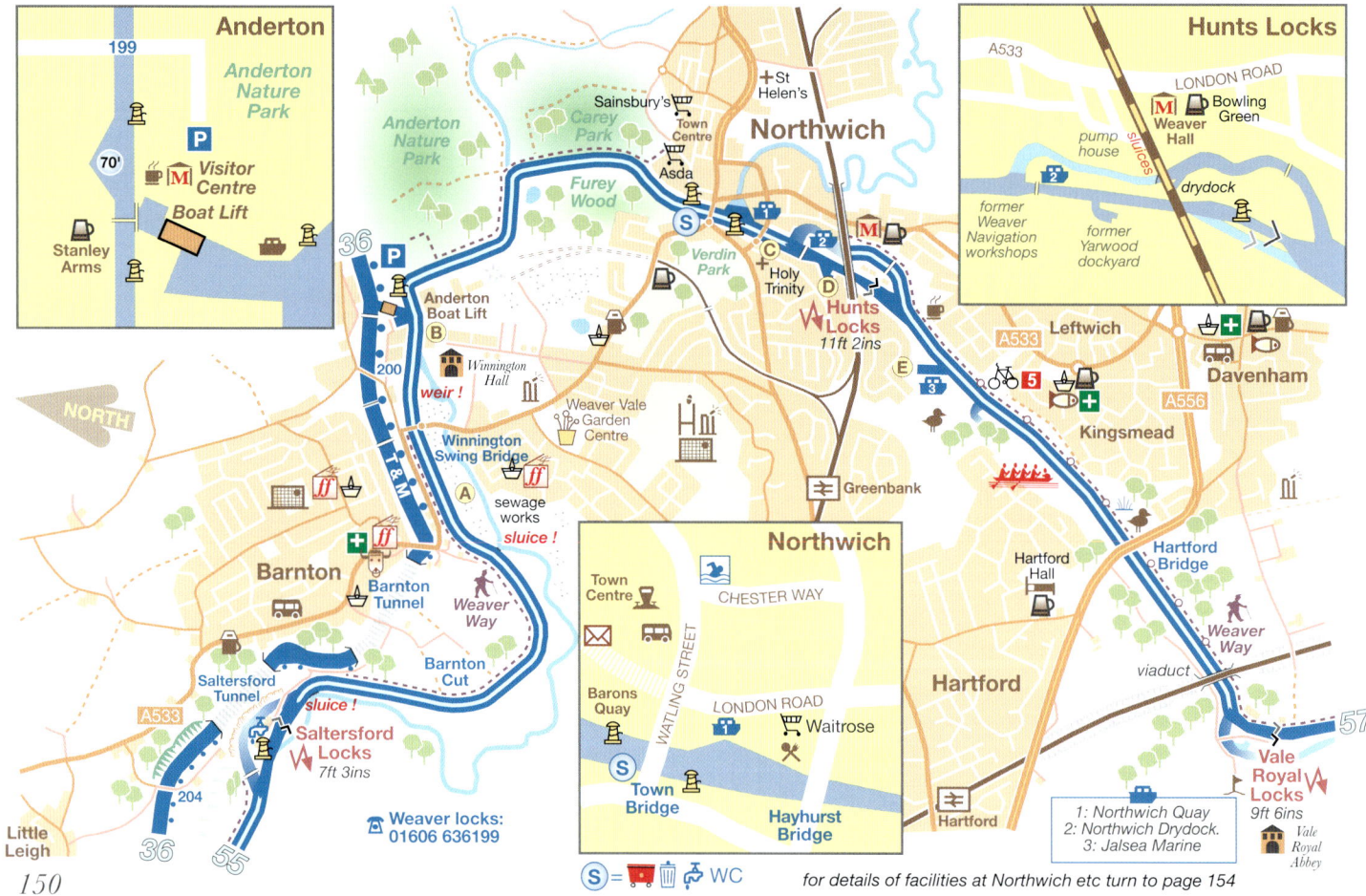

WERE you intrigued by the presence of the railway-like semaphore signals guarding Dutton Locks? You'll get used to them, such pleasing survivals, once used to indicate when and which chamber to enter. Their provenance is something of a mystery, for the Weaver was never, unlike so many canals, railway-owned. Perhaps someone cleverly got them cheap from Crewe.

Saltersford Locks are idyllically located beneath a wooded bluff. They date from 1874 and Lock-wheeler was delighted to find evidence that their machinery emanated from the Scottish engineering firm Hanna, Donald & Wilson of Paisley, his 'hame-toon': see also page 121. The larger chamber (to starboard) is in use today. You could fit twenty narrowboats in it and half a million gallons of precious water will disappear down towards the Mersey estuary when you pass through.

The river proper meanders off to the west as the navigation traverses Barnton Cut, an improvement dating from the 1830s. How rural everything feels, yet you are soon to encounter the remaining vestiges of the industry which once made the Weaver a viable commercial waterway. If, however, you are of a 'dark satanic' persuasion, go soon, because such scenes are inevitably earmarked for redevelopment in this post-industrial age. Wallerscote Works, for example, have already been razed to the ground, and housing is being erected on their site.

Winnington Swing Bridge - a rather dull and charisma-lacking structure compared to its sisters - separates Wallerscote from Winnington, where the vast soda ash plant is due to be demolished and replaced by fifteen hundred houses. Well, that's the plan, though a stumbling block concerns the government funding (or lack of it) of a replacement for the traffic-light controlled, single-laned, pinch-point of that swing-bridge, which would struggle to cope with all the extra traffic emanating from so many homes.

While it still stands, Winnington Works attracts urban explorers. One can understand the attraction, there is a magnificent element to its gaunt unloveliness. Clearly Anderton's Boat Lift will lose much of its inherent drama when all it looks over is an unremitting sea of low-rise rooftops. The works can trace its history back to 1873 and the birth of a partnership between John Tomlinson Brunner and Ludwig Mond. By 1926 it was part of Imperial Chemical Industries' mighty portfolio. Polythene was discovered 'accidentally' in an on-site laboratory seven years later. Life-size statues of messrs Brunner (whose father was Swiss) and Mond (of German birth) hitherto located at the entrance to the works' office block, are due to be relocated to Northwich town centre just as soon as the cash-strapped council can find £50k.

Another hostage of time's relentless march is Winnington Hall, a 16th century half-timbered structure, as imposing in its somewhat overshadowed way as Little Moreton Hall (Map 53). ICI used it incongruously as a social club - one pictures bacchanalian nights - but now it's a suite of offices, all a far cry from its early 19th century status as a girls finishing school where Halle gave recitals and Ruskin readings.

Reference to the Ordnance Survey's six inch map of 1882 reveals a bewildering amount of change. Not only in the plethora of salt and chemical works, but in the shape of the river and its adjoining flashes. Interestingly, at that time, there were locks at Winnington; whilst, upstream of the newly constructed boat lift, lay Witton Flashes, a veritable inland sea of subsidence-induced flood water, across which even a private ferry plied. An adjoining expanse of water was known demonically as Fury Pond. Even the salt works held nomenclatural appeal: Warbur's Eye Works, Byeflat Works, Island Works, Eureka Works. Naturally, all this phenomena - man-made and otherwise - is in the past tense and the landscape beside the banks of the Weaver has evolved into Anderton Nature Park; a fair result, most will assume.

Lulled into a bucolic state of bliss, one comes upon Northwich unexpectedly. The dull blank wall of Barons Quay retail park does not necessarily bode well, but one shouldn't judge a book by its cover (though the Canal Companions have always contradicted that notion) or a town by its contemporary architecture. A pair of handsome swing-bridges hastily

○ **Key**
A site of Wallerscote Works
    (under redevelopment)
B former Winnington Works
    (proposed for redevelopment)
C former Weaver Navigation
    workshops and offices
D site of Yarwoods dockyard
E site of Pimblotts dockyard

151

make amends, and form a more reliable character assessment in the process. Constructed by Handyside & Co. of Derby, they were erected within six months of each other in 1899. Fortunately for posterity, both they and their picturesque control cabins are Grade II listed, and their occasional operation makes for compelling viewing if you are fortunate enough to see them being swung for larger than average vessels; not that impatient motorists will necessarily share your appreciation.

Between them the river widens at the confluence of our old chum the River Dane (Maps 34/51). Northwich Quay, together with its attendant retail park, is the modern manifestation of a once extensive boat repair yard. The Canal & River Trust placed Navigation Yard, former headquarters and workshops of the Weaver Navigation Trustees, up for sale whilst we were researching this edition. There are concerns that the site will simply be redeveloped, and its historic character forfeited in the process. Amongst its most valuable buildings is a waterside clock tower circa 1830 boasting a cupola mounted on four Doric columns. The neighbouring offices on Navigation Road are equally handsome, and we sadly watched mahogany furniture being taken out of the building and loaded into a van. For safe-keeping? We were sceptical. That CRT should chose to have their HQ in a tower block in Milton Keynes, rather than here, or similarly historic buildings in their rapidly dwindling portfolio of historic/handsome properties, does little for their credibility as guardians of our inland waterway heritage.

Northwich once made a living not only from salt and chemicals, but from shipbuilding too. Several busy yards were based here turning out narrowboats, wide beam barges, tugs, coasters, river steamers and ferries. Some of ICI's 'Brunners' were built by Yarwoods. In 1980 Lock-wheeler was fortunate enough to journey downstream aboard *Marbury* just as the fleet was being disbanded. Yarwoods also built a good many narrowboats for the Grand Union Canal Carrying Company's fleet. But perhaps one of their most curious commissions was the RAF's auxilary vessel *Aquarius* launched in 1934, a 'spy ship' whose construction was overseen by 'Lawrence of Arabia' shortly before his fatal motorcycle accident.

A vertitable cornucopia of preserved vessels lurks along the narrow cut which ensues beyond Navigation Yard. Hunts Locks are framed by an equally lengthy and lofty railway viaduct carrying the old Cheshire Lines Committee's route from Manchester to Chester. The Weaver Trustees insisted on a minimum clearance of 69 feet, a demand which resulted in Northwich's railway station being consigned to the eastern fringe of the town. In amongst the humdrum schedule of hourly passenger services, lengthy trains of imported biomass pellets, unloaded from ships at Seaforth on the Mersey, trundle east for Drax power station in Yorkshire. The river channel is navigable downstream from above the locks to a drydock (pictured on page 4) sepulchrally located beneath one of the viaduct's forty-eight stone arches.

Upstream of Hunts, the channel, by-passing old meanders, is long and relatively straight as far as the Vale Royal railway bridge. This reach is used for rowing and, with footpaths on either bank, is also popular with pedestrians and runners. Fishermen favour this length too, finding it well stocked with good-sized roach, perch, pike, tench and bream. Jalsea Marine's yard used to belong to Pimblotts who built 'Brunners', wide boats for the Leeds & Liverpool Canal, barges for the Bridgewater Department of the MSC, and some of the distinctive steel hulled 'Admiral' class narrowboats.

Hartford (or 'Blue') Bridge carries the frenetically busy Northwich by-pass across the navigation. It is built, uninspiringly but practically, of concrete piers with a steel span. Beyond it the Weaver finally begins to justify its reputation for beauty. Trees spill down to the water's edge, their higher branches framing a lofty sandstone viaduct erected by the Grand Junction Railway in 1837 and now carrying the electrified West Coast Main Line across the Weaver Navigation. From these hurrying trains you catch tantalising glimpses of the Weaver luxuriating in its wooded cutting, but by water the journey is so much slower and the sense of intimacy correspondingly deeper. Set on a bend - so that, whichever way you are travelling, it remains out of sight until the last moment - Vale Royal Locks are amongst the loveliest on the inland waterways.

57 WEAVER NAVIGATION Winsford 4mls/0lks/1½ hrs

CONNOISSEURS regard the Vale Royal Cut as the prettiest stretch of the Weaver, and their opinion is difficult to refute. Leek Tunnel Pool (Map 29) notwithstanding, the visitor moorings upstream of Vale Royal Locks must qualify as one of the most idyllic on the inland waterways network. In medieval times there was a huge Cistercian abbey hereabouts. It had been founded by King Edward I in 1277 in his gratitude for being spared on a perilous voyage back from the Holy Land. In subsidence induced flashes grebes and coots nest on floating lily pads and yellow iris are abundant.

New Bridge was the scene in 1892 of riots during a prolonged waterman's strike. In the end, order was restored when a crack regiment of Hussars was brought in by train from Manchester. Beware the swing-bridge's low headroom, it may have to be swung even for some narrow boats. The bosky charm of Vale Royal gives way to Little Siberia as the Weaver negotiates a reach overlooked by a massive rock salt mine. An enigmatic vertical structure looks as it must be used for the launching of rockets, but in all likelihood contains winding gear akin to a colliery headstock. Five hundred feet down, the salt mine's galleries extend for well over a hundred miles. The bulk of the mine's production is used for road de-icing, but its worked-out seams now provide useful storage space for all manner of data, records and valuable artefacts.

Crumbling timber quays recall the Weaver's part in the transportation of mid-Cheshire salt products. Two railway companies vied for this business as well. You had to be on the ball when booking a ticket: the Cheshire Lines Committee called their station, Winsford & Over, the London & North Western, Over & Wharton; shades of Weston and Ingestre on Map 22. The CLC route has been converted into the Whitegate Way, a six mile long public bridleway and wildlife haven.

The town of Winsford uninspiringly straddles both banks of the Weaver; an industrial abyss dropped in the midst of Cheshire pastures. Colonised by post war overspill schemes, its economy now seems in the lap of baleful business parks. Winsford Bridges mark the end of the Canal & River Trust's jurisdiction of the river, but the local authority indulgently permit gratis exploration of Winsford Bottom Flash. Prudence is required if so tempted, and wisely undertaken in company. Leaving the river's confines and heading out into the flash is like going out to sea, and we were reminded, a little chillingly, of Elizabeth Jane Howard's short story *Three Miles Up*. Gulls enhance maritime illusion, as do the sailing dinghies. Red buoys mark the shallows, yellow buoys mark the racing zone. Local boaters will tell you that it is possible to drop anchor and moor midstream, though for peace of mind you may prefer to return to the more orthodox confines of the river: too much excitement isn't always good for you.

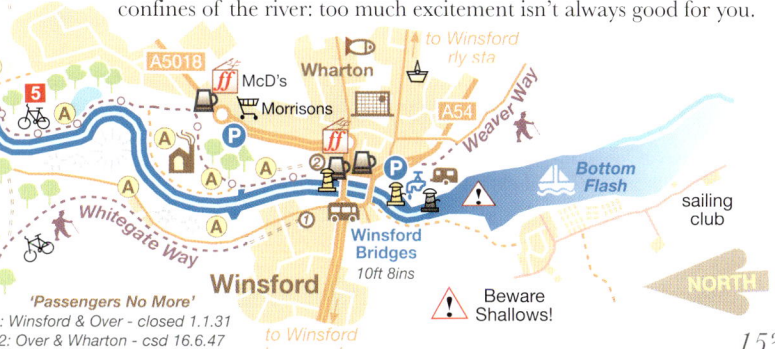

153

Acton Bridge   Maps 37/ 55

Scattered community on hillside overlooking the Trent & Mersey Canal and the River Weaver.

Eating & Drinking
DAVENPORTS - Warrington Road. (Bridge 209). Tel: 01606 853241. Award-winning tea room open Fri-Mon but pre-booking essential. CW8 4QU

HAZEL PEAR - adjacent Acton Bridge railway station. Tel: 01606 854434. Charming and comfortably refurbished inn whose name recalls fruit being grown commercially in the district. Food served daily from noon throughout. CW8 3RA

LEIGH ARMS - Warrington Road. Tel: 01606 853327. Comfortable Robinson's outpost overlooking Acton Swing Bridge. Intriguing painted windows featuring local scenes, not least the Weaver Navigation. CW8 4QT

RIVERSIDE INN - Warrington Road. Tel: 01606 852310. Marston's 'Two for One' restaurant with customer moorings and waterside patio. Food served from noon daily. CW8 3QD

Connections
TRAINS - Acton Bridge railway station can be a useful staging point for towpath walkers. It hosts an hourly service of London Northwestern Railway trains between Birmingham and Liverpool daily.

Northwich   Map 56

Surprisingly large, and unexpectedly likeable, you can tell that Northwich is off the beaten track because it still retains a good number of five figure telephone numbers. Handy moorings offer instant access to the town's pedestrianised shopping streets characterized by handsome but ersatz half-timber buildings erected to compensate for salt-mining wrought subsidence. Raise your eyes above their customary horizontality to admire the fascinating figurines which adorn the upper frontages of many black & white buildings.

Verdin Park stretches enticingly west of the Weaver Navigation on its way through the town. It contains a statue to Robert Verdin, a salt manufacturing philanthropist who gifted the park to the town in 1887. Nearby stands Holy Trinity church, erected (along with those at Weston Point and Winsford) by the Weaver Trustees. We found it locked, of course.

Eating & Drinking
BOMBAY QUAY - Hayhurst Quay. Tel: 01606 249911. Modern riverside Indian open from 5pm Mon-Thur and from noon Fri-Sun. CW9 5EU

BOWLING GREEN - London Road. Tel: 01606 352491. 17th century half-timbered pub easily accessed from Hunts Locks. Open from 3pm Mon & Tue; from noon the rest of the week. Food served 12-3pm and 4-7.45pm Wed-Sat and 12-6pm Sun. CW9 8AA

HUSH BREWING TAP - Navigation Road. CW8 1BE

PENNY BLACK - Witton Street. Tel: 01606 42029. Wetherspoons housed in former post office dating from 1914. Open daily from 8am. CW9 5AB

SALTY DOG - High Street. Micro pub with emphasis on live music. Open from noon daily. CW9 5BY

SALTHOUSE NW - Hayhurst Quay. Tel: 01606 624385. Contemporary cafe bar open from 5pm Mon-Thur, and from 3pm Fri-Sun. CW9 5HD

Shopping
Indoor retail market Tue, Fri & Sat. Carbon footprint-free fruit and veg from First Choice Fruit on Leicester Street. Fine butchers called Webb & Son (est 1929) on Witton Street whose motto is 'maintain thine honour and extend thy fame', and whose warm, jelly-running pork pies are mouth-watering. Asda supermarket at Barons Quay, Sainsbury's supermarket on Venables Road. Branch of Waitrose alongside Hayhurst Quay. Bratts department store on the High Street sadly closed in 2021, notwithstanding its familial connections with Pimblotts boatbuilding dynasty. Sacrilege!

Things to Do
WEAVER HALL MUSEUM - London Road (handy for Hunts Locks). Tel: 01606 271640. Heritage of mid-Cheshire housed in a former workhouse. CW9 8AB

Connections
BUSES - D&G 37 operates hourly (ex Sun) to/from Northwich, Middlewich, Sandbach and Crewe. D&G 48 links Northwich and Frodsham via Acton Bridge. TRAINS - local services to/from Chester, Stockport & Manchester along the scenic mid-Cheshire line from station approx one mile east of town centre. Take the train to Delamere and walk in the woods. TAXIS - JJ's. Tel: 01606 76262.

Davenham   Map 56

Suburbanised village which once gave its name to a steam-powered Brunner. The centre lies a twenty minute walk from Vale Royal Locks and hosts a useful array of shops and eating/drinking establishments.

Winsford   Map 57

Winsford's modern centre lies to the west of the river, a turgid hike from the visitor moorings at Winsford Bridges. Unforgivably, the Weaver Trustees' Christ Church was demolished in 2005.

Eating & Drinking
RED LION - Wharton Road (adjacent Winsford Bridges). Tel: 01565 748217. Refurbished red-brick pub beside the Weaver. Open from noon. Food served 12-3pm and 5-8pm Mon-Sat and 12-6pm Sun. CW7 3AA

Fast food outlet by bridge; fish & chips in Wharton

Shopping
Morrisons supermarket east of Winsford Bridges and Asda in town centre to the west

Connections
BUSES - D&G 37 operates hourly (ex Sun) to/from Northwich, Middlewich, Sandbach and Crewe.

INFORMATION

This Guide
Pearson's Canal Companions are a long established, independently produced series of guide books devoted to the inland waterways and designed to appeal equally to boaters, walkers, cyclists and other, less readily pigeon-holed members of society. Considerable pride is taken to make these guides as up to date, accurate, entertaining and inspirational as possible. A good guide book should fulfil three functions: make you want to go; interpret the lie of the land when you're there; and provide a lasting souvenir of your journeys.

The Maps
There are sixty-four numbered maps whose layout is shown by the Route Planner inside the front cover. Maps 1 to 27 cover the Four Counties Ring, a popular circular route of 109 miles including sections of the Shropshire Union, Trent & Mersey and Staffordshire & Worcestershire canals. Maps 28 to 30 portray the Caldon Canal, an off-shoot of the Trent & Mersey.

Maps 31 to 53 cover the Cheshire Ring, another circular route of 97 miles. Maps 54 to 57 portray the Weaver Navigation, a navigable river linked to the Trent & Mersey Canal by the Anderton Lift. A number of extra maps with alphabetical suffixes cover useful neighbouring canals.

The maps - measured imperially like the waterways they depict, and not being slavishly north-facing - are easily read in either direction. Users will thus find most itineraries progressing smoothly and logically from left to right or vice versa. Figures quoted at the top of each map refer to distance per map, locks per map and average cruising time. An alternative indication of timings from centre to centre can be found on the Route Planner. Obviously, cruising times vary with the nature of your boat and the number of crew at your disposal, so quoted times should be taken only as an estimate. Neither do times quoted take into account any delays which might occur at lock flights in high season, or the need to slow when passing lengthy lines of moored boats. The wise boater factors in an hour or two extra per day for such contingencies. Walking and cycling times will depend very much on the state of individual sections of towpath and the stamina of those concerned.

The Text
Each map is accompanied by a route commentary placing the waterway in its historic, cultural, and topographical context. As close to each map as is feasible, gazetteer-like entries are given for places passed through, listing, where appropriate, facilities of significance to users of this guide. Every effort is made to ensure these details are as up to date as possible, but - especially where pubs/restaurants are concerned - we suggest you telephone ahead if relying upon an entry to provide you with a meal at any given time.

Walking
The simplest way to go canal exploring is on foot along the towpaths originally provided so that horses could 'tow' boats. Walking costs little more than the price of shoe leather and you are free to concentrate on the passing scene; something that boaters, with the responsibilities of navigation thrust upon them, are not always at liberty to do. The maps set out to give some idea of the quality of the towpath on any given section of canal. More of an art than a science to be sure, but at least it reflects our personal experiences, and whilst it does vary from area to area, none of it should prove problematical for anyone inured to the vicissitudes of country walking. We recommend the use of public transport to facilitate 'one-way' itineraries but stress the advisability of checking up to date details on the telephone numbers quoted, or on the websites of National Rail Enquiries or Traveline for trains and buses respectively.

Cycling
Bicycling along towpaths - like walking, free of charge - is an increasingly popular pastime, though one not always equally popular with other waterway users such as boaters, anglers and pedestrians. Some sections of towpath are designated cycle routes and part of the National Cycle Network and these are depicted on the maps. It is important to remember that you are sharing the towpath with other people out for their own form of enjoyment, and to treat them with the respect and politeness they deserve. A bell is a useful form of diplomacy; failing that, a stentorian cough.

Boating
Boating on inland waterways is an established, though relatively small, facet of the UK tourist industry. It is also, increasingly, a chosen lifestyle. There are 38,000 privately owned boats registered on the canals - many of which never *seem* to move. But in addition to these, numerous firms offer boats for hire. These range from small operators with a handful of boats to sizeable fleets run by companies with several bases.

Most hire craft have all the creature comforts you are likely to expect. In the excitement of planning a boating holiday you may give scant thought to the contents of your hire boat, but at the end of a hard day's boating such matters take on more significance, and a well equipped, comfortable boat, large enough to accommodate your crew with something to spare, can make the difference between a good holiday and one which will be shudderingly remembered for the wrong reasons.

Traditionally, hire boats are booked out by the week or fortnight, though many firms now offer more flexible short breaks or extended weeks. All reputable hire firms give newcomers tuition in boat handling and lock working, and first-timers soon find themselves adapting to the pace of things 'on the cut'.

Navigational Advice

Newcomers, hiring a boat on the inland waterways for the first time, have every right to expect sympathetic and thorough tuition from the company providing their boat. Boat-owners are, by definition, likely to be already adept at navigating. The following, however, may prove useful points of reference.

Locks are part of the charm of canal cruising, but they are potentially dangerous environments for children, pets and careless adults. Use of them should be methodical and unhurried, whilst special care should be exercised in rain, frost and snow when slippery hazards abound. At busy or popular locks, Canal & River Trust volunteers are often present to help.

The majority of locks featured in this guide are of the narrow variety, though on the Rochdale Canal in central Manchester they are widebeam. On the Weaver Navigation they are very large and manned and we would urge newcomers to the river to seek advice from the keepers on duty until they become familiar with procedures.

Some locks, in areas perceived as prone to vandalism, are fitted with 'Water Conservation (T) Keys' which can be obtained from chandleries and CRT offices.

Finally, it behoves us all to be on our best behaviour at locks. Remember to exercise a little 'give and take'. The use of foul mouths or fists to decide precedence at locks is one canal tradition not worthy of preservation.

Mooring on the canals featured in this guide is per usual practice - ie on the towpath side, away from sharp bends, bridge-holes and narrows. A 'yellow' bollard symbol represents visitor mooring sites; either as designated officially or, in some cases derived from personal experience. Of course, one of the great joys of canal boating has always been the ability to moor wherever (sensibly) you like. And whilst this is still the case, in recent years it has become obvious - particularly in urban areas - that there are an increasing number of undesirable locations where mooring is not to be recommended for fear of vandalism, theft or abuse. It would be nice if local authorities would see their way to providing pleasant, secure, overnight facilities for passing boaters who, after all, bring the commerce of tourism in their wake. Few boaters would object to making a payment in such circumstances, as is the custom on rivers.

Turning points on the canals are known as 'winding holes'; pronounced as the thing which blows because in the old days the wind was expected to do much of the work rather than the boatman. Winding holes capable of taking a full length boat of around seventy foot length are marked where appropriate on the maps. Winding holes capable of turning shorter craft are marked with the approximate length. It is of course also possible to turn boats at junctions and at most boatyards, though in the case of the latter it is considered polite to request permission before attempting to do so. Given their predilection for signage, CRT should consider erecting signs at official winding holes stating the maximum length of boats which can be turned. Silting and vegetation can adversely affect the practicality of such sites.

Tunnels occur at a number of points on the canals and are great fun to negotiate, but to be on the safe side pets and young children should be kept 'below'. Don't forget to put your headlight on as you enter and to turn it off when you emerge at the other end. Many tunnels 'leak', so remove your Canal Companion to a place of safety!

Boating facilities are provided at regular intervals along the inland waterways, and range from a simple water tap or refuse disposal skip, to the provision of sewage disposal, showers and laundry. Such vital features are also obtainable at boatyards and marinas along with repairs and servicing. An alphabetical list of hire bases and boatyards appears on pages 158-159.

Closures (or 'stoppages' in canal parlance) traditionally occur on the inland waterways between November and April, during which time most of the heavy maintenance work is undertaken. Increasingly, however, an emergency stoppage, or perhaps water restriction, may be imposed at short notice, closing part of the route you intend to use. Up to date details are available on www.canalrivertrust.org.uk or from hire bases.

Moveable Bridges are an occasional feature of the routes included in this guide. Some 'swing', some 'lift', some are manually or windlass-operated, some mechanised. Most require either a CRT facilities key and/or 'handcuff' key to facilitate their moving. Always return them to the position you found them in after use unless it is obvious that another boat is approaching to use them.

Waterway Authorities

Canal & River Trust
The Canal & River Trust controls the bulk of the inland waterways network. Their Head Office is located at: First Floor North, Station House, 500 Elder Gate, Milton Keynes. MK9 1BB Tel: 0303 040 4040
www.canalrivertrust.org.uk

Bridgewater Canal
The Bridgewater Canal (Maps 38-43) is an integral part of the Cheshire Ring. A reciprocal arrangement with the Canal & River Trust allows boats to pass through (for a maximum of 10 days) without extra charge, though passages must be booked in advance on CRT's website or by telephoning 0303 040 4040. Should you need to contact the Bridgewater Canal Co. their address is: Bridgewater Canal Company, Venus Building, 1 Old Park Lane, Trafford City, Manchester M41 7HA. Tel: 0161 629 8432.

Manchester Ship Canal (Peel Ports)
There is access to the Manchester Ship Canal at Pomona Lock (Map 43) and Weston Marsh Lock (Map 54). Private pleasure craft may use the MSC only if they comply with a number of strict conditions, such as Third Party insurance and a Certificate of Seaworthiness. A pdf is available from the ship canal's owners www.peelports.com. Or telephone the MSC Maritime Centre on 0151 949 6000.

Societies
The Inland Waterways Association was founded in 1946. Many routes now open to pleasure boaters may not have been so but for this organisation. Membership details, together with details of the IWA's regional branches, may be obtained from: Inland Waterways Association. Tel: 01494 783453. Other support groups include: Bugsworth Basin Heritage Trust; Lichfield & Hatherton Canals Restoration Trust; Macclesfield Canal Society; Manchester Bolton & Bury Canal Society; River Weaver Navigation Society; Rochdale Canal Group; Shropshire Union Canal Society; Staffordshire & Worcestershire Canal Society; Trent & Mersey Canal Society; and Whaley Bridge Canal Group. Further details can be found via the internet or through the Inland Waterways Association.

Public Transport
Public transport can be of great use in getting to or from one's boat, or effecting one-way walks or bicycle rides. We urge readers, however, to source 'up to date' details in advance of their journeys, either via the internet, or on the following telephone numbers:
National Rail Enquiries - Tel: 0345 748 4950.
Traveline (bus services) - Tel: 0871 200 2233.

Amendments
Updates to current editions can be found on our website: www.jmpearson.co.uk. Feel free to email us if you spot anything worth notifying others about.

Uncaptioned Photographs
Page 1: Bridge 148, T&M Canal, Maps 15/32.
Page 2: Bottle kilns, Cliffe Vale, T&M Canal, Map 18.
Page 3: Backstreet Manchester, Map 44
Page 4: Northwich Dry Dock, Map 56.
Page 5: Penkridge, S&W Canal, Map 25.
Page 69: Stockton Brook, Caldon Canal, Map 28.
Page 81: Bartington, T&M Canal, Map 37.
Page 147: Acton Bridge, Weaver Navigation, Map 55.

Maximum Dimensions

Ashton Canal
Length: 71ft 5ins
Width: 7ft 0ins
Draught: 3ft 0ins
Headroom: 5ft 11ins

Bridgewater Canal
Length: 70ft 0ins
Width: 14ft 0ins
Draught: 3ft 6ins
Headroom: 8ft 6ins

Caldon Canal
Length: 72ft
Width: 6ft 8ins
Draught: 3ft 11ins
Headroom: 5ft

Macclesfield Canal
Length: 72ft 0ins
Width: 7ft 0ins
Draught: 3ft 3ins
Headroom: 6ft 10ins

Peak Forest Canal
Length: 72ft 0ins
Width: 7ft 0ins
Draught: 4ft 0ins
Headroom: 6ft 0ins

Rochdale Canal
Length: 72ft 0ins
Width: 9ft 5ins
Draught: 3ft 9ins
Headroom: 6ft 0ins

Shropshire Union Canal
Length: 72ft 0ins
Width: 7ft 0ins
Draught: 3ft 6ins
Headroom: 8ft 0ins

Staffs & Worcs Canal
Length: 70ft 0ins
Width: 7ft 0ins
Draught: 3ft 3ins
Headroom: 6ft 0ins

Trent & Mersey Canal
Length: 72ft 0ins
Width: 7ft 0ins
Draught: 3ft 3ins
Headroom: 5ft 9ins

Weaver Navigation
Length: 196ft 10ins
Width: 35ft 1ins
Draught: 9ft 6ins
Headroom: 29ft 6ins

BOATING DIRECTORY

Boat Hire

ABC BOAT HIRE - Nantwich, Shropshire Union Canal, Map 11. Tel: 0808 303 8712. CW5 8LB
www.abcboathire.com

ABC BOAT HIRE - Gailey, Staffs & Worcs Canal, Map 26. Tel: 0808 303 8712. ST19 5PR
www.abcboathire.com

ABC BOAT HIRE - Anderton, Trent & Mersey Canal, Map 36. Tel: 0808 303 8712. CW9 6AJ
www.abcboathire.com

ANDERSEN BOATS - Middlewich, Trent & Mersey, Maps 14/34. Tel: 01606 833668. CW10 9BQ
www.andersenboats.com

ANGLO WELSH - Bunbury Wharf, Shropshire Union Canal, Map 11A. Tel: 0117 304 1122. CW6 9QB www.anglowelsh.co.uk

ANGLO WELSH - Great Haywood, Trent & Mersey Canal, Map 23. Tel: 0117 304 1122. ST18 0RJ
www.anglowelsh.co.uk

BAILEY'S TRADING POST - Macclesfield Canal, Map 48. Tel: 01625 872277. SK12 1TH
www.baileystradingpost.com **Day Hire Only**

BOLLINGTON WHARF - Bollington, Macclesfield Canal, Map 50. Tel: 0779 134 5004. SK10 5JB www.bollington-wharf.com **Day Hire Only**

BLACK PRINCE HOLIDAYS - Etruria, Trent & Mersey, Map 18. ST1 5PA Tel: 01527 575115.
www.black-prince.com

BLACK PRINCE HOLIDAYS - Bartington Wharf, Trent & Mersey, Map 37. Tel: 01527 575115. CW8 4QU www.black-prince.com

CANAL CRUISING - Stone, Trent & Mersey Canal, Map 20. Tel: 01785 813982. ST15 8QN
www.canalcruising.co.uk

CHAS HARDERN - Beeston, Shropshire Union Canal, Map 11A. Tel: 01829 732595. CW6 9NH
www.chashardern.co.uk

CHESHIRE CAT - Audlem, Shropshire Union, Canal, Map 9. Tel: 0786 779 0195. CW5 8AY
www.cheshirecatnarrowboats.co.uk

COUNTRYWIDE CRUISERS - Brewood, Shropshire Union Canal, Map 2. Tel: 01902 850166. ST19 9BG www.countrywide-cruisers.com

EVIE - Bollington, Macclesfield Canal, Map 49. Tel: 0776 088 9093. SK10 5JB **Day Hire Only**

FLOATING HOLIDAYS - Middlewich, Trent & Mersey Canal, Maps 14/34. Tel: 0790 158 8364. CW10 9BD www.floating-holidays.co.uk

FREEDOM BOATS - Macclesfield, Macclesfield Canal, Map 50. Tel: 01625 420042. SK11 7AW
www.freedomboats.co.uk **Day Hire Only**

HERITAGE NARROW BOATS - Scholar Green, Macclesfield Canal, Map 53. Tel: 01782 785700. ST7 3JZ www.heritagenarrowboats.co.uk

NAPTON NARROWBOATS - Autherley, Shropshire Union Canal, Map 1. Tel: 01902 789942. WV5 9HW www.napton-marina.co.uk

NORBURY WHARF - Norbury, Shropshire Union Canal, Map 5. Tel: 01785 284292. ST20 0PN
www.norburyhire.co.uk

OAKWOOD MARINA - Davenham, Trent & Mersey Canal, Map 35. Tel: 01606 331961. CW9 7RY
www.oakwoodmarina.co.uk **Day Hire Only**

PHOENIX DAY BOAT - Whaley Bridge, Peak Forest Canal, Map 47B. Tel:0775 927 2632. SK23 7LS
www.phoenixdayboat.co.uk **Day Hire Only**

PORTLAND BASIN MARINA - Ashton-under-Lyne, Peak Forest Canal, Map 46. Tel: 0161 330 3133. SK16 4SQ
www.portlandbasinmarina.co.uk

THORN MARINE - Stockton Heath, Bridgewater Canal, Map 39. Tel: 01925 265129. WA4 6LE
www.thornmarine.co.uk

VENETIAN - Venetian Marina, Middlewich Arm, Map 12. Tel: 01270 528122. CW5 6DD
www.venetianhireboats.co.uk

Boatyards

ANDERTON MARINA (ABC) - Anderton, Trent & Mersey Canal, Map 36. Tel: 01606 79642. CW9 6AJ

ANGLO-WELSH (GT. HAYWOOD) - Trent & Mersey Canal, Map 23. Tel: 01889 881711. ST18 0RJ;

ANGLO-WELSH (BUNBURY) - Shropshire Union Canal, Map 11A. Tel: 01829 260957. CW6 9QB

ASTON MARINA - Aston-on-Trent, Trent & Mersey Canal, Map 20. Tel: 01785 819702. ST15 8QU

AQUEDUCT MARINA - Church Minshull, Shropshire Union, Middlewich Branch, Map 13. Tel: 01270 525040. CW5 6DX

BARBRIDGE MARINE - Barbridge, Shropshire Union Canal, Map 11. Tel: 01270 528682. CW5 6BE

BLACK PRINCE (BARTINGTON) - Trent & Mersey, Map 37. Tel: 01606 852945. CW8 4QU

BLACK PRINCE (STOKE) - Etruria, Trent & Mersey Canal, Map 18. Tel: 01782 201981. ST1 5PA

BOLLINGTON WHARF - Bollington, Macclesfield Canal, Map 50. Tel: 01625 575811. SK10 5JB

BOURNE BOAT BUILDERS - Penkridge, Staffs & Worcs Canal, Map 24. Tel: 01785 714692. ST19 5RH

BRAIDBAR - Higher Poynton, Macclesfield Canal, Map 48. Tel: 01625 873471. SK12 1TH

CANAL CRUISING - Stone, Trent & Mersey Canal, Map 20. Tel: 01785 813982. ST15 8QN

DOLPHIN BOATS - Stoke-on-Trent, Trent & Mersey Canal, Map 18. Tel: 01782 849390. ST4 4HW

FRADLEY MARINA - Fradley, Trent & Mersey Canal, Map 23C. Tel: 0794 116 7087. DE13 7EW

FRADLEY MARINE SERVICES Fradley, T&M Canal, Map 23C. Tel: 0797 1686516. DE14 7DN

FURNESS VALE MARINA - Furness Vale, Peak Forest Canal, Map 47B. Tel: 01663 742971. SK23 7QA

GREAT HAYWOOD MARINA - Trent & Mersey Canal, Map 23. Tel: 01889 883713. ST18 0RQ

HESFORD MARINE - Lymm, Bridgewater Canal, Map 41. Tel: 01925 754639. WA13 0SW

INDUSTRY NARROWBOATS - Stretton, Wharf, SUC, Map 2. Tel: 0791 225 9338. ST19 9QX

JD BOAT SERVICES - Gailey, Staffs & Worcs Canal, Map 26. Tel: 01902 791811. ST19 5PR

KERRIDGE DRYDOCK - Kerridge, Macclesfield Canal, Map 19. Tel: 01625 574347. SK10 5AP

KINGS BROMLEY MARINA - Kings Bromley, T&M Canal, Map 23B. Tel: 01543 417209. WS13 8HT

KINGS LOCK CHANDLERY - Middlewich, T&M Canal, Maps 14/34. Tel: 01606 737564. CW10 0J

LYME VIEW MARINA - Wood Lanes, Macclesfield Canal, Map 18. Tel: 01625 858176. SK10 4PH

MIDDLEWICH CANAL CENTRE - Trent & Mersey, Maps 14/34. Tel: 01606 610610. CW10 0JJ

MIDDLEWICH WHARF - Trent & Mersey Canal, Maps 14/34. Tel: 0330 043 0547. CW10 9BD

MIDWAY BOATS - Barbridge, Shropshire Union Canal, Map 11. Tel: 01270 528482. CW5 6BE

M R MARINE - Wincham, T&M Canal, Map 35. Tel: 0774 125 3988. CW9 7NT

NANTWICH CANAL CENTRE (ABC) - Nantwich, Shropshire Union Canal, Map 11. Tel: 01270 625122. CW5 8LB

NEW ISLINGTON MARINA - Manchester, Ashton/Rochdale canals, Map 45. Tel: 0746 968 2736. M4 6EA

NEW MILLS MARINA (ABC) - New Mills, Peak Forest Canal, Map 47A. Tel: 01663 741310. SK22 3JJ

NORBURY WHARF - Norbury Jnct., Shropshire Union, Map 5. Tel: 01785 284292. ST20 0PN

NORTHWICH DRYDOCK - Northwich, Weaver Navigation, Map 56. Tel: 0739 397 8654. CW8 1BE

NORTHWICH QUAY - Northwich, Weaver Navigation, Map 56. Tel: 0796 746 1038. CW9 5HD

OAKWOOD MARINA - Rudheath, Trent & Mersey Canal, Map 35. Tel: 01606 331961. CW9 7RY

OTHERTON BOAT HAVEN - Penkridge, Staffs & Worcs Canal, Map 25. Tel: 01785 712515. ST19 5NX

OVERWATER MARINA - Audlem, Shropshire Union Canal, Map 9. Tel: 01270 812677. CW5 8AY

OXLEY MARINE - Autherley, Staffs & Worcs Canal, Maps 1/27. Tel: 01902 789522. WV10 6TZ

PARK FARM MARINA - Rudheath, Trent & Mersey Canal, Map 35. Tel: 01606 44672. CW9 7RY

PORTLAND BASIN MARINA - Ashton-under-Lyne, Peak Forest Canal, Map 46. Tel: 0161 330 3133. SK16 4SQ

PRESTON BROOK MARINA - Preston Brook, Bridgewater Canal, Map 38. Tel: 01928 719081. WA7 3AF

PRESTON BROOK WHARF - Preston on the Hill, Bridgewater Canal, Map 38. Tel: 0774 895 8303. WA4 4BA

STOKE BOATS - Longport, Trent & Mersey Canal, Map 18. Tel: 01782 813831. ST6 4NB

STRETFORD MARINE - Stretford, Bridgewater Canal, Map 43. Tel: 0161 866 8419. M32 0NQ

TALBOT WHARF - Market Drayton, Shropshire Union Canal, Map 8. Tel: 01630 652641. TF9 1HN

TRAFALGAR MARINE SERVICES - Newtown, Peak Forest Canal, Map 47A. Tel: 01663 747808. SK22 3HF

UPLANDS BASIN MARINA - Anderton, Trent & Mersey Canal, Map 36. Tel: 01606 782986. CW9 6AJ

VENETIAN MARINA - Cholmondeston, SU Canal, Map 12. Tel: 01270 528122. CW5 6DD

WINCHAM BOAT SERVICES - Wincham, T&M Canal, Map 35. Tel: 01606 47078. CW9 7NT

Selected Trip Boats

ANDERTON BOAT LIFT - Weaver/Trent & Mersey trips including passage through the lift. Maps 36/56. Tel: 01606 786777.

CITY CENTRE CRUISES - Manchester & Salford, Bridgewater Canal and Manchester Ship Canal, Maps 43/44. Tel: 0161 902 0222.

THE DANNY - Cruises on the Weaver Navigation aboard the steam powered tug *Daniel Adamson*. www.thedanny.co.uk

JUDITH MARY II - Whaley Bridge, Peak Forest Canal, Map 47B. Tel: 0754 089 5615.

MERSEY FERRIES - Public cruises on the Manchester Ship Canal. Tel: 0151 330 1003.

NORBURY WHARF - Public and chartered trips on the Shropshire Union from Norbury Junction. Map 5. Tel: 01785 284292.

Selected Fuel Boats

ALTON - Macclesfield and Peak Forest Canals. Tel: 0779 134 5004.

HALSALL - Four Counties Ring. Tel: 0749 114 9149.

MOUNTBATTEN - Shropshire Union Canal. Tel: 0794 623 9778.

THE CANAL COMPANIONS

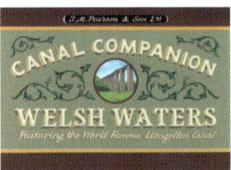
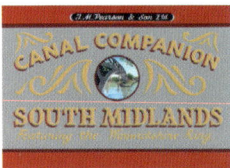